Awakening *
Twenty-First Centu...

SPIRITUAL PILGRIM

A MEMOIR

WISE *Ink*
CREATIVE ★ PUBLISHING

REV. DR. JIM SHERBLOM

SPIRITUAL PILGRIM
TESTIMONIALS:

"Jim Sherblom took me on a journey of heart and mind. By weaving pilgrimage practices from various religions with his own searching, Sherblom shows us both the agony and the ecstasy of following God."

- Rev. Howard Dana,
senior minister, First Parish Unitarian Universalist in Concord

"Establishments hate mystics. We seekers of unity both love and need them. They remind us that there is no One Way. We need others, whose vision is deeper and broader than ours, to nudge us back onto the Path to spiritual maturity, compassion, wisdom, and a more universal vision of salvation for all. Jim Sherblom here offers not just his own personal experience, but the counsel of the wisest of all ages."

- Rev. John Buehrens,
past president, Unitarian Universalist Association

"Many come to religion with a sense that there is something happening in their lives that is beyond what they can explain or even fully understand. The language of mysticism that Jim Sherblom teaches in his clear, concrete, and yet ephemeral book provides the tools a community needs to have a conversation about that which could be otherwise beyond words."

- Rev. Sarah Drummond,
academic dean, Andover Newton Theological School

"In this enchanting book, Jim Sherblom relates his experience of pilgrimage in different religious traditions, and his encounters with mystics who reveal and embody the mystery that crackles just below the surface of life. Sherblom tells his story with such insight and wonder that he turns from pilgrim to guide for the reader, and reading the book itself becomes a kind of pilgrimage."

—Rev. Martin B. Copenhaver,
President of Andover Newton Theological School
and author of *This Odd and Wondrous Calling*

"Are you seeking a living mystic guide? In his new book you'll find Jim is sparkling and wonderfully accessible as he channels the wisdom of the Sages of the Ages. What a pleasure to walk with him as he shares with us his spirited spiritual adventures."

- Steven Cadwell,
Ph.D., psychotherapist, educator, performer, filmmaker, activist

"*Spiritual Pilgrim* is an odyssey to the shores of the world's mystic traditions. With knowledge and self-revealing honesty, Jim Sherblom will deepen your understanding of the transcending and unifying power of mysticism. His insights will then guide you home into the depth and wonder of your next breath."

- Rev. Stephen Shick,
poet, minister and author of *Be the Change* and *Consider the Lilies*

"Equal parts memoir and guidebook, *Spiritual Pilgrim* entrances with stories that reveal Jim's unabashedly open heart and deep well of knowledge."

- Doug Stone and **Sheila Heen,**
coauthors of *New York Times* bestselling *Difficult Conversations*

"Reading this book, I felt myself illuminating from the inside out. Reverend Jim knows just where to lead us so that the lights of the many mystics before us can touch, warm, and awaken our inner light."

- Anna Huckabee Tull, Author, *Living the Deeper YES*

ISBN 13: 978-1-63489-140-0

Library of Congress Catalog Number: 2018947881
Printed in the United States of America
First Printing: 2018
22 21 20 19 18   5 4 3 2 1

Cover design by Nupoor Gordon
Interior design by Dan Pitts

Wise Ink Creative Publishing
807 Broadway Street NE, Suite #46
Minneapolis, MN 55413
wiseinkpub.com

To order, visit ItascaBooks.com. Reseller discounts available

This book is dedicated to the many mystics
of this world and no longer of this world
who over decades helped me find my Way.

CONTENTS

FOREWORD

However it comes to us, transcending mystery is the spark that starts us on our way, in a search for our path along the Way:

> *Direct experience of that transcending mystery and won-*
> *der, affirmed in all cultures, which moves us to a renewal*
> *of the spirit and an openness to the forces which create and*
> *uphold life.*

These words are the first of six sources affirmed by the faith that I love and call home—Unitarian Universalism. They are words that matter to us; many of us first found our way to this religious community because of the promise imbedded in them. There is something so much greater than we are, found among all peoples of the earth, that can lead us to abundant and regenerative life—and it is accessible to each of us. Many of us have felt this way for as long as we can remember; some of us find ourselves surprised by this realization in the midst of our "regular" lives.

It's that direct experience, and the continuous search for it, that guides Jim Sherblom in this engaging work of universalist pilgrimage. Not every person gets to travel the world in search of the Holy, but that is not what makes this book worth your time. Even among those of us who consider ourselves deeply religious, there are few of us with the courage to realize the demands of the path we seek, few of us willing to place ourselves amid unfamiliar rituals led by people of different faiths and culture. But that is part of the wonder of this book.

For the new seeker, this book will inform your search and enlarge your heart. It is, in part, a survey course in miniature on world religions—Jim serves as teacher as well as seeker in these pages, as he [re]introduces the reader to Rumi and Shams in Sufi Islam, and shamanic figures unfamiliar to many of us. He is moved by the Interior Castle of Teresa of Avila, enters into the Dark Night of the Soul with John of the Cross, and is transformed by the Buddhist realization of life as suffering. This is not a tourist visitation, but a painful, joy-filled, deeply felt experience of the Way. And for those willing and able to seek the holy in the company of others, Jim has created a set of prompts at the end of each chapter that are fertile materials for gratifying spiritual practice.

Every true seeker knows by heart that the Holy is unexplainable, and so I will not try. As Jim does, I invite you to dive in, with a receptive mind and heart. Prepare yourself for a renewal of your own spirit, and perhaps the opening of your own way forward.

Spiritual Pilgrim is a worthy guide as you pursue the Way for yourself.

The Rev. Rosemary Bray McNatt, President
Starr King School for Ministry, Berkeley, CA

FINDING MY WAY

I should begin by telling you what I know about mystics. Over several decades, I have traveled to distant lands, traversing diverse cultures and ways of being human, answering the question of how to live transcendentally as a transient spiritual pilgrim.

Mystics occupy a liminal space between two realities, two worlds. Many mystics grew up different, somehow set apart from others, often on the fringes of society. They developed an unusually intense relationship to divine mystery. Confucius, Buddha, Moses, Jesus, Madonna, Muhammad, and Rumi were all mystics, and each influenced my own spiritual journey.

Mystics experience realities beyond what can be described by the rational mind. The inadequate ways we have to describe those experiences include such words as *awe*, *transcendence*, *mystery*, and *wonder*. Every human being can experience such realities, but the mystic uses meditation, austerities, and spiritual disciplines to cultivate them on a more intense and more frequent basis. While everyone probably has the ability to become a mystic, very few people actually want to do so. Even though their experiences are largely indescribable, mystics' reports of realities are often perceived as phantasmagorical.

There have been many famous spiritual seekers as well as unknown mystics. Each left signs and wisdom for the Way. It is said the Buddha, Siddhartha Gautama, was born a prince destined to be either a great ruler or a great spiritual being. At age twenty-nine, even though he was happily married with a small child, he chose to pursue the mystical path. For Buddha, that led to awakening and dedicating his life to helping others awaken to reality.

Happily married and living in Midian, Moses was in his late twenties when divine mystery—despite Moses's verbal objections—called him to lead the Israelites out of Egypt and into the promised land. Moses seems to have had a particularly intimate and tumultuous experience of divine mystery. The Bible says he saw God face-to-face, or perhaps only God's backside, but it transfigured him.

Jesus of Nazareth was in his early thirties when John the Baptist baptized him in the Jordan River and he began preaching the kingdom of God. Jesus had such an intimate relationship with God that he addressed God by the affectionate term Abba, meaning "Daddy." Jesus seemed to hold a unique position, as much the son of God as he was the son of Mary. Jesus's journeys with divine mystery—and the religions that would eventually emerge in his name—would transform the practice of religion on the planet Earth.

I am a spiritual pilgrim traveling mystic journeys. A pilgrimage is a metaphysical journey to seek spiritual significance. Some pilgrimages are metaphorical, but in most faith traditions, undertaking a physical pilgrimage might happen once in a person's lifetime. I have embarked upon a dozen pilgrim journeys to seek spiritual awakening. I am drawn to how each spiritual journey has changed me. I began as a naive young adult, and my spiritual maturity ripened over time. This book tells the stories of the surprising inner journeys of my maturing soul.

Every faith tradition draws upon certain sources. I am an ordained Unitarian Universalist minister and mystic, and Unitarian Universalists draw upon six such sources. The first of these is the principle of "direct experience of that transcending mystery and wonder, affirmed in all cultures, which moves us to a renewal of the spirit and an openness to the forces that create and uphold life."

Faith traditions often have porous boundaries, especially among mystics. Over three decades, I have traveled with Unitarian Universalist mystics, Islamic mystics, Chinese mystics, shamanic mystics, Buddhist mystics, Christian mystics, and transcendentalist mystics. All have warmly welcomed me into their path, taught me their Way, and encouraged me to find my own Way to spiritual enlightenment. The Way of the pilgrim is the Way of the transient seeker of truth.

There are as many types of pilgrimages as there are pilgrims, but spiritual pilgrims generally seek some combination of transcendence, atonement, and wisdom. Transcendence by experiencing even glimpses of the ultimate reality beyond our mundane existence. Atonement by being forgiven for our sins. Wisdom in learning something important about ourselves. A spiritual pilgrim seeks spiritual transformation. Only then are we traveling *à la sainte terre*—to a holy land—wherever it may be, physically or metaphysically, or even if only in our minds. We go forth as spiritual pilgrims.

I never consciously chose to embark upon any of the pilgrimages described in this book; they chose me. As the pilgrim and poet David Whyte writes,

> *There are places that seem to expect us:*
> *to take us in like pilgrims*
> *from the way ahead to tell us suddenly*
> *and without fanfare*
> *of a new beginning*
> *made out of nothing*
> *but the way we got here,*
> *as if the hard road of difficulty and despair*
> *and minor triumph that brought us here*
> *could make sense simply by the nature*
> *of a particular geographic welcome.*

I simply learned to say yes whenever spiritual adventure is offered.

INTERRELIGIOUS MYSTICISM

*In the beginning was the WORD, and the WORD was with God,
and the WORD was God. All things came into being through the
WORD, the indwelling of divine mystery, and without the WORD not
one thing came into being. What has come into being was life, and the
spirit of life was the light of all people. The light shines the Way in the
darkness, and the darkness did not overcome it.*

—Gospel of John 1:1–5 (my rendering)

The Mystery of the Way

This is the mystery of the Word, of the Way, and of my awakening. I
was born in 1955 and grew up in a small New England town, the fifth
of ten children in a working-class American Baptist minister's family.
Nobody I knew was an admitted mystic, yet there were detailed descriptions of mystical experiences in the Bible. It fascinated me. It seemed
to me that the spiritual Way Jesus and his followers taught began as a
first-century, mystical form of Judaism.

The first followers of Jesus Christ were simply called the followers of the Way. There is a deep psychospiritual teaching in Jesus's
commands to "sleep not" and "awake, for you know not the hour,"
and his proclamation that "the Kingdom of God is within." I devoured
mystics' writings, beginning by examining the ancient mystic roots of

Christianity. I particularly focused on the miracles of Jesus Christ, in pursuit of the miraculous and seeking transcendence and spiritual awakening.

After the 70 CE destruction of Jerusalem and the scattering of the Jews into the Diaspora, this emerging religious tradition thrived in urban centers throughout the eastern Mediterranean. But by the second century, the religion became more organized, with bishops, priests, and deacons, and it focused more on liturgical forms and formalities. This led some mystics to seek to experience the spiritual Way taught by Jesus in monastic communities or hermitages. In the second century, Jewish and Christian mystics had a reluctant parting of the Way, becoming separate religions, but both would always draw from the same living waters.

Growing up, it seemed to me that the Roman Catholics still venerated mystics in their cults of the saints and practice of pilgrimage and penance. And I was fascinated by the Desert Fathers, known as saints of solitude. One of the earliest was Antony of Egypt (251–356), who at age twenty fled a life of wealth and luxury to live in tombs carved out of caves. He took very literally Jesus's comment to the rich young man in the Gospel of Matthew: "If you want to be perfect, go and sell everything you have and give the money to the poor."

Antony devoted his life to loving God, fasting for days, eating only bread and water, often praying through the night, and practicing spiritual exercises that opened his heart to the divine mystery. His biographers said he fought devils and wild beasts, waging a silent, solitary battle for his soul that lasted twenty years before emerging victorious and awakened to the love of God and all humanity. His solitary pilgrimage became a model for Christian mystical wisdom teachers. When I read about him, I deeply admired him. He is considered the father of Christian monasticism, with many devoted disciples. I wondered what it might be like to become a Christian mystic like him.

In high school, I began to discover other spiritual adventurers. Perhaps the most famous—or perhaps the most notorious—spiritual pilgrim in the beginning of the twentieth century was the rascal sage George Ivanovich Gurdjieff. Gurdjieff's spiritual curiosity led him to travel over decades to central Asia, Egypt, Iran, India, Tibet, Russia, and Rome. He taught his followers how to attain unity of body, mind, and spirit such that they could awaken, as if from a hypnotic sleep, to transcend to a higher state of consciousness. He called this discipline the Work or the Method, but most mystics simply call it the Way.

His disciple P. D. Ouspensky described the Work as a journey seeking the miraculous. In his master work, *Tertium Organum*, Ouspensky explored the mystic teachings of Immanuel Kant's idealism, transcendentalism, and concepts of space and time; the mathematical basis of being; the eternal now; the core teachings of Indian philosophy; reality and illusion; dimensionality; the limits of our perception; and the possibility of psychospiritual transformation.

Three generations after these spiritual adventurers, I would embark on a similar journey of becoming. Initially, I journeyed only through the word, using my imagination and my reading. Eventually, I would travel widely with mystics in many religious traditions. To understand these mystics' realities, I needed to understand the mystic roots of my own religion of birth and then travel outside and beyond that foundation. Only then could I explore the mystic teachings of the world's major wisdom traditions. Traveling as a spiritual pilgrim, I set out on the Way.

The Way is a mystery. The key to discerning a mystery, as any spiritual detective knows, is to understand the context and perspective within which the mystery unfolds. So, on my spiritual journey from rational Christianity to mystical awakening, I began with Judaism and the early Christianity described in the Bible. I developed a love affair with early Christian mystics. And when I later discovered Islam, the third Abrahamic faith, it led me even further back into the mists of time, to understand the Zoroastrian roots of all Abrahamic faiths. That became the key to understanding the interreligious roots of the mystics I followed.

Roots of Faith

One of the earliest historically validated messengers of God was a young Persian priest named Zoroaster (also known as Zarathustra) born in the late seventh century BCE. He is often claimed to be much more ancient, because his followers recorded their sacred texts in an archaic form of the Indo-Iranian language, similar to the archaic Sanskrit of the Rig Veda in India. This gives his message an atmosphere of greater antiquity. He seems to have preached and taught in Babylon during the final years of the Babylonian Empire in the early sixth century BCE.

Zoroaster taught about the eternal battle between good and evil, humanity's free will to choose, an individual judgment at the end of each person's life leading to heaven or hell, and bodily resurrection in paradise at the end of time. He opposed polytheism, animal sacrifice, ritualized religious services, the use of hallucinogenic plants in religious rituals, and any oppressive class system that privileged the rich and powerful.

When the Persian king Cyrus the Great conquered Babylon in 538 BCE, he adopted Zoroastrianism as the Persian state religion, which it would remain for the next thousand years. This also impacted what would become Judaism—many decades earlier, the Babylonians had conquered Jerusalem and taken the Judean elite in exile to Babylon. There the Judeans lived, strangers in a strange land, under Zoroastrian culture and religion for three generations.

In the Hebrew Bible, Second Chronicles tells of how the Jewish people came to be. The book ends with King Cyrus claiming to be the world's savior, saying, "The LORD, the God of heaven, has given me all the kingdoms of the earth, and he has charged me to build him a house at Jerusalem, which is in Judah." Cyrus sent what would become the Jewish people home to build a new house of God.

Writing in the middle of the sixth century BCE, after his own epiphany of the divine mystery, the Jewish prophet known to scholars today as Deutero-Isaiah (second Isaiah) seems to have absorbed many Zoroastrian teachings into the proto-Jewish faith. Yahweh's claim in Isaiah 44:6 that "I am the first and I am the last, besides me there is no god" is the first statement of monotheism in the entire Hebrew Bible. This becomes foundational to postexilic Judaism and subsequently the other two great Abrahamic faiths: Christianity and Islam. The Abrahamic faiths all appear to have at least some roots in Zoroastrianism.

Zoroaster seems to have been the first prophet to use I AM for what God calls himself. In the Avesta, God says, "I AM the Creator, I AM the Sustainer, I AM the Discerner, I AM the Beneficent." In fact, the Jewish book of Leviticus, revealed shortly after the Jews returned from Babylonian exile, looks very similar to a Zoroastrian liturgical sacrifice manual. I AM—as a name for the divine, as a tool for understanding your own Thouness, or as the spark of the divine within each of us—would become the mystic discipline for awakening to the nature of the divine mystery.

The Gospel of John appears to clearly identify Jesus as the world savior portrayed in Second Isaiah when it has him claim: "I AM the bread of life," "I AM the light of the world," "I AM the resurrection and the life," "I AM the Way, the Truth, and the Life." The synoptic Gospels even recount some of Jesus's travels to Zoroastrian religious centers such as Tyre and Sidon, in what is now Lebanon, and Greco-Roman religious centers such as Caesarea Philipi and the Decapolis. Jesus taught in a very diverse religious culture with strong influences from the surrounding Zoroastrian areas comprising modern Syria, Jordan, and Iran.

Western European Mystics

I went on to study at Yale, where I had many misadventures that ultimately led me to true love. Loretta and I have been together now for over forty years. My misadventures also led to my spending a fifth year at Yale to rewrite my senior thesis. During this time, I studied the mystics in Sterling Memorial Library. This is how I learned to love God as a mystic and to love mystic descriptions of the Way. I would carry this understanding of the divine mystery into my mystic's quest.

The Desert Fathers' mystical devotion to loving God spread across Western Christianity in the beginning of the second millennium. Then Christianity saw a resurrection and renewal of mysticism, with one of the most extraordinary teachers being Bernard of Clairvaux (1090–1153). Born to French nobility, Bernard joined a small Cistercian monastery in Burgundy at age seventeen while mourning his mother's death. Bernard combined Western Christianity's rationality with Eastern Christianity's devotion to divine mystery in order to create a rational mystic's Way to loving and being loved by God.

He wrote, "Love is the fountain of life, and the soul which does not drink from it cannot be called alive." Bernard even entitled his spiritual guide *On Loving God*. In this guide for young monks, he described four degrees of love in relationship to God and ourselves:

1. Loving yourself for your own sake, which is the most selfish kind of love;

2. Loving God for your own benefit, which is the most selfish love of God;

3. Loving God for God's sake alone, which brings us into intimacy with God;

4. Loving yourself as a child of God, which unites us with God through love.

Bernard was a spiritual athlete so respected for his disciplines that three years later, at the age of twenty, he was appointed abbot of a new monastery at Clairvaux. His teaching attracted so many new monks that over the next forty years of his life, Bernard founded seventy more Cistercian monasteries. Another hundred were founded by his followers during his lifetime.

He also wrote the Primitive Rule for the Knights Templar, the new monastic military order. The Knights Templar took monastic vows, fought in the Crusades, and swore to defend the Holy Land militarily. I would come to love and seek out stories of the Knights Templar.

After Yale, I attended Harvard Business School, married Loretta, and joined Bain and Company as an international management consultant. They relocated us to London, where our daughter was born. They then taught me German so I could help found a German office for Bain. So, at the age of twenty-seven, I was living and working in Munich, West Germany, with Loretta and our thirteen-month-old daughter. I was earning more than I had ever imagined I would earn, working a crazy, stressful job. Having grown up poor and now happily married to Loretta, the daughter of well-educated Chinese immigrants, I was enjoying the good life in Europe. But something was missing. I was feeling a shallowness in my spiritual journey. I felt a call to pilgrimage.

I resumed my study of medieval European Christian mystics, beginning with Hildegard of Bingen (1098–1179), a Benedictine abbess who revolutionized Christian mysticism in Germany. Descended from German nobility, Hildegard experienced visions from an early age and recorded twenty-six of them in her book *Scivias*, which is short for *Scito vias Domini*, or "know the ways of the Lord." In one, she describes "a fiery light, flashing intensely, coming from the open vault of heaven and poured through my whole brain. Like a flame that is hot without burning, it kindled my heart and . . . suddenly I could understand." This is a mystic's description of awakening to the nature of divine mystery. It felt far more exciting and meaningful than traditional worship services to me.

About that same time, Francis of Assisi (1182–1226), the mystic who founded the Franciscan order of monks, also had dreams and visions following a grave illness. Born to a wealthy Italian family, he heard the voice of God commanding him to repair the church, God's house. Like Antony of Egypt, he renounced all his worldly goods and practiced extreme spiritual austerities. Yet he was known to his friends and followers for his amazing joy in life.

Francis was a Christian nature mystic, as can be clearly seen in his most famous prayer, Canticle of the Sun:

Be praised, my Lord, for all your creatures,
And first for brother sun, who makes the day bright

and luminous.
And he is beautiful and radiant, with great
*   splendor,*
He is the image of you, Most High.

Be praised, my Lord, for sister moon and the stars,
In the sky you have made them brilliant and
*   precious and beautiful.*
Be praised, my Lord, for brother wind and for the
*   air both cloudy and serene,*
And every kind of weather, through which you give
*   nourishment to your creatures.*

Be praised, my Lord, for sister water,
Who is very useful and humble and precious and
*   chaste.*
Be praised, my Lord, for brother fire, through whom
*   you illuminate the night.*
And he is beautiful and joyous and robust and
*   strong.*

Be praised, my Lord, for our sister, mother earth,
Who nourishes us and watches over us
And brings forth various fruits with colored flowers
*   and herbs . . .*
Praise and bless my Lord and give thanks to him
*   and serve him with great humility.*

Lastly, I fell deeply in love with Meister Eckhart (1260–1328). Slightly later and more scholarly than Francis, Eckhart would preach some of German Christianity's most mystical sermons on the divine mystery and the love of God. He was the prior of the Dominican monastery at Erfurt, a professor of sacred theology in Paris and then Cologne, and the Roman Catholic vicar general for Bohemia. Yet he too was a nature mystic, now remembered more for his moving mystical writings than for his administration or theology.

> *When I was the stream, when I was the forest, when I*
> *was still a field,*
> *When I was every hoof, foot, fin, and wing, when I was*
> *the sky itself,*
> *No one ever asked me did I have a purpose,*
> *No one ever wondered was there anything I might*
> *need,*
> *For there was nothing I could not love.*
>
> *It was when I left all we once were that the agony*
> *began,*
> *The fear and questions came, and I wept, I wept.*
> *And tears I had never known before.*
> *So I returned to the river, I returned to the mountains.*
>
> *I asked for their hand in marriage again, I begged,*
> *I begged to wed every object and creature, and when*
> *they accepted,*
> *God was ever present in my arms. And he did not say,*
> *"Where have you been?"*
> *For then I knew my soul—every soul—has always held*
> *Him.*

Mystics at Religious Borders

Through my reading and meditation, I discovered that the most interesting mystics were often those practicing interreligious mysticism, drawing upon two or more religious traditions simultaneously.

The mystics of central Europe drew upon Christian as well as Sufi disciplines, from which Eastern Orthodox mysticism emerges. The German mystics Hildegard of Bingen and Meister Eckhart drew upon

German nature mysticism as well as Christianity to create a distinctive form of northern European Volk (people's) mysticism. Francis of Assisi in Italy and Brother Lawrence in France, both veterans of Mediterranean wars of religion, created an ecstatic southern European form of mysticism.

But perhaps most distinctive were the mystics of Mozarabic Spain, drawing upon Jewish, Moorish, and Christian practices to create an intimate union with God. These mystic saints of the Way were Teresa of Ávila and Saint John of the Cross.

Following a prolonged illness, Teresa of Ávila (1515–1582), a young Carmelite nun, wrote of her direct experience of profound mystical raptures and dwelling in the divine mystery. In her autobiography, she said one day she was walking down a hallway when her eyes fell upon a statue of Jesus, and his abiding love for her through her own inconstancy broke her heart open. Gently but powerfully, Jesus taught her to love God and to recognize that our souls are part of God. She wrote of this experience in lyric poetry:

> *We bloomed in spring. Our bodies are leaves of God.*
> *The apparent seasons of life and death our eyes can*
> *   suffer;*
> *But our souls, dear, I will just say this forthright:*
> *They are God Himself, we will never perish unless*
> *   He does.*

Over the years, Teresa reformed the Carmelite order and founded fourteen new monasteries that she helped administer. Her superiors insisted she write spiritual guides for these new Carmelite sisters, so Teresa wrote three books: her autobiography, then *The Way of Perfection*, and finally *The Interior Castle*. These are among the finest guides for Christian mystics.

Ultimately, nothing separated Teresa from God. She wrote:

> *God dissolved my mind – my separation.*
> *I cannot describe now my intimacy with Him.*
> *How dependent is your body's life on water and*
> *   food and air?*

I said to God, "I will always be unless you cease to be,"
And my Beloved replied, "And I would cease to Be if
    you died."

Teresa was in her early fifties and at the height of her spiritual power and insight when John of the Cross (1542–1591), a twenty-five-year-old Carmelite friar, met her and became her closest friend. Just like Teresa's family, his family were conversos—Jews who had been forced to become Christians—though his mother also seems to have been of Moorish descent. Some of Teresa and John's shared sense of intimacy with God reflects Jewish and Sufi mysticism as well.

Five years later, John became the priestly confessor for the convent in Ávila, of which Teresa was now the prioress. Teresa and John spent many hours together, exchanging spiritual poetry in their shared love of God. John wrote, "I did not have to ask my heart what it wanted, because of all the desires I have ever known, just one did I cling to, for it is the essence of all desire: to hold beauty in my soul's arms." John practiced fasts and other established physical spiritual practices, such as beatings and whippings, to try to transcend his mortal body.

From Saint John, I would learn to endure the dark night of the soul. John joined in Teresa's work of reforming the Carmelite order. But jealous church authorities kidnapped John and imprisoned him for nine months in a small, windowless cell with a ceiling so low he couldn't stand up straight. It was from this experience that he wrote some of his finest spiritual poetry, including his instructions on encountering the dark night of the soul:

> *My soul is a candle that burned away the veil;*
> *Only the glorious duties of light I now have.*
> *The sufferings I knew initiated me into God.*
> *I am a holy confessor for men.*

> *When I see their tears running down their cheeks*
> *And falling into His hands,*

What can I say to their great sorrow
That I too have known.

The soul is a candle that will burn away the
darkness,
Only the glorious duties of love we will have.
The sufferings I knew initiated me into God.
Only his glorious cares I now have.

After escaping from his prison cell and returning to teaching male
Carmelite novices, he wrote *Ascent of Mount Carmel,* a series of
prose commentaries on his poetry, explaining the mystic journey to
help seekers of the Way on their spiritual pilgrimage. He wrote:
If you want, the Virgin will come walking down the
road pregnant with the holy, and say,
"I need shelter for the night, please take me inside
your heart, my time is so close."

Then, under the roof of your soul, you will witness
the sublime intimacy, the divine,
The Christ taking birth forever, as she grasps your
hand for help,
For each of us is the midwife of God, each of us.

Yet there, under the dome of your being does
creation come into existence eternally,
Through your womb, dear pilgrim—the sacred
womb of your soul,
As God grasps our arms for help; for each of us is
His beloved servant never far.

If you want, the Virgin will come walking down the
street pregnant with Light and sing . . .

These mystics fascinated me. Yet through my reading and my own mystical experiences, I knew I had found only a small Christocentric window into the divine mystery's role in human flourishing. I suspected there was much more that mystics knew from their own experience of the divine mystery. I began to devour sacred texts from many other spiritual traditions: the Upanishads, the Bhagavad Gita, the *Dhammapada,* the I Ching, and the Tao Te Ching. I felt ready to more deeply explore interreligious spirituality. I wanted to see more of the world and experience it more deeply.

Hindu Mystics

So, in the summer of 1983, I resigned from my wonderful but stressful position at Bain and Company, and they offered me a transition package that allowed me and my wife to purchase round-the-world air tickets and head off for our first interreligious spiritual journey. I was an aspiring mystic traveling with a family. Thus began the first of my many spiritual pilgrimages. It set my expectations for traveling as a pilgrim and pursuing a long, hard journey along a spiritual path toward awakening and human flourishing.

In August 1983, we embarked on our pilgrimage. We started our trip by driving through Liechtenstein and Switzerland, then flew to Bombay (now Mumbai). After years of reading and studying, I was eager to explore Hinduism, the world's third largest religion, in India.

Lord Krishna, the face of the divine mystery in the Bhagavad Gita, presents himself to Hindus in many human forms, including a baby, a mischievous child, a mother, a friend, a lover, a divine ruler, and a being supremely transcending all these identities. Female Hindu mystic Mirabai of Jodhpur (1498–1546) even goes so far as to say, "God has a special interest in women, for they can lift this world to their breast and help Him comfort." God wants to comfort us like a mother nursing her child. This was a new aspect of the divine for me.

In a Daniel Ladinsky translation, Mirabai uses very explicit and coarse language to advise women to be cautious in embracing the love of the divine, because it requires complete surrender.

Girls, think twice before inviting God near.
His charms will turn you into a slave—are you ready
   for such
a wonderful bondage?

Everyone may think you are worshipping a mirage.

And what if God asked you to give all your gold
   bangles
and fine cloths to the next
beggar you see?

Giving God our body to shape is one thing,
for this can excite us,

but when our jewelry and silk are at risk,
surely it is time to seriously ask,

is all this God stuff—
real?

The divine mystery is awesome and inexplicable. The Hindu mystics' concept of intimate union with the divine felt different to me than Christian concepts. But as I went deeper into the mystic, I left my childhood faith further and further behind. I engaged with mystics in multiple traditions. Along the way, I found ecstatic joy, love, and intimacy with the divine mystery.

Kabir (1440–1518), another Hindu mystic and poet contemporary with Mirabai, wrote (also in a Ladinsky translation):

If I told the truth about God, you might think I was an idiot.
If I lied to you about the Beautiful One
You might parade me through the streets shouting,
*   "This guy is a genius!"*

The world has its pants on backwards.
Most carry their values and knowledge in a jug that
*   has a big hole in it.*
Thus having a clear grasp of the situation if I am asked
*   anything these days I just laugh!*

On my spiritual journey, I encountered the ancient Hindu Vedas and could not help but notice that all 114 hymns of the ninth book of the Rig-Veda speak of the power of Soma, a mystical drink that can bring humans feelings of immortality, at least for a moment. It led me to consider the possibility that hallucinogenic plants and potions could be important accelerators of certain kinds of mystical experiences.

We have drunk Soma, have become immortal,
Gone to the light have we, the gods discovered.
What can hostility do against us?
What, O Immortal One, mortal man's fell purpose?

Joy to our heart be thou, when drunk, O Indu [highest
*   god],*
Like father to a son, most kind, O Soma;
Thoughtful like friend to friend, O thou of wide fame,
Prolong our years that we may live, O Soma . . .

Ailments have fled away, diseases vanished,
The powers of darkness have become affrighted.
With might hath Soma mounted up within us;
The dawn we've reached, where men renew existence.

I had eagerly read the ancient lessons for soul liberation in the Upanishads, which traditionally were delivered only orally from master to student. I was eager to see how people lived these lessons in practice in late twentieth-century India. Finally, I had meditated long and earnestly on the Bhagavad Gita, the epic poem on the meaning of human life.

I had been introduced to the Upanishads by my brilliant high school English teacher a decade before. I knew these meditation guides to individual enlightenment had aided many seekers on the path, and now I wanted to travel to where they had been inspired. As the Kena Upanishad teaches:

> *Rising above the senses and the mind, and*
> *renouncing separate existence, the wise realize*
> *the deathless Self.*
> *The divine mystery our eyes cannot see nor do*
> *words express.*
> *It cannot be grasped by the mind.*
> *We do not know, we cannot understand . . . thus we*
> *have heard from the illumined ones.*

I accepted the Hindu notion that the yoga, or path of knowledge and wisdom, is the shortest route to divine realization, though it's also the steepest, requiring a combination of reason, spiritual practice, and divine intuition.

I was ready to immerse myself in the Hindu mystic experience when we touched down in Bombay. After a few days, we went on to New Delhi and then the Taj Mahal. It felt like stepping into another world in India. There was deep joy but also deep sorrow. We were startled by the enormous poverty, learning that mothers sometimes maimed their children so they would be more sympathetic and successful as street beggars.

Beggars were everywhere. Our taxi driver told us the street beggars weren't really hungry and we shouldn't give them any money, but

Loretta would roll down the window and offer the crackers she had for our daughter. Sometimes the crackers were rejected, perhaps proving our driver right. But other times, children hungrily grabbed at the crackers and consumed them desperately. We were deeply saddened by the extent of the poverty and its impact on human flourishing.

With its strong sounds and smells, traveling in India was like stepping into a very different way of being human. Hinduism does not attempt to change our life circumstances so much as change the way we experience those circumstances. It is a religion of harmony in the midst of change, adaptation to the world as it is, and finding peace in the midst of turbulence. The divine is in everything, so there is nothing that is not holy, not even poverty.

In his book *Meeting God*, cultural anthropologist Stephen Huyler says, "Hinduism is a religion of ultimate individuality and personal choice. Both good and evil are believed to be of God, and the purpose of most rituals is to maintain a balance between such opposites: creation and destruction, light and dark, masculine and feminine. For the Hindu, as every aspect of existence has a purpose, human meaning involves a fundamental sense of duty and conscientious accountability." On our journey, we were immediately plunged into this phantasmagorical way of being human. Great joy often shines forth, only following great sorrow.

The deeply moving philosophical teachings of the Upanishads and Bhagavad Gita had not prepared me for the poverty and despair of this enormous postcolonial country. In these overcrowded cities, with their beggars and desperate poverty, I tried mightily to reconcile sensation-rich India with its material poverty. I failed miserably.

In 1983, India offered much to see, but the wisdom for my path was not yet apparent to me. I would return thirty years later, older and wiser, and have better luck.

Buddhist Mystics

Despite its beginnings in India, Buddhism now seemed mostly absent there—at least in 1983, by our observation. So we flew next to Kathmandu in Nepal, where a form of Buddhism was very much alive.

Buddhism blazed forth as a spiritual fire from the poorest and most remote parts of India 2,600 years ago. Over the millennia, Buddhism emerged in many forms across very different cultures. The dominant form of Buddhism in the world today is Mahayana Buddhism, the so-called greater vehicle that seeks the enlightenment of all sentient beings. Theravada Buddhism, the so-called lesser vehicle, helps Buddhist monks achieve enlightenment in this lifetime. This tradition is strongest in Southeast Asia. In my studies, I also began to understand the similarities and differences between Tibetan, or Tantric, Buddhism, which retains a shamanic folk tradition; Chinese Ch'an Buddhism, with its strong Taoist flavor; and its descendent Japanese Zen Buddhism, which offers seekers a direct path to enlightenment. Many paths; all are one.

All forms of Buddhism can be traced to Siddhartha Gautama's awakening and his vow to awaken all sentient beings. Siddhartha Gautama (circa 563–483 BCE) was a minor prince of the Shakya clan at the foot of the Himalayas, an area that today represents the border between Nepal and India. He achieved enlightenment through meditation in what is now Bihar province in India, and then taught his Middle Way to awakening for all with ears to hear. He taught the four noble truths and the noble eightfold path to awakening (here translated by Thanissaro Bhikkhu from the Samyutta Nikaya):

> *Just this noble eightfold path: right view, right*
> *aspiration, right speech, right action, right*
> *livelihood, right effort, right mindfulness, right*
> *concentration. This is the ancient path, the ancient*
> *road, traveled by the Rightly Self-Awakened Ones*
> *of former times. I followed that path.*

Following it, I came to direct knowledge of aging & death,
direct knowledge of the origination of aging & death,
direct knowledge of the cessation of aging & death,
direct knowledge of the path leading to the cessation of
aging & death. I followed that path.
Following it, I came to direct knowledge of birth . . .
becoming . . . clinging . . . craving . . . feeling . . .
contact . . . the six sense media . . . name and
form . . . consciousness, direct knowledge of the
origination of consciousness, direct knowledge of
the cessation of consciousness, direct knowledge of
the path leading to the cessation of consciousness. I
followed that path.

I experienced an archaic form of enlightenment within the truly breath-taking Himalayan landscape. I was fascinated by the embodied and sensual nature of the Tantric path into divine mystery. This was intimate knowledge of God through meditation. The passion and joy with which young monks continuously twirled their prayer cylinders and rattles, walking barefoot through the streets with a constant chant in their mouths, was extraordinarily compelling. The Buddhist prayer wheels for continuous praying were everywhere honored and omnipresent.

Even I could perhaps find enlightenment in such a setting, but I would first have to learn to guide myself. As the Dhammapada teaches:

Learn what is right, then teach others, as the wise do.
Before trying to guide others, be your own guide first.
It is hard to learn to guide oneself.

However, enlightenment was not yet to be for one so young, so ambitious, and so spiritually immature. I was a novice on this spiritual path. As the Dhammapada warns the immature seeker:

The immature who know they are immature have a
little wisdom.

But the immature who look on themselves as wise
are utterly foolish.
They cannot understand the dharma even if they
spend their whole life with the wise.
How can the spoon know the taste of soup?
If the mature spend even a short time with the wise,
they will understand dharma,
Just as the tongue knows the taste of soup.

And so I embarked upon what would become my lifelong journey toward spiritual maturity.

Nirvana Interlude

After Nepal, we went to the Maldives, an archipelagic nation in the Indian Ocean. We were in heaven. In 1983, there was no more beautiful place on earth. Our resort was on a small island. From our bed, we had a 180-degree view of the ocean with its constantly changing colors.

After lunch, our daughter could toddle across our short stretch of beach to feed the tropical fish. They would swim up and nibble bread out of her hand. We played in the sand and the surf, we ate well, we slept well, and we had our souls restored. Sometimes just being at rest, at peace, can roughly replicate the equanimity of enlightenment. For two very young, overscheduled, and overstressed householders, this felt like nirvana. Such bliss!

A German diving guide taught me how to scuba dive with sharks. That drew upon my competitive and risk-taking nature. I swam with sharks, though not without trepidation.

Stepping away from working so intensely helped me learn how to breathe again, to awaken to a sunrise and glory in the sunset, to appreciate a simple meal well prepared, and to dwell within the circle of love of my wife and daughter. I began to learn how to surrender to whatever life had to offer, to fully immerse myself in life, and to be grateful for it. In spiritual pilgrimage my mystic nature began to blossom and bloom.

Chinese Mystics

Next, we flew to Hong Kong and visited the tourist sights of this impressive former British colonial trading capital. It was in Hong Kong that I first learned how China often distinguishes six faiths: Confucianism, Taoism, Buddhism, Catholicism, Protestantism, and Islamism. All of these were in 1983 officially discouraged as superstitions, carefully regulated by the state, and often practiced only in secret.

I vowed to one day come back to study with the Chinese mystics, particularly the seemingly inscrutable Taoists and the austere Zen and Ch'an Buddhists. The instant enlightenment theoretically offered by Japanese Zen teachers held great appeal for me.

Ever since I'd first read D. T. Suzuki's *Introduction to Zen Buddhism* in college, with its foreword and affirmation by Dr. Carl Jung, I had dreamed of practicing the path of Zen, of becoming, as the Buddha described, a rightly self-awakened one. I had an earnest desire to awaken, though without seeking a particular teacher, community, or doctrine. It would require tremendous spiritual discipline over an extended period of time. I set my heart upon that journey.

Traveling on to mainland China, we joined a China Travel Service tour. We entered another world, another reality. Foreigners traveling in China were still quite restricted in the 1980s, but through the travel service we were able to visit the major tourist sites.

When we went to Shanghai, our tour guide helped connect us with Loretta's aunt. Loretta's maternal grandfather had been a capitalist in Shanghai. Loretta's mother grew up surrounded by luxury. As the Communist insurgents overturned the Nationalist government, Loretta's grandfather took precautions. He sent his son and wife, with some of his readily liquid assets, to live in Taiwan in case he needed to flee the Communists. He sent his two middle daughters, including Loretta's mom, to be educated in Catholic schools in America. These two daughters could build a life in America in case even Taiwan fell. This is how my wife came to be born in Butte, Montana. Her father was from a very rural part of China, with an engineering degree from Columbia, and her mother had an MBA from New York University. Loretta's maternal grandfather kept his youngest daughter with him in Shanghai to care for him. When the government fell, he was moved to a small apartment, and the family's mansion turned into housing for eight families. It was this aunt we would finally meet.

Before we departed Germany, Loretta had asked her mother what we should bring her aunt, who was now married to the chief engineer at a Shanghai chemical plant. They had two children somewhat younger than Loretta. Her mom said to take fifteen new US $20 bills and present them upon first meeting her aunt. For us, it was relatively insignificant; for them, it was about six months' income.

When we rang the doorbell for their tiny apartment, Loretta's aunt quickly answered with great joy at meeting her niece for the first time, along with her niece's husband and baby. Loretta spoke minimal Mandarin, learned in one year of intensive Chinese-language classes at Yale, but fortunately her aunt remembered her English.

Loretta presented the cash gift at the front door. Her aunt deftly stuffed half the bills into her bra before she turned around to her husband and children to essentially say, "See how generous my rich niece and her husband are!"

We had long conversations over Shanghai Chinese cooking. They took us to the old family mansion and showed us where Loretta's mother had gone to school under Catholic nuns before leaving for the United States. Loretta's mother had hated Catholic school, thought poorly of white people in general, and had little or no use for Christianity or its beliefs. As an immigrant to America, she was disdainful of American Christianity and was a confirmed atheist. We got the impression the government discouraged religious expression in Communist China.

Heading Homeward

We ended our seven-week around-the-world pilgrimage with a week relaxing on Hawaii's beaches—another nirvana. Spiritual life seemed particularly diverse on the Hawaiian Islands. Chinese Confucian culture mixed with Japanese Zen Buddhist thought. These were blended with indigenous Polynesian spirituality and an overlay of Christianity brought by the missionaries. All this was surrounded by the hedonistic behavior of sun-worshiping vacationers. When we told the Hawaii Congregational church that I was directly descended from Asa and Lucy Thurston, the missionaries who founded that church, they treated us like long-lost cousins. Clearly, my journey would be synchronistic, involving a lot of interreligious spirituality.

Next, we traveled to California to visit Loretta's mom in Sunnyvale, and then we headed back to Boston to introduce our daughter to America. After two years of urbane and cosmopolitan European living and international travel, we were somewhat apprehensive about returning to our own violent and soul-sick country and its politics.

Yet we had tired of traveling and were eager to return home. We had surrendered ourselves to whatever the world had to offer, and it was far more remarkable than anything we ourselves could have conceived of. The world I had spent so many hours reading and studying about was so much more interesting than I had ever imagined.

Now the question was, what could I learn from these ancient traditions I had experienced on our pilgrimage? How could their spiritual disciplines be useful when adapted to my own journey, to my postmodern pilgrimages in late twentieth- and early twenty-first-century spirituality? Our travels had fixed in my mind a determination to follow my bliss, wherever it might lead. I longed to experience life as a pilgrim, wherever the spirit should lead me.

Interreligious Mysticism
BOOK GROUP DISCUSSION GUIDE

Author's Comment

If you were, as I was, brought up within late twentieth-century American rational Christianity, it can be quite disorienting when first encountering religious mystics. This becomes even more the case when you travel with mystics across religious traditions. It requires a certain suspension of disbelief to hear of mystics' experiences and begin to make sense of how they might impact your own faith.

Questions to Encourage Conversation

1. What do you think of the Christian mystical teachings of Antony of Egypt and the Desert Fathers? Why are they considered doctors of the church?

2. How does your heart respond to Francis of Assisi's or Meister Eckhart's nature mysticism?

3. Would you have liked to be a Carmelite serving under Saint Teresa of Ávila and her spiritual confessor, Saint John of the Cross?

4. How disorienting for you is Mirabai of Jodhpur's intimate talk of God?

5. What do you make of the role of Soma in ancient spiritual techniques?

6. What do you think of the many paths of Buddhist mystics or the distinctive Way of Chinese mystics?

7. Are you in any way attracted to the pilgrim's Way?

Reflection

As a group, reflect upon the mystical paths that might most resonate for you.

UNITARIAN
UNIVERSALIST MYSTICS

Everything that lives is holy. If the doors of perception were cleansed,
everything would appear to man as it is, infinite . . . Matter is holy,
the matrix of existence. Immerse yourself in that ocean, plunge into it
where it is deepest, struggle in its currents. For it cradled you long ago
in your pre-conscious existence, and it can lift you up to God.

—Jacob Trapp, UU minister, *The Light of a Thousand Suns*

Householder Pilgrim

Everything that lives is holy when we perceive it as such, swimming deep within the ocean of cosmic consciousness, being nursed on the bosom of God. This is the perennial philosophy and journey of the spiritual mystic within Unitarian Universalism as much as any other mystic faith. However, because of our religious tradition, Unitarian Universalist mystics follow the path of reason into mystery, embracing the wonder in all religions and accepting that all human beings are capable of experiencing God's love, however they may conceive of it.

We moved to Concord, Massachusetts, in early 1986 and joined the First Parish Concord Unitarian Universalist church. I began to teach in their religious education program. Mindful of the four Hindu stages of life—student, warrior, householder, and sage—I was passionately engaged with the householder stage.

As my meditation became increasingly transcendentalist, my spiritual pilgrimages became quite local, mostly around Concord and Walden Pond. I spent my spiritual energy paddling on the Concord and Assabet Rivers, but my work life and home life took precedence over further exotic spiritual pilgrimages, confining me to local journeys of the spirit. However, I did continue my study of diverse mystic ways into divine mystery, and I continued to mature as a spiritual being.

One of my favorite short pilgrimages during this period was to a very conservative Roman Catholic monastery in Still River, Massachusetts. Affiliated with the Benedictines, they followed a medieval monastic schedule, singing Gregorian chants at their seven short worship services each day. As part of the First Parish adult programs, we created a spiritual support group for men seeking recovery of our lost selves. I led several retreats at this beautifully rural monastery. We participated in the monks' worship services from dawn to dusk, attending workshops and taking walking meditations in between.

I remember one winter weekend workshop in particular. Our group was trying to cover some fairly deep and complicated material on Sunday morning, with a plan to join the monks for worship and lunch before heading back to Concord. The local Catholic bishop was visiting the monastery and would be attending worship and lunch as well, so the monks were very busy.

It had snowed quite heavily the night before, and we were hoping the roads would be plowed and cleared by lunchtime. I rushed through our material in order to give the men enough time to pack, clear the snow off their cars, and be ready to leave immediately following lunch.

But when we broke from our workshop, we discovered the monks had taken time from their meditations to clean the snow off all our cars. I expressed my surprise to the guest master, and he said simply, "Christ stayed here last night, and we wished to clear the snow from his cars to speed him on his way." This was the true spirit of Jesus Christ.

This is living in the perpetual presence of God, which became one of my core spiritual practices. This practice was best represented by Brother Lawrence (1614–1691), a modest Catholic monk in seventeenth-century France. He was born Nicholas Herman to peasant parents in Lorraine, France. Family poverty forced him to join the army, but in the midst of war, his mystical visions created an alternate reality for his day-to-day living. He encountered God daily through practicing God's presence.

His biographer wrote: "In the deep of winter, Herman looked at a barren tree, stripped of leaves and fruit, waiting silently and patiently for the sure hope of summer abundance. Gazing at the tree, Herman grasped for the first time the extravagance of God's grace and the unfailing sovereignty of divine providence. Like the tree, he himself was seemingly dead, but God had life waiting for him, and the turn of the seasons would bring fullness." Injured in combat, he was released by the army. He spent some time working as a footman for a wealthy family, but then he joined a Carmelite monastery in Paris as Brother Lawrence.

Through deep meditation, Brother Lawrence centered his heart upon God such that the love of God made every last detail of his life surpassing bliss. He ran errands, cooked meals, scrubbed pots, and did the simplest tasks, all in the presence of God, making him a model for beloved mystics ever since. In his *Spiritual Maxims,* published late in his life, Brother Lawrence says, "I began to live as if there were no one save God and me in the world."

I too began to live in the presence of divine mystery. Here I offer a passage from one of my early journals to illustrate living as a spiritual pilgrim while fully engaged as an entrepreneur and householder. This entry is from August 1, 1995:

> It was early in the morning, with the diffuse predawn light the only indication that it was no longer night. I was driving to the airport along the as-yet-lightly traveled roads, headed for the first flight out of Boston to Detroit in time for me to chair a 9:30 a.m. board-of-directors meeting in Ann Arbor, Michigan. But for

now, all that mattered was life renewed as the sun
was preparing to arise in the east.

I opened my car window to feel the morning air. It was cool and comforting. I knew that it
would be hot and humid later in the day, and the
day would be tense and full, but for now I cherished
the cool darkness. The earth was quiet, except for
the rhythmic pulse of my car's engine beating in
syncopation with my heart. As the sun began to
peek above the horizon, birds broke out in song as
if on cue. (Sunrise, cue the birds.) Nature sprang
to life as the long day began. I was a part of this
emergent nature. I knew this in my heart, and it
gave me peace.

As I passed the nearby reservoir, heavy clouds
of mist clung to the still water's surface—the water giving back its accumulated heat of the previous day in great swirls of mist that looked like dry
ice melting. Through this lingering mist, I saw a
group of ducks going about their morning chores.

I didn't know why or when, but I had chosen
this lifestyle. It seems I was forever getting up too
early and too frequently on my way to catch the early
plane. Nothing in my upbringing would have defined this as the good life. Perhaps most people still
would not today.

But I have always felt a need to succeed, to be
wealthy, and to leave my mark on this life. This is
probably, at least partly, my response to growing
up in poverty. By now I have earned a goodly measure of all that I desired, but of course it still required that I sometimes must catch the early plane.
Some mornings, I think it would be easier to turn

back over and snuggle down in the covers when the
alarm goes off. Certainly, the early alarm makes the
nights too short. Yet I am called to passionately live a
life of purpose. This is my life, and I am glad for it.

There never seems to be time anymore for that
comfortable haze between sleeping and waking, or
waking gently and rested without the need for an
alarm clock. Instead, it's getting up before the sun
to shower and shave in the predawn darkness, trying hard not to disturb my wife's slumber. She will
need her rest later for the demands of her work and
the children, who sleep now so peacefully. I am often
alone with the morning. I am alone with God.

As the car tops the rise, I have a panoramic view
of Boston before me. Boston looks sleepy, with the
sun rising in the outer harbor. The traffic becomes
heavier. I now must maneuver through traffic lights
and rotaries. In a few minutes, I will pass through
the tunnel under Boston Harbor and emerge at the
frenetic activity of the early-morning airport.

I know this way by heart. But for a last few minutes, I am alone with the sunrise, my ambitions, and
the birth of a new day. For me to successfully navigate
through a busy day of leadership and conflicting re-
sponsibilities, I must maintain a sense of nonattachment. I am just one small being on this overcrowded
planet, and this planet is just one small speck in the
universe. Yet the wellbeing of the entire planet becomes my spiritual concern. I wish my own wellbeing. I wish your wellbeing. I wish the wellbeing of all
sentient beings. It isn't much, but it is what we have to
work with, and hence it is everything. All will be well.

Nonattachment would become one of my spiritual yoga practices. As Ravi Ravindra writes in *The Wisdom of Patañjali's Yoga Sutras*: "As spiritual searchers we need to become freer of the attachment of our own smallness in which we get occupied with me-me-me. Pondering on large ideas or standing in front of things which remind us of a vast scale can free us from acquisitiveness and competitiveness and from our likes and dislikes . . . recalling our own experiences in which we acted generously or with compassion for the simple delight of it without expectation of any gain can give us more confidence in the existence of a deeper goodness."

Unitarian Universalist Vision Quests

As Unitarian Universalists, we affirm direct experience of that transcending wonder which moves us to renewal of the spirit and an openness to the forces that create and uphold life. So, in order to embody direct experience of transcending wonder, our men's group, like many mystics before us, felt called to the woods.

In our search for direct experiences of meaning, we eventually discovered a small retreat center on a mountain in Vermont. The center was run by Arthur, a retired UU minister, and his wife, Ellen, who had trained with both a Celtic shaman and a Native American mystic. There, we could individually and collectively experience what we came to call a vision quest. We could experience our interior spiritual journeys together while each confronting our own reality alone.

I personally participated in six of these vision quests over seven years, giving them up only after my ordination as a UU minister. My calling to ministry was an outgrowth of these vision quests. Many of the men who came to the center for more than one or two years were similarly transformed, each gradually growing to become more clearly and dearly his truest self as a result of the mystical experiences these quests entailed.

The first vision quest was in August 1998. Eight of us made our way to this Vermont mountain retreat, which we came to call Blessing Wood. We made the several-hour journey together up to the mountain, maximizing our bonhomie and comradeship. It would become a pattern every summer.

I was forty-two at the time, and my spiritual pilgrimages were going deeper. God was calling me to a deeper experience of life. I was excited, even if a little anxious, for this experience. They said Native Americans had performed solo vision quests on this mountain for generations before white settlers came to the mountain.

Upon arrival, we began to prepare ourselves for the ordeal of the next several days. Arthur and Ellen would act as caretakers, guides, and shamans on our inward journey. After preparatory meditation and centering exercises and a simple meal, we slept in rough cabins that first night. We headed to our prepared separate meditation sites at first light in the morning.

That first day, we each picked a site on which to spend the next four days. We would be out of sight of each other, but we would have adequate water, wood for burning, and some simple shelter from the weather. We would have earth, wind, fire, and water enough for four days, but we would go without food until we returned to the base camp. We wanted to be part of nature and embrace it in its fullness.

We discovered early on that our questing was far more successful when we fasted for the entire four days. Our visions became far more colorful and seemingly more meaningful when the glucose levels in our circulating blood dropped to miniscule amounts and our brains shifted over to ketone chemistry to fuel our minds. Please don't ask which perception of reality is more real. Often by the fourth day of each quest, the barrier between self and other would become blurred, opening the possibility of becoming one with all being, resulting in exultations of joy.

Our vision quests were inspired by the desert monastics of early Christianity, by the monastic practices of eastern European Christian monks, and by the shamanic practices of various indigenous peoples, some of whom may even have encountered the divine mystery in this way on this very location in the distant past. Such rite of passages from one way of being in the world to quite another, of learning to live between two worlds, can be disorienting. Deep meditation and fasting alone on a sacred site in nature is a potent force for spiritual awakening.

My prayer commencing this first vision quest was, "Oh Great Spirit, help me know your holy way. I surrender to you my soul, come what may." That first night, I dreamed I was alone on a poorly constructed raft floating down a swiftly flowing river. I passed through forest, then jungle. The river became turbulent as the raft approached a large waterfall, and I lost all control. The raft was utterly destroyed, and I began to drown. As I surrendered to death, the feeling of panic and desperation swept away.

Then, in my dream, I found myself washed ashore on a little beach, deserted and hot. I saw a wise owl and called to it, but it flew away. I followed a small trail that led through the forest to a glade, where there was a little chipmunk. He was full of energy and life, chattering away. But the owl swooped down and killed the chipmunk before flying away with it. I was horrified at the owl's cruel taking of life, yet somehow knew I would eventually befriend it. Life and death were woven finely together.

I awoke from this dream just as the sun was beginning to rise. Feeling deeply disturbed, I climbed to the top of the mountain. The mountain offered majestic views, the morning air was cool and fresh, and mist rose in the valleys. My spirit lifted! A strong, clear voice said to me, "*We all start out in the mist. Some of us use all our energy to conquer mountains, where we can be above others and superior, alone in our barrenness. Pay attention instead to the mists. That is where your salvation lies.*" I understood.

Settling into my vision site later that morning, I marked out the six directions and the boundaries of this small site. I prepared myself for a long, slow process. Arthur had left seasoned wood for me, so I practiced and explored the secrets of fire.

There was a small stream running through the site. The steady, gurgling sound of water over rocks created a syncopated pulse that reflected the rhythm of life. I vowed to try to be more like water, flowing, dropping, eddying, creating a small backwater, and then continuing downstream. Too often, I tried to push the river. Now I would relax and go with the flow.

A particularly gorgeous butterfly landed next to me. It was black, with white dots on its outer wings and blue dots on its lower wings. Since childhood, butterflies have always held a mystic meaning for me. I was at peace with the butterfly, flitting its wings so carelessly in the sun. Later, a dragonfly came to join our little community. It was less showy than the butterfly, but perhaps more purposeful. I could be a dragonfly, or even just a firefly.

A water bug practiced his effortless dancing across the surface tension of the stream. Life is most deeply experienced and lived in the tension on the surface. In the stream was a small fish. He darted between the rocks. The stream sang its multipart harmonies as the little fish struggled to not be swept downstream and over the waterfalls. I was visited at dusk by the frantic fluttering of a small black bat. The world transformed once again from day into night.

Sleeping alone in the wild, even such a domesticated wild as that Vermont hilltop, was a strange and glorious experience. The night was full of sound, yet without sight one can only imagine who or what is making that sound. It was a night full of horror or delight. As Mary Oliver says in her poem "Sleeping in the Forest": "All night I heard the small kingdoms breathing around me, the insects, and the birds who do their work in darkness." I slumbered in their midst.

The next day, I felt more at one with the forest, with its birds, spiders, bugs, with a little red-tailed squirrel. The forest seemed to gradually adapt to me. As I sat naked in the stream with water passing over and around me, a noisy chipmunk visited and made me think of foraging owls. I wondered at the meaning of my vivid dreams. The cool breeze and damp weather brought mosquitos at midday. Butterflies frolicked. I observed tiny flowers, toads, flies. This small piece of forest was teeming with life. I began to laugh and play with Gaia, the Spirit of this forest.

I watched a small worm working away at a decomposing leaf, releasing its substance back to the earth, from which it was borrowed. The worm, the leaf—all manifestations of Gaia. I watched a long, green, articulated centipede climb up the side of a rock, stumble, lose its grip, and tumble back into the dirt. Awkwardly, it fumbled around, twisting and turning its long body, but then it found its bearings and continued on. All of us make such journeys.

Suddenly, a terrified, small black mole, nearly blind, slammed into me, then scurried away. I looked up to see a large, female great horned owl, gray in color and quite majestic for a predator, marking the closing of my second day. What did the mole have to teach me about male helplessness? What could the owl teach me about the power of feminine energy? I had come here to learn. These woods had much to teach me.

When my quest was completed, I returned from the forest tired, hungry, yet prepared to take my life in a new, if uncertain, direction.

Conversations with God

Seven of the eight men returned to Blessing Wood in August 1999. We wanted to see if guided meditation and fasting for more days, within an appropriate sense and setting, could lead to even deeper visions. I also wanted to explore what had led me to commit to raising a third ten-year venture fund for Seaflower Ventures, where I was managing partner, even while enrolling at Andover Newton Theological School (ANTS) for the next five years to become an ordained UU minister. My spiritual journey was becoming far more intense, taking me from being an entrepreneurial venture capitalist into becoming a spiritual catalyst for divine mystery. At age forty-three, life was calling me into new adventures.

We traveled up to Vermont on Sunday and agreed to each spend Monday through Friday at our vision sites, fasting the whole time. We were rational mystics. We had learned from advancing brain chemistry research that fasting—no food, just water—was key to the mystical vision of experiencing oneness with the universe.

I chose a site on the side of a small hill. I marked the six directions and my boundaries, then set up my altar on a low tree stump. I had my meditation candle, some Tibetan incense, and the clay head of a wild-man mystic I had made in high school. I also had a small pup tent, a backpack, water, a change of clothes, and provisions for making a fire.

Sitting under some shade trees, I was deeply enjoying the view over the valley when I heard a large animal wandering in the woods. It noisily thrashed about but stayed well away from me. Many more birds visited and serenaded me than when I was at the river bottom the year before. A hawk circled overhead. Two woodpeckers attacked trees behind me like jackhammers.

Life was abundant here. The site was teeming with it. Every square inch was thick with life—four different kinds of inchworms, three different kinds of flies, and a multitude of bugs, bees, hornets, crickets, and grasshoppers. There was even a hopping, flying little brown bug that looked like a chip of wood. Life is ubiquitous.

Watching the beginnings of a beautiful sunset, I heard young deer in the distance giving their surprised barks and making their rustling way through the thick brush. Only when the sun set did I finally light the fire. As day darkened into night, an owl hooted in the dark.

I had recently learned an ancient Eastern Orthodox Christian prayer: "Lord Jesus Christ, have mercy on me, a sinner." When prayed repeatedly five thousand times or more in a day, it is said that it will yield insight into divine mystery. My Tuesday was devoted to testing this perpetual prayer technique. Using hash marks in my journal to keep track, I prayed this prayer many more than five thousand times before the sun went down.

By midday the next day, I had my first direct epiphany of God. My journal records our conversation as follows:

ME: What do you ask of me?

GOD: To do justice, love kindness, and walk humbly with me.

Me: What may I ask in return?

God: That which is your deepest desire.

Me: And what is that?

God: You must find it for yourself. But it is deeply connected with who you are.

Me: What shall I do with Loretta's and my wealth?

God: Do good works, live responsibly, use it as a tool to free yourself from sin and shortcomings. Do not worship it, but do not waste it either. Use it to make the world a better place, to build community rather than loneliness, to free yourself to be what you were born to be.

Me: Who am I?

God: One of my children.

Me: Lord Jesus Christ, have mercy on me, a sinner.

God: Serve my children.

My heart soared! This experience of epiphany brought forth a hymn of my childhood called "In the Garden":

I come to the garden alone,
while the dew is still on the roses,
and the voice I hear, falling on my ear,
the Son of Man discloses.
And he walks with me, and he talks with me,
and he tells me I am his own,
and the joy we share as we tarry there,
none other has ever known.
He speaks and the sound of his voice
is so sweet the birds stop their singing,
and the melody that he gave to me,
within my heart is ringing.
And he walks with me . . .

My eyes filled with tears of joy, and my heart filled with gratitude. I wrote down these further lessons as I heard them from the divine mystery:

> "When you light a flame, consecrate it, and it will be consecrated."

> "When you eat food, pause to give thanks, and it will do you no harm."

> "When you do good works, dedicate them to God, and you need no other recognition."

> "Behave well toward your wife and children, and you will have goodwill enough for the world."

> "Don't agonize over your shortcomings. You were chosen because you are good enough to do my work. Therefore, you need to be no better than you are."

> "I am with you always."

> "Be not troubled. Be not afraid. Anxieties and mishaps are there to help you become who you are becoming and are an integral part of the unfolding of life in the universe."

This conversation with God went on seemingly for hours, filling my heart and several pages of my spiritual journal. For all that time, the sun seemed to stand still. The sky was clear, then gradually became cloudy. Eventually, it became overcast and threatened rain, and then cleared again. I needed to interrupt our conversation five or six different times to add fresh wood to the fire that damp day. Yet the sun stood unchanged, holding one spot in the sky, while God spoke.

Finally, I found myself incredibly sleepy, so I lay down to take a nap. Upon awakening some time later, the fire was out and the sun had moved markedly across the sky.

It was as if time did not exist during those hours in which I talked with God. Of course, I didn't have a watch or computer with me, so I don't know objectively what happened. But this experience would later plunge me into reading and talking about quantum physics, the nature of the space-time continuum, and the eternal now. We are located within the space-time continuum and subject to its physical laws; God is not. Deep communion with God may be the answer for what seemingly disrupted the space-time continuum in my immediate presence. Or perhaps it just wreaked havoc with my own sense of time. It is all a mystery. Blessed be the mystery.

On Thursday, I practiced the presence of God. Waking in gratitude before dawn, I stretched, enjoying the animal nature of my body. Wildflowers were abundant on the hill. I discovered it is true: you can see the whole universe in a flower.

I needed a time of withdrawal and introspection before embarking on training for ordained ministry at ANTS. This vision quest created that space for me to be alone with God.

Talking to My Dad

Many shamanic traditions, as well as traditional Chinese Confucianism, honor communing with one's ancestors. Communing with the spirits of ancestors is described by mystics in Asian, African, European, Aboriginal Australian, and indigenous North American cultures.

Talking with dead ancestors had never been a big part of my spiritual practice, though. Rhode Island Baptists don't do that—except for one day, when my dead dad decided to show up.

It happened the summer of 2000, when I took a break from my seminary classes to return with the men's group to the woods. The forest made a very nice setting for a retreat. It helped reunite me with the cycles of the earth and all of nature. This year, I was on a hilltop.

I awoke to discover fresh deer tracks passing right through my site. They had visited me in the night. It was an overcast and dreary day. I moved everything that needed to stay dry into my little pup tent. This damp wetness didn't feel particularly uplifting spiritually. Uninspired, I waited out the rain. I tried meditating while sitting on a pack towel but could not concentrate. Rain kept coming down.

I missed my family. I felt foolish. I missed rainy afternoons spent playing cards with my wife and kids. Instead, I was here in the cold and damp. The sun was setting, but I could not see it through the fog. I sat alone, listening to the steady drumming of the rain.

I also missed my father. I was now following him into the path of parish ministry, and he was much on my mind. He had been dead for more than eight years. He'd had a hard life, losing his childhood home in the Great Depression at the age of ten, then having far too many children. He was fired by his church at age thirty-six, nearly died of lymphoma when I was in college, and lived much of his life among the working-class poor.

In the dreariness of the gathering gloom, I experienced a vision of my father. So I spoke with him:

ME: Dad, why did you choose to be a minister?

ED: I didn't actually choose the ministry. It chose me. As you will discover, when God calls, you can procrastinate, you can prevaricate, and you can pontificate, but you will ultimately have no peace until you respond . . . do ministry with an open heart, and there's no telling where it can take you.

ME: Why were your relationships with your children so difficult?

ED: I was a proud man, an educated man, from a very different culture than the one you grew up in. I grew up in the Depression-era Swedish immigrant community. I only felt useful when working. I tried to meet the changing demands of the times. I guess I failed. But most of my children failed to meet me even halfway. Maybe you'll do better with your own children.

ME: What is the experience after death really like?

ED: You'll find out soon enough when you get here. People and societies too focused on the hereafter don't do well with the here and now. You are alive for a short time—do your best, love your children and

your wife, help the needy, and try to live your life
as much as possible in the here and now. The hereafter will take care of itself.

ME: Am I a good father?

ED: Yes, you are!

ME: Thank you!

ED: You're welcome.

This communing with my long-dead father broke open my heart to
new levels of transformational healing—perhaps even more so because I was traveling the path to ordained ministry. I could be a better person and did not need to wait until the journey following death
to become so. The first step would involve becoming more vulner-
ably open to the person I had chosen to be. My mystic teachers had
taught me that with God's help, even this was possible.

Dark Night of the Soul

On the third evening, nighttime brought thunder and lightning to
the mountain. As I tried to settle down to sleep, a small, frightened
deer crashed into my little tent, temporarily knocking himself off
his feet. He was followed by what sounded like a larger deer—they
dashed off into the dark.

A heavy fog settled over the night. It suddenly turned freezing
cold. I built a large fire just outside my tent and scrunched down under what dry clothes were left to try to get some sleep.

My dark night of the soul began. A critical synopsis of my life
unfolded, unbidden, behind my closed eyes. It began with my misadventures at age seventeen. These feelings and images illustrated,
catalogued, and reviewed every major mistake of my adult life. I recalled every time I hurt someone deeply. It physically pained me every time I saw my audacity or ego somehow trample over someone's
reasonable right to fair treatment.

Many of these events were long forgotten. Some I hadn't thought about in twenty years. Other events I hadn't sufficiently regretted at the time. Yet they all piled up, one after another. I saw my behavior from a different perspective. I had strong-willed my way through life, often disregarding other people's feelings and sometimes not being there for them when they needed me.

I moved from the fire to a quiet stump in the dark and let the sordid story unfold. My life had many redeeming parts, but that was not what this night was about. I was deeply humbled. Hot tears of remorse did not go far enough to make it right. I had often fallen short as a sibling, as a friend, as a husband, as a father, as a coworker, as an employer, and as a neighbor. I was a wretched human being.

The sum of my worst offenses portrayed a truly detestable person. I was shocked and deeply grieved. I had never seen the extent of my mistakes in undiluted form. As every major error was dredged up, I could feel the other person's pain. This left me drained. Mortified. It left me seeking forgiveness, reconciliation, and redemption.

I rebuilt the fire so I could take more time for thought. This aspect of me was all ego: self-centered, callous, willful, and uncaring. This was a perspective I had never seriously considered before. How could such a person become a minister of God?

After what seemed many hours, the fire died to just red ashes, so I went to bed to get what sleep I could. My sleep was filled with bad dreams. Suddenly there was no comfort to be had. The ground I lay upon had somehow become uneven, full of rocks and sticks. The same spot where I had slept peacefully the two previous nights was now hard and barren. I slept fitfully. In my dreams, every mistake or sin I committed had consequences—some ruining other people's lives and some ruining my own. God judged me very severely that night.

Increasingly, my dreams pointed to horrible consequences if I did not change my behavior. I might end up divorced, estranged from my children, friendless, drinking too much, unsatisfied, and cynical. I could end up hurting and damaging—at times irreparably—people who I loved, who trusted me, who deserved better. I couldn't get warm. I was morose. The possible consequences of my callous pursuit of success were more than I could bear. My life was probably already more than half over. I was in despair.

Finally, I threw off my covers and my clothes and stood naked in the night.

"I am here, God," I shouted to the night. "Wherever and whenever you need me, send me."

Suddenly, the sky was full of stars! One was so clear, bright, and low in the sky it must have been Saturn. There were more stars than I had ever seen in a night sky.

Transformed and inspired, I no longer felt the cold. God was in this place, and I hadn't been mindful of him. Having wrestled with divine mystery, I had struggled mightily and then yielded my ego to God. I was finally at peace.

I climbed back into my tent and fell into a deep sleep. I woke with the sunrise and with clear memories of the night before. My little tent looked as though a great battle had been fought within.

I tried to make sense of this dark night of the soul. Yes, I was every bit as horrible as I had felt myself to be. But now I could choose to be different. I could trust and obey. With God's grace, I would live differently, becoming the person I aspired to be. I could be a better human being. The peace that surpasses understanding was worth the entire struggle. I was standing on holy ground and had the opportunity to once again reinvent myself.

As morning turned into day, I packed up and began the hike back to our base camp. There was a spring in my step. Joy filled my heart unlike any I had known. It would take years for me to process it all, but already I knew this was a turning point. Mystically, I was redeemed.

Deeper Wisdom

Each August, I continued these weeklong vision quests with my First Parish men's group. One reflection from August 2001 reads: "There is no wisdom hidden from those who have ears to hear and eyes to see. There are surprising paths through the forest that lead to incredible places, but you can't follow every path. So pick one, cultivate its fruit well over time, and then suck the juiciness out of it and be glad." Over the years, I had become quieter, more grounded in God, less so in my own ego. My spiritual journey was leading toward equanimity.

That quest of 2001, however, was the first year when it had already rained heavily for hours before we headed out to our isolated sites. The mountainside grove of trees I had selected for my site was now muddy, and so windy I couldn't start a fire. My meditations were scattered and unsatisfying. I was in a deep fog.

I prayed six thousand times another variation on the perpetual prayer I had so productively prayed in my 1999 vision quest. This version was "Sweet Jesus, yours is the Way. Grant my mind your peace and my heart your love." But even this yielded very little comfort or insight. I was cold, wet, and thoroughly miserable. Sincere mystic seekers sometimes simply encounter emptiness.

I awakened the next morning to the reality that this was not about spiritual fireworks. It was about opening my third eye, seeing the sacred in the mundane, being awake, aware. Seeing beneath and beyond what is. God was in this place.

On the third day, after another sleepless night spent wrestling with angels and my own mortality, I noticed it was getting lighter in the east, signaling predawn. As dawn rose, I went to the mountaintop and talked with God.

He didn't give me Ten Commandments—only one, "Follow the Way." That is all that is required of me. And I will discover the Way in walking it. That is all anyone can achieve. By covenanting with God, I was transformed. Then I slept the sleep of pure surrender.

I named that place Harmony Grove because it was the site of my final surrender of my will to God. Thank you, God. Thank you for teaching me a generosity of the spirit. Generosity of the spirit ultimately moves mountains.

Beyond Self

We began our August 2002 vision quest with our UU shaman leading us in a guided meditation. In this meditation-induced vision, I was visited by a lone dove, traditionally a sign of the Holy Spirit descending. Talk about a powerful harbinger of creative change, peace, and wellbeing.

As I walked to my new vision site for this year, I knew this dove signaled a time of new cycles and new worlds opening to me. It brought me a tremendous sense of peace and love. Frustration would pass and be replaced by peace of mind. All would be well. It was time to awaken to the promise of the future, beyond self, and to be greeted with loving kindness. The dove looked directly into my eyes before it flew away. I understood. I was at peace.

I prayed, "O Divine Mystery, whom I know when I breathe or laugh, pause to reflect or relax—sometimes I fear your power, your judgment, your absence, or even your amazing grace operating in my life. Why do I often feel so alone? Are you truly sometimes not present? Do you not love me?"

In that moment, gratitude washed over me. Blessed assurance. I felt beloved. I prayed, "Thank you for comforting me when I am distressed, teaching me when I am complacent, and greeting me when I come home to myself. O Divine Mystery, thank you for my life."

I also prayed, "Sweet Jesus, teach me loving kindness." I decided to make this my perpetual prayer for the rest of this quest, grounding my being in loving kindness. The hash marks in my spiritual diary indicate I prayed that simple prayer more than six thousand times over the next three days. My being was transformed, making me a manifestation of the Happy Buddha, just pleased to be. I wondered why I didn't do this more often—take the opportunity to just be!

Life is suffering. We move through this suffering to pure being. We must first engage the world before we can truly transcend it. But getting stuck in the world robs life of its transcendent joy. Joy and suffering are the yin and yang of existence: not in conflict as we suppose, but two halves of the whole. Neither can exist and prosper for long without the other. Life is about balance. A being grounded in balance can achieve far more than one out of kilter, even if the imbalance seems to favor achievement. Balance requires equanimity.

Contemplating the misery of the world made my heart ache. There was too much suffering for one heart to hold, to heal. Yet ignoring the suffering would make one grow hard-hearted and estranged from the world, estranged from the essence of life. We must each take on our share of suffering in order to transform the world.

I was visited by my guardian angel, Michael, who said, "Our world is full of love, but also fear and anxiety. It is full of opportunities for connection, but also for loneliness and estrangement." Michael said I was being groomed to do God's work in the world by responding to fear and anxiety with loving kindness. He said, "To do this requires you to be totally grounded, psychologically as well as physically, in a power greater than yours."

I was startled out of this contemplation of divine mystery by a juvenile moose crashing through a forest trail that crossed my meditation site. He had not sensed my presence. I rose up in horror, startling the moose, who, in turn, ran away in the other direction. A woodpecker diligently pecked out his breakfast from a dead tree, keeping me company as I calmed myself. My sleeping bag was twisted and covered with leaves despite resting on a plastic ground cover, looking again as though I had been wrestling with angels all night. Perhaps I had indeed.

I now knew the difference between righteousness and self-righteousness. With one, the energy flows from and is grounded in the divine mystery; with the other, it flows from my ego self. Righteousness helps set the world right so that events unfold in accordance with the divine. Self-righteousness creates more pain and suffering. Too often, even what begins as righteous action eventually slips over into self-righteous action as ego gets involved.

I was simply sitting and meditating on the nature of the divine when I heard something coming toward me. I looked up to see two magnificent young deer bucks—their antlers gorgeous—making their way down my hill, stopping to feed just in front of me. It seems when I am in a deep meditative state, I am often perceived as no threat to the other beings of the forest. It appears I am less noticeable, giving off fewer vibrations, when lost in meditation.

I put down my prayer beads and watched the deer feed. One somehow caught a whiff of me and froze, causing the second to freeze also. Then, after what seemed like many minutes with none of us moving, barely breathing, the young deer turned and ambled off beyond the edge of my vision. I was again at peace, at home in the universe.

I spent most of my final night of this quest again battling my ego self. I was seeking death of my ego, letting go of desires and needs, letting go of ambitions and aspirations, opening up more fully to what others need and want, opening up to the will of God. I was seeking annihilation of that which appeared to be most central to my being, in exchange for what was truly ultimate: to more fully participate in the divine mystery. I'd started down this path before, but the brain rewiring was especially painful this time. Most of the night coyotes serenaded me.

I ambled forth from this vision quest feeling much closer to God—a God with a circumference as big as the universe yet with its center at each and every point. We are the center of the universe, and so is everything. Everything is an axis mundi. God was in this place, and I did not know it until I came to experience Him directly for myself. I worshiped in the presence of God before walking out to join my friends and making our Way back home.

Dwelling in God

I went on a final vision quest with my men's group in August 2004. I spent the entire fourth day of that quest in a state of euphoria— euphoria over the goodness of life, even while hungry, sitting on a mountaintop. I felt the cool morning air as a call to rejoice in the new day. I marveled at the chickadee singing near me. I greeted the summer rain with a grin. When the rain passed, I also greeted the reemerging sun with a grin.

Feeling no limits on potential happiness—when outward circumstances no longer dictate attitude—is a blessing. When it rains and you don't get sick from the wet, it is a blessing. When you get soaked but can see the sources of new life abounding, that is a blessing too. Everything is a blessing!

Blessings are joyous ways of being, of experiencing our circumstances, rather than circumstances themselves. We cannot control circumstances. It does no good to wish for other circumstances. The many blessings in our lives come from what we do with those circumstances. This is also a blessing.

For the next seven years, I devoted my time and my spiritual life as co-senior minister at the Unitarian Universalist congregation of First Parish in Brookline, Massachusetts. Being an ordained, professional religious leader left me little time or energy for solo spiritual pilgrimage. For those seven years, serving God in the parish was my pilgrimage. My spiritual life was focused upon meeting the needs of my congregation.

But my contract stipulated that in my seventh year of parish ministry, I could take a paid sabbatical to renew my spirit and replenish my soul. So as that time approached, I opened myself to the universe to creative serendipity, to show me the best use of this time away.

Two years earlier, I had enrolled in the part-time doctor of ministry program at ANTS. My sabbatical seemed like a great time to spend a few months writing the first draft of my doctoral thesis. I wanted to be productive, but I also wanted to travel again with mystics as a sort of pilgrimage.

Through a seminary professor, I met a Chinese Christian teacher who offered to guide me in studying Taoism for a month at his retreat center in the mountains of the Chinese New Territories. But as my sabbatical plan began to fall into place, creative serendipity introduced yet another possibility—one which would transform my spiritual practice and relationship to the divine forever.

At the Unitarian Universalist Association general assembly that June, an old friend who was a UU seminary president suggested I more deeply explore the Sufi mystic Jalaludin Rumi by traveling to Konya, Turkey, with her provost and students that next December. I had been experimenting with saying yes to any and all callings of the spirit. So I said yes, moved my sabbatical forward a month, and booked a flight to Istanbul.

Unitarian Universalist Mystics
BOOK GROUP DISCUSSION GUIDE

Author's Comment

I have been more candid here about my early mystical experiences—many of them transcribed directly from my spiritual journals—than I could be in a scholarly setting. I seek to show you what has been true for me and allow you to decide what resonates with your own lived experience of the divine mystery.

Questions to Encourage Conversation

1. Have you ever tried to practice the Way of a householder pilgrim?

2. Can you potentially see Christ (God) in every person?

3. What do you think about Brother Lawrence's practice of the perpetual presence of God?

4. Does joyous nonattachment resonate for your spiritual path?

5. What do you make of the author's conversations with God?

6. Have you ever communed with your dearly departed ones?

7. Have you experienced any kind of dark night of the soul?

8. How does the author choose to "Follow the Way"?

9. Do you believe in guardian angels?

10. Have your prayers and meditations ever led you beyond self?

11. Do you ever experience everything that lives as holy?

12. Can you simply dwell in the presence of divine mystery?

Reflection

As a group, discuss which of these many spiritual disciplines feels most appropriate for your individual spiritual practice.

ISLAMIC MYSTICS

We have not come into this exquisite world to hold ourselves hostage from love. Run, my dear, from anything that may not strengthen your precious, budding wings... For we have not come here to take prisoners or to confine our wondrous spirits, but to experience ever and ever more deeply our divine courage, freedom, and light.

—Hafiz, fourteenth-century Sufi mystic

Sufi Mysticism

In the name of Allah, the Most Merciful and the Most Compassionate, I arrived in Istanbul on a December Monday in 2011. This transcontinental city—strategically located between two worlds, linking Western European culture and Eastern Islamic culture—had seen the rise and fall of empires. Its architecture and its people reflecting both East and West.

It was a Greek city until 330 CE, when the Roman emperor Constantine named it Constantinople and made it the capital of the Byzantine Empire, which was the eastern half of the Roman Empire. With the city under Byzantine rule, Christianity spread throughout the Middle East and North Africa. In 1453, the city fell to the Ottoman Empire. It became an Islamic stronghold—a key strategic and richly rewarded point on the historic east-west trade route called the Silk Road.

Istanbul has been recognized for millennia as a holy city, an axis mundi, a mixing place for world religions. While adjusting to jet lag, I walked the old city, absorbing its diverse and complex history. I visited the Sultan Ahmed Mosque, also known as the Blue Mosque, whose beauty dominates the skyline. It was once the center of the Sunni Islam faith in the Ottoman Empire. From here, I would embark with a group of Sufis and scholars to explore the teachings of Jalaludin Rumi.

Sufism is a branch of Islamic learning that deals with purification of the heart. Its influence within Islam is like a vast underground stream. For several weeks, I would travel with Sufis, practicing their Way, learning their disciplines to thread this spiritual path.

Often described as followers of the Way or the Real (*Al-Haqq*), Sufis seek to apprehend divine reality and then enter into an intimate relationship with the divine, known as Allah in Arabic. Allah, which is Truth or Ultimate Reality, is known by many names, but Sufis prefer *Al-Haqq.* They teach that all mystical experiences meet at paradise, but paradise assumes widely different aspects, depending upon the mystic's religion, culture, and temperament. Each finds their Way beyond contingent reality.

Sufism blossomed beautifully and ecstatically within Islam at the borders between classical Greek culture, Christian mysticism, and Islamic faith. The English word *mystic* is translated as "Sufi" in Arabic, Persian, and Turkish. Etymologically, the term appears to be derived from the Arabic word *suf,* or "wool." In Syria, Egypt, and the deserts of North Africa, early Sufis wore coarse, woolen garments as a sign of penitence and renunciation of worldly vanities.

I was first introduced to Sufis in the mid-1990s. I began with Coleman Barks's wonderful renditions of the mystical poetry of the thirteenth-century medieval Sufi master Jalaludin Rumi. My understanding deepened as I next discovered Andrew Harvey's marvelously insightful *Teachings of Rumi.* And it expanded greatly upon discovering Daniel Ladinsky's wonderful translations of poems by Hafiz as well as the anthology *Love Poems from God*, which juxtaposed the poetry of Christian, Muslim, and Hindu mystics. I was in paradise, talking to and listening to God directly!

When I arrived in Istanbul, it was with my copy of *The Essential Rumi* by Coleman Barks. Ibrahim—my *shaykh*, or spiritual teacher—told me Barks's translation was okay for UU worship, but it missed much of the spiritual radicalism of this Sufi saint. Ibrahim belonged to the Mevlevi Order, which followed the teachings of Rumi, who was also known as Mevlana. To truly understand Rumi, Ibrahim explained, one must read him in Persian and Arabic, or at least in Reynold Nicholson's wonderful out-of-print English translation.

So I went to the Istanbul English-language bookstore in search of this obscure book, only to discover a newly published copy of a Nicholson anthology on sale next to the cash register. This had to be the translation Ibrahim wanted me to get. I was being guided by serendipity.

On Tuesday, Ibrahim led us to the Şakirin Mosque to experience noon prayer. Then we boarded a ferry at the Üsküdar Quay to visit the historic and spectacular Eyüp Sultan Mosque. But our journey was not primarily about sightseeing. The purpose of these mosques (places of prostration) was to help us practice the presence of, and surrender to, God on our pilgrimage.

Sufis believe that for gnosis (divine knowledge) to transfigure the spiritual seeker, one must see with an inner light—their mystic heart. One must see the beauty, goodness, and grace of the divine, so that every brightness on earth becomes dark beside the splendor of God.

One Sufi prayer is, "O God, I never listen to the cry of animals, or the quivering of trees, or the murmuring of water, or the warbling of birds, or the rustling wind, or crashing thunder, without feeling them to be evidence of Thy unity and a proof that there is nothing unto Thou." Mystics commune and dance with the Beloved, thereby becoming one with Ultimate Reality.

Sufi mystics teach that their wisdom includes the perennial wisdom passed down from teacher to student for millennia. There was no time when human mystic communion with the divine mystery *wasn't*. Sufis worship God (Allah) and celebrate the prophet Mohammad, as well as those who are the heirs and guardians of the prophet Mohammed's teachings. Yet their mystic techniques precede the rise of Islam by millennia. That said, it is impossible to truly understand Sufism without understanding Islam and the Zoroastrian roots behind all three Abrahamic faiths: Judaism, Christianity, and Islam.

Submission (*Islam*), Faith (*Imam*), and Beauty (*Ihsan*) are the keynotes of Sufism. Early Sufi texts include the sayings of *rahib*, or Christian anchorites, giving religious instruction and advice to wandering Muslim ascetics. Sufi rituals and vows appear to have their roots in Christian mysticism, but they developed their own distinctive patterns and flavors over time. Here is one such distinctive teaching in which their wisdom teacher is Jesus:

> *Jesus passed by three men. Their bodies were lean*
> *and their faces pale. He asked them, "What has*
> *brought you to this plight?"*

> *They answered, "Fear of hell."*

> *Jesus said, "You fear a thing created, and it behooves*
> *God to save those in fear."*

> *Then he left them and passed by three others, whose faces*
> *were paler and their bodies leaner still. He asked them,*
> *"What has brought you to this plight?"*

> *They answered, "Longing for paradise."*

> *Jesus said, "You desire a thing created, and it behooves*
> *God to give you your heart's desire."*

> *Then he went on and passed by three others of*
> *exceeding paleness and leanness so that their faces*
> *were as mirrors of light. He asked, "What has*
> *brought you to this plight?"*

They answered, "Our love of God."

Jesus said, "You are the nearest and dearest to God himself."

A core teaching of Islam is to surrender oneself, the ego-self (*naifs*), to God. This is both the core of the religion and a great paradox. Sufis say the cosmic irony is that our independent ego-self doesn't actually exist. Even if it did, it could not control reality. So there is no self to surrender. No self who can. The surrender demanded by Islam is the surrender of a contingent reality in pursuit of coming to know what is Real (God). Traveling with Sufis, I learned ever more deeply to surrender my ego-self.

Between Worlds

On Wednesday, Ibrahim introduced our small band of pilgrims to the complex religious history of Istanbul. We walked to Ayasofya, also known as Hagia Sophia, the heart of Eastern Orthodox Christianity. This site was consecrated as a Christian church by the Byzantine emperor Justinian in 537, converted to an Islamic mosque by Mehmed the Conqueror in 1453, and declared a national museum by President Atatürk in 1835. It holds the complex wisdom of this ancient city with Greek, Roman, Byzantine, Ottoman, Islamic, and secular roots.

Entering the building, we were immediately in the inner narthex, with its brilliant mosaic of Christ Pantocrator ("ruler of all") over the Emperor Door. I felt humble and small under its huge dome and spacious nave with abundant gold mosaics. The Byzantine emperors intended this effect; they were crowned seated on a huge throne in the Omphalion at its center.

A magnificent ninth-century mosaic of the Virgin Mary (Madonna) and Christ Child dominates the church's apse. Mosaics above the apse once depicted the archangels Gabriel and Michael, but they were destroyed during the Ottoman era.

Ottoman additions include a *minbar*, an imam's pulpit for leading prayer; a *mihrab*, an ornate marker indicating the direction of Mecca; large gilt letters in Arabic; and an ornate Muslim library behind the Omphalion. This interreligious repurposing of beauty and layering of meaning continues throughout the building.

In the afternoon, we visited other historic Christian churches, again, not as tourists but as spiritual travelers seeking clues to the divine mystery. The Christianity Muslims first encountered was primarily gnostic in nature. Gnostic Christianity seeks divine knowledge to enter into awareness of God's unconditional love, which is often called heaven or paradise.

Because Istanbul was once a Greek city, Pythagorean and Platonic thought also greatly influenced the Islam of the Ottomans. Doctrines of emanation, illumination, gnosis, and ecstasy were all transmitted to *siddique*, or spiritual adepts. This became cosmic consciousness.

On Thursday, Ibrahim took us to pray alongside the few remaining Istanbul Jews at the synagogues in Balat and Galata. We learned to pray: "*Barukh atah Adonai, Eloheinu, melekh ha'olam,*" which means "Blessed are you, Lord, our God, sovereign of the universe." We also invoked a simple reminder, based upon Genesis 2:2–3, to rest in divine mystery: "On the seventh day, God was finished with all the work of making, but lingered, resting from the work of making, blessing the seventh day and making it holy; for in it, God added rest, not doing, above all the works which were created by God for doing." Blessed assurance, blessed rest.

In medieval times, these were vibrant Jewish communities. Now only a small remnant remained. We visited a Jewish history museum to better understand five hundred years of Islamic tolerance and support of Judaism in its midst. We sang mystical Jewish songs. I loved one by Rabbi Shlomo Carlebach that goes: "Return again, return again, return to the land of your soul . . . Return to who you are, return to what you are, return to where you are, born and reborn again." Seek the fire of spiritual passion, and your soul will emerge transformed.

During this medieval period, there were also flourishing Buddhist monasteries in Balkh, the metropolis of ancient Bactria, which became a major Sufi center of learning. It is said that Sufi self-culture, ascetic meditation, and intellectual abstraction owe a good deal to Buddhism. Some Sufis even adopted the practice of meditation using Hindu or Buddhist prayer beads. But while Buddhists sit quietly, Sufis use recitation, music, dance, and trance to reach God.

For Muslims, the Prophet Mohammad is the perfected human being whose relationship to God is the spiritual standard, par excellence. The Qu'ran, the revelation that the Prophet Mohammad taught, says God is nearer to the human being than the jugular vein, that is, nearer than consciousness itself. Our relationship to divine mystery is both intimate and omnipresent. But we must be willing to tame our baser instincts in order to dance in ecstasy with the Divine.

During the medieval period, Sufism gradually formalized itself into separate religious orders growing up around great spiritual teachers. For Sufis, the direct transmission of divine light from the teacher's heart into the heart of the student—not worldly knowledge—allows the spiritual seeker to progress. So, a Sufi *shaykh* transforms the spiritual seeker by planting love of the divine in their heart. Rumi taught, "Wisdom is like the rain. Your currency on the Path of God is courage and faith, and you will be taught according to your courage and faith."

And so I traveled for weeks on pilgrimage with Ibrahim, my Mevlevi *shaykh*, and other Islamic mystics. Incredible, unbelievable things happened to me and around me. It left me with amazing stories, some of which were truly unbelievable, but all of which were deeply transformative. Going beyond self, we discovered how to dance with divine mystery.

Singing and Whirling with Sufis

The Mevlevi Order follows Rumi's teachings, including humility, self-control, and abstinence from worldly desires. A key teaching is that of engaging in *dhikr*, a special form of moving meditation to practice consciousness of the divine mystery while seeking the presence of the divine through all-encompassing love. The core dhikr ceremony of the Mevlevis is called Sema, which can include whirling, singing, instrumental music, incense, meditative dance, ecstasy, and trance. In Sema, one surrenders ego-self to become one with the Real, with Ultimate Reality.

I had already spent many hours trying to understand these Sufis and their love of the divine mystery. Now they would teach me to whirl. I bought a pair of black leather dancing boots in anticipation.

On Friday, Ibrahim introduced us to dhikr. He showed me how to whirl on one foot, using the other to gain and maintain momentum. I was to focus on one hand outstretched before me, my other hand flung skyward. Awkward but spiritually transcendent. I felt like a twirling ballet dancer riding a bucking bronco. That idea alone made me giggle with God.

Ibrahim taught us that the first stage of dhikr is to forget oneself in complete absorption into worship. One of the chants we used was the 112th surah of the Qur'an, called the Al-Ikhlas:

> *We take refuge with Allah the All-Merciful from the*
> *source of all negativity.*
> *In the name of Allah, the Tenderly Compassionate and*
> *Infinitely Merciful One.*
> *Allah is the Uncaused Cause of all that exists; Allah*
> *does not give birth,*
> *and nothing gave birth to Allah, and there is none like*
> *unto Allah.*

> *Perfect praise flows to Allah alone, Lover and*
> *Sustainer of all worlds,*

> *most intimately called the Tenderly Compassionate One*
>   *and the infinitely*
> *merciful one presiding magnificently over the Day of*
>   *Divine Awakening.*
>
> *O Beloved Lord, you alone do we worship and upon*
>   *you alone do we rely.*
> *Keep us in your direct path, the Mystic way of those who*
>   *through*
> *your Mercy have received and truly taken in your*
>   *sublime guidance*
> *and not the path of those who have constricted hearts,*
> *nor the path of those who have moved away from the*
>   *Path of Return.*

Sufis distinguish three ways of knowing God: through the mind's contemplation, which they term *sir*, or "secret soul"; through ecstatic experiences, which they call *ruh*, or "spirit"; and through love, which they call *qalb*, or "heart." We might call this approaching divine mystery through mindfulness, ecstasy, and love, with love being the highest state. Over the course of our pilgrimage travels, we would explore all three paths and discover that they work synergistically. I practiced all three paths and never felt nearer to God.

As the Persian Sufi poet Baba Kuhi of Shiraz wrote:

> *In the market, in the cloister—only God I saw.*
> *In the valley and on the mountain—only God I saw.*
> *Him I have seen beside me often in tribulation;*
> *in favor and in fortune—only God I saw.*
> *In prayer and fasting, in praise and contemplation,*
> *in the religion of the prophet—only God I saw...*
> *Myself with mine own eyes I saw most clearly,*
> *but when I looked with God's eyes—only God I saw.*
> *I passed away into nothingness, I vanished,*
> *and lo, I was the All-living—only God I saw.*

On Saturday, we departed Istanbul on the overnight train, heading for the city of Konya. All through the night, I read the Nicholson anthology I had purchased in Istanbul. When Ibrahim saw it the next morning, he explained that this wasn't the Nicholson work he had been referring to earlier in our trip. Rather, he encouraged me to get *The Mathnawi of Jalaluddin Rumi*, Nicholson's six-volume translation of Rumi's masterpiece. But Ibrahim said sadly it wasn't available in English in Konya or even Istanbul. I would need to buy it from Amazon backlists upon finally returning to Boston.

Even if I didn't have the definitive Nicholson translation, Rumi seemed to be already walking with me, dancing with me, leading me. This sense of being guided by mystic masters—some of this world and others no longer of this world—became an explicit part of my mystic understanding when I traveled with the Sufis. This is what mystics call living between two worlds, two complementary realities. Rumi writes:

> *Look for the moon in the sky, not in the water!*
> *If you wish to rise above mere names and letters,*
> *make yourself free from self at one stroke.*
> *Become pure, from all attributes of self,*
> *that you may see your own bright essence,*
> *Yea, see in your own heart the knowledge of the prophet,*
> *without book, without tutor, without a guide.*

However, I still felt unprepared to find my way without book, without tutor, without a guide. Sufis speak of three kinds of spiritual seekers: first, those who worship God and hope for paradise; second, those who make meaning of God, such as philosophers and theologians; and last, the gnostics, who ecstatically love God with all their hearts. I had now joined the third group. Yet these are not independent paths; they interconnect and work with each other.

That Sunday afternoon found me wandering aimlessly around Konya, waiting for our next evening session to start. As I came upon a rug shop, the merchant waved me in. I waved him off. I didn't need a rug. But he continued, claiming he had exactly what I needed. He swore he had my book in English. I was intrigued. I hadn't said a word about any book.

The merchant sent a dirty young man dashing down the street before urging me to enter the shop. We drank Turkish tea and talked about each other's families, but no books were apparent. Finally, I insisted on seeing this book he wanted to sell me. He showed me to a small alcove of books in Arabic and Turkish!

I was very annoyed and about to leave when the young man returned carrying a dusty, poorly printed six-volume set of the *Mathnawi* as translated by Nicholson. The rug merchant sold it to me for twenty dollars without any haggling, half what I paid for the Nicholson anthology in Istanbul.

That night, Ibrahim saw me reading the *Mathnawi*, and I shared the story of how I came to acquire it. He said it was the surest sign of being on my best spiritual path. Serendipity paves the Way. Such fortuitous happenings are what Jungians call synchronicity. Sufis simply call it the hand of God.

Dancing with Divine Mystery

Konya has built contemplation mosques around the tombs of Rumi and his soul companion, Shams of Tabriz. In those mosques, Sufis practice meditation, melodious chanting, and whirling, usually late at night.

Our Sunday evening spiritual gathering included Sufis from Turkey, Syria, Iraq, Iran, Afghanistan, Russia, Estonia, England, France, Mexico, and the USA. The rest of our week was devoted to practicing Sema to align ourselves with the movement of the universe.

Turning, or whirling, is a fundamental aspect of our conditioned existence. Everything turns. By turning, each Semazen, or participant in these group rituals, seeks to align the mind with truth, align the heart with love, abandon the ego-self, and submerge in the divine mystery.

The first turning, or stage of the ceremony, begins with a eulogy exalting the prophet Muhammad as a manifestation of divine love. The second turning is to align with our fundamental being. The third turning is to align with the breath of God, which gives life to everything. Thus, we turn into alignment with God's messenger, with our own being, and with God's living breath. Breath is all.

The next turning stage involves greeting one another in a ritualized form of soul sharing. This involves rising up in knowledge, awe, and amazement of God's power, sacrificing oneself to love, and completing the spiritual journey. When done properly—which takes a lot of practice, and I never did do it properly—it brings the Semazen to a state of whirling ecstasy. In this state, the Semazen drowns in bliss and can bring all the participants into that spiritual state as well. The ceremony ends with a benediction for all believers, martyrs, and faithful.

The Sufi whirling dervish performances are great for Turkish tourism, so the government tolerates the Sufi dhikrs and even substitutes stylized secular dancers dressed as Sufis for tourists. On Monday evening, we attended one such stylized performance, with sixteen men dressed as Sufis whirling away on the dance floor of Konya's largest stage. It was like watching a particularly lovely, somber, but boring ballet. It held no religious significance for most of the tourists and performers. It was just local color.

Afterward, Ibrahim took us down a back alley, where an ancient wooden door was sunk into a wall. We entered a room filled only with street shoes. We changed into our whirling boots and entered another room, where everyone was drinking Turkish tea. From there, we entered into a large room, where everyone was doing dhikr. There was nothing somber or boring about the kaleidoscopic movement and energy in that vast room.

After a few hours, I fell away, as did growing numbers of the participants. Finally, only one young man was whirling away. As he seemingly rose into the air, his eyes rolled up inside his head, he drew the entire room into his trance with the divine. It was ecstasy! I was told later that he is famous among Sufis for his dancing, and that back in Mexico, where few know or care that he is a Sufi, he is a popular singer. Such is the divine mystery.

We developed a pattern of sleeping late into the morning, reading and studying through the day, and then practicing our dhikr all through the evening and well into the night. Many nights, we would chant and sing and whirl into the early hours of the morning. While the rest of us would collapse in exhaustion, one particular, joyous, blind Sufi would continue to whirl.

One glorious night, this man joined our group and asked us to call him Ismael. He was enchanting! He played music on a Sufi sitar that could make angels weep, he chanted in Arabic in a voice akin to the voice of God, and he told incredible stories about his travels with the Beloved. We knew we were traveling with someone who traveled with the Beloved.

When the student is ready, the new teacher arrives. Ismael became my Shams, my soul companion.

On these nights when everyone but Ismael was exhausted, I'd ask, "Ismael, where are you going?"

"To meditate with friends no longer of this world," he would say.

"But aren't you tired?" I'd ask.

"When the Beloved calls," he'd say, "the greatest Sufi whirling meditation can be found in the tombs and mosques of the lovers of God."

I went with him one time, even though I was bone tired, to the mosque that held Shams's tomb. We were met by Russian, Iranian, Iraqi, Afghanistan, and Turkish Sufis who wished only to chant, sing, and whirl until they achieved ecstatic union with the divine. Shams knew how to connect with the Beloved through poetry, singing, and dancing. Shams taught that becoming one with the Beloved brings us to a blissful state called "heart's ease."

We had been whirling and meditating all night, and it was nearly four in the morning when a Sufi saint called Baba—a term of endearment—approached me. He was Ismael's teacher. Baba placed his hand on my chest. He infused my Ka'ba—the temple within my heart—with loving kindness. Energy exploded from all my extremities. I felt the incredible power of God's love. I have never before felt so thoroughly engulfed by the dynamic energy of love. My heart was broken open.

The next morning, it still left a large red circle over my heart. Thereafter, the mystics treated me differently.

Rumi said, "All other joys and pursuits are like a ladder. You cannot stay on any of the rungs of a ladder; the really happy person is the one who is vigilant and understands this." Traveling with Sufis, I came to understand we are all on a journey guided by love. And when the Beloved says "Dance," we not only dance, we dance *ecstatically* if we understand anything about God's nature!

Sufis teach that if a man regards himself as existing only through God, then that which is godly in him predominates; he sees nothing but God. But if he regards himself as independently existent, then his ego predominates; God becomes hidden to him. When that happens, it doesn't matter how often you pray or what rituals you pursue—you cannot know God.

The Sufi Imam Junayd illustrated this when instructing a Muslim returning from his hajj pilgrimage to see the Ka'ba, the sacred heart of the Great Mosque at Mecca.

Junayd asked the pilgrim, "When you circumambulated the Ka'ba, did you behold the immaterial beauty of God?"

"No."

"Then you have not circumambulated the Ka'ba as required. When you reached the slaughter place and offered sacrifice, did you sacrifice the objects of your worldly desire?"

"No."

"Then you have not done the required sacrifice. When you threw the stones against evil, did you throw away whatever sensual thoughts block your mind from God?"

"No."

"Then you have not thrown the required stones against evil, and you have not performed the hajj pilgrimage. All of your journey was for naught."

As part of our own pilgrimage, we would be celebrating Şeb-i Arus, the anniversary of Rumi's union with the divine, and we would do it with a mystic heart. Mevlevi Sufis come to Konya for dhikr annually for this ceremony. Though pilgrims honor Rumi's death, the epitaph over his tomb reads: "When we are dead, seek not our tomb in the earth, but find it in the hearts of men." The spiritual ecstasy I experienced with these Sufis was beyond belief. I experienced oneness with divine mystery not in the mosques (*masajid*) but in the hearts of mystics.

Historical Islam

My understanding of historical Islam was shaped by Mevlevi Sufis and my shayhk Ibrahim. I recognize that many Sunni would tell the story quite differently. But this is my understanding. Born circa 570 CE, Muhammad was orphaned at an early age. He was a mystic, spending many hours in silent prayer and taking an annual silent retreat in a mountain cave called Hira.

During meditation at the age of forty, he experienced an epiphany of the divine mystery in the form of the archangel Gabriel, who sought for him to become a holy prophet, a praiseworthy messenger of Allah. One tradition says Muhammad was so discombobulated by this vision and this divine command that he discontinued his meditation retreats for three years.

Eventually, Muhammad confirmed the reality of his divine realization: he was born to be Allah's messenger, and all monotheistic descriptions of God were one. He surrendered to divine mystery—hence the name Islam, which means "submission." He began to recite what the angel dictated to him. It became the Qur'an, the basis of Islam, and transformed his life and people.

The Arabian Peninsula of his day had been devastated by a long series of wars between the Persian and Byzantine Empires, leaving many warring tribes battling in a state of relative poverty. Muhammad created his first Muslim army from these warring tribes and also organized a growing tribal empire. He combined spiritual, military, and civic leadership. This three-part legacy of completely surrendering to divine mystery, leading a growing economy, and deploying a diverse army is uniquely reflected in the legacy of Islam. Muhammed was a prophet and a general, and also deeply involved in state building.

To accomplish all this, Muhammad relied upon his dear wife Khadija, who financed and supported him, and his oldest and most trusted friend, Abu Bakr, to rule these recently united Arab tribal leaders, and upon his friend Umar as his most trusted military general. And he chose his son-in-law and nephew, 'Alī, as his spiritual heir. Each with a unique role.

But upon Muhammad's death, the tribal chiefs chose Abū Bakr as the first caliph (successor of the prophet) of Islam. While seemingly not a particularly religious leader, he quickly earned the tribal leaders' faith. He imposed fair and equitable governance across the growing Islamic empire, putting down local rebellions. He invited General 'Umar to lead the Islamic army as "Commander of the Faithful" against the Byzantine Empire. Wealth and power would follow.

When Abū Bakr died two years later, he nominated General 'Umar as the second caliph. During the ten years of his reign, 'Umar led the Muslim armies to conquer all of ancient Mesopotamia, Byzantine Syria, Byzantine Egypt, and large parts of the former Persian Empire.

Upon his death, the tribal leaders chose 'Uthmān, the wealthy leader of the important Umayya clan, as the third caliph. During his twelve-year reign, he standardized what it meant to be Muslim, expanding sharia law and persecuting any who refused to become Muslim.

When 'Uthmān was himself murdered, Muhammad's designated successor and spiritual heir, 'Alī, finally seized control of the caliphate. In the first decades after Muhammed's death, some of his most prominent friends and followers seemed to choose worldly power for the growing empire over spiritual attainment. 'Alī now tried to restore Islam's heart. But the Shia say by then it was perhaps too late.

Though a devoted mystic, and incredible person in his own right, and a friend of God, 'Alī unfortunately did not become a great leader of this diverse and expansive empire. He was not a great statesman like Abū Bakr, nor a great military leader like 'Umar. But he was Muhammad's chosen successor and a great imam, or spiritual leader. He had married Muhammad's daughter Fāṭimah, so their children were the direct lineal descendants of God's last prophet. 'Alī felt many Muslims had abandoned, or at least unwisely modified, many of the prophet's important teachings in the twenty-five years since Muhammad's death. Now, God willing, Muslims would surrender themselves fully and completely to God.

'Alī tried to reform Islam by reining in the power of territorial governors and tribal leaders, but the Muslim empire had grown too fast and was too diverse. It instead plunged the Muslims into civil war. In 661, while 'Alī was devotedly saying the dawn prayer at the Great Mosque of Kufa, an assassin slaughtered him, hacking into his skull with a poisoned sword.

Mu'awiya, the Arabic governor of Syria, seized the caliphate. Mu'awiya moved the Muslim capital from Medina in Arabia to Damascus in Syria, and turned it into the Umayyad dynasty, a hereditary monarchy for his family. This dynasty would last nearly one hundred years. They would conquer North Africa, much of Spain and Portugal, and western India. They even attacked Constantinople, making it one of the world's largest and richest empires.

As I combined this understanding of Muslim history with my own experiences, it seemed to me that much of the spiritual heart of Islam had been abandoned by many Muslims in pursuit of worldly wealth and power. The Shia view 'Alī's murder as Sunni Islam's original sin at the very heart of their faith.

Yet Sufis offered me a way to learn how to dance in ecstasy with the Beloved, with Ultimate Reality. Rumi would be my universalist guide to understanding this mystic Way to joyous oneness with the divine mystery. In this Way I would find my heart's ease.

Rumi the Universalist

On Saturday, after nearly two weeks of preparation and practice, we were finally ready to participate in Rumi's Şeb-i Arus, the mystical celebration of his unity with the divine mystery.

Mevlana Jalāl al-Dīn Muhammad Rumi was born in 1207 CE to a Persian-speaking family. They lived in a part of the former Byzantine Empire under Turkish Muslim rule in what is present-day Afghanistan. His father, Bahā' al-Dīn Walad, also known as Bahauddin, was a respected Islamic preacher, theologian, jurist, and mystic. They were non-Arabic Muslims living in the mixed religious borderlands between Persian Zoroastrians, Byzantine Christians, pagan Mongols, and Arabic Muslims. Rumi's spiritual universalism results from this diverse mix of cultures and religious expectations.

As Rumi recounts, he began experiencing altered realities by fasting for as long as three or four days as early as the age of six. Rumi was eight years old when Mongols invaded, forcing his father to take his family and students to flee west through Iran and on to Baghdad.

The Mongol invaders overturned the government, burned down the libraries, smashed dams and dikes so an oasis turned back into desert, and committed genocide by exterminating up to 90 percent of the local Persian population. Rumi's family fled on pilgrimage to Mecca, eventually settling in Karaman, where the sixteen-year-old Rumi agreed to an arranged marriage that would yield two sons.

Rumi was twenty-one when his father led the growing family, including Rumi's wife and sons, and other students to Konya in Anatolia. There, Bahauddin founded a madrassa, or religious school, and began to greatly expand his number of followers.

In his book *Rumi's Secret*, Brad Gooch explains how Rumi's universalizing tendencies owe much to the Anatolian milieu:

> *Anatolia was territory defined in the imagination of*
> *Muslims as the outer limits of their civilization,*
> *the borderlands of Christian Rome, or Rum. The*
> *term Rumi was used sometimes as a synonym for*

Christian, this shadow meaning still clinging to
the name used for the poet after his death. From
now on [Rumi's family] would be living in
cities where they were greatly outnumbered by
mostly Greek-speaking or Armenian Christians,
with Muslims in Anatolia estimated at ten
percent of the population.

Bahauddin intended Rumi to take his place as a respected Islamic theologian, jurist, and mystic, but Rumi was only twenty-four when his father died in 1231. So, one of Bahauddin's most prominent students, Burhān al-Dīn Muḥaqqiq, led the madrassa and trained Rumi for the next nine years.

At the age of thirty-four, Rumi finally became the imam, issuing fatwas, or religious decrees; giving sermons in the mosques of Konya; and teaching in the madrassa. His initial teachings roughly followed those of his father.

Three years later, Rumi formed a mystical friendship with Shams of Tabriz, a wandering Sufi dervish. This took Rumi's faith to a deeper level.

Shams said most religious teachers were comfortable describing the appearance of things, such as moonlight—how soft and beautiful it was—without realizing it was merely a reflection of the sun. Shams's own name means "sun." He embraced the sun, the divine mystery, directly. He had little patience with abstract debates over theology. He preferred music, poetry, and movement as ways to connect with the divine mystery. Shams taught Rumi how to whirl in ecstasy and meditate in communion with God.

Shams said, "I do not know why they fear to interact with the main source. They think, what if they were stricken by that light; what if their eyes were dazzled by that very light; what if all they thought they knew were not true . . . What if all they wrote were mere illusion?"

Rumi was dazzled by Shams's teachings of direct experience of the divine mystery. Shams taught that in order to experience God's love, you need to establish resilience and audacity, and finally your heart will be broken open with a perfect love of divine mystery. Rumi became my teacher; Shams, my life coach. These ancient mystics could together teach me to dance with God.

Rumi and Shams were constant spiritual companions and mystical friends for the next four years. Unlike Rumi, Shams had no official authority for his radical teaching, having never received the cloak of authority from any living Sufi master. Shams's authority was of the heart.

Rumi's students, and perhaps even his sons and wife, grew jealous of Shams's great influence and friendship with Rumi. When Shams disappeared suddenly one night, some said he was killed by the jealous students. This brought an abrupt end to this deep spiritual friendship.

Rumi was heartbroken. He wandered the world in grief until he experienced a great spiritual awakening. Rumi's spiritual love for Shams became the Ka'ba at the core of his faith. In one of his poems, he writes:

> *Oh you who've gone on hajj—where, oh where, are you?*
> *Here, here is the beloved! Oh come now, come, oh come!*
> *You, lost in the desert—what air of love is this?*
> *You are the house, the master, you are the Ka'ba, you!*

> *Why should I seek Shams? I am the same as He.*
> *His essence speaks through me. I have been looking for*
> *myself.*

Through his love, Shams turned a preacher into a poet and a pious man into a singing, dancing fool for God. Rumi found union with God through Shams.

Over the next twenty-five years, Rumi wrote the most moving poetry about love and the divine mystery:

> *Through love bitter things become sweet...*
> *Through love agonies are healing balms.*
> *Through love thorns become roses...*
> *Through love disaster becomes good fortune.*
> *Through love a prison becomes a rose garden...*

Through love the dead are resurrected.
Through love the emperor becomes a slave.

If destiny comes to help you, love will come to meet
*   you.*
A life without love isn't a life. God doesn't take it
*   into account.*

Through his mystical experiences, Rumi deepened his liberal Islamic faith even while transcending it. Describing his emergent faith, he wrote, "Not Christian or Jew or Muslim, not Hindu, Buddhist, Sufi, or Zen. Not any religion or cultural system. I am not from the east or the west, not out of the ocean or up from the ground, not natural or ethereal, not composed of elements at all. I do not exist . . . I belong to the Beloved, have seen the two worlds as one . . . first, last, outer, inner, only that breath breathing human being." This is the essence of love.

Ismael's Story

Our last day in Konya was spent at the Şeb-i Arus ceremony, paying our respect to Rumi. Rumi's mosque was built to hold thousands of pilgrims, but the gathered crowd far exceeded its capacity.

Ismael asked me to take his arm and guide him through the crush of the crowd. But push as I might, the crowd pushed back. We were falling farther and farther behind Ibrahim in making our way toward the mosque.

When Ismael realized this, he began to sing. Suddenly, everyone stepped out of our way. We caught up with our group just as we entered the mosque.

A booming voice came over a loud speaker, asking, "Is that Ismael?"

When Ismael responded, they invited him to ascend a high platform and lead the assembled masses in prayers, singing, and recitations from the Qur'an. This humble, blind Sufi was the rock star of Rumi's Şeb-i Arus ceremony. I learned to more deeply love and trust God through him. Ismael and I became fast friends of divine mystery and each other.

After the ceremony, we traveled back to Istanbul by bus. During the journey, Ibrahim's son told me about something that had happened earlier during our pilgrimage. When we were visiting an eight-hundred-year-old Sufi mosque made from the cedars of Lebanon, Ibrahim had sensed a spiritual presence in another part of the mosque. He'd sent his son to investigate. His son said Ibrahim was surprised to learn it was me, communing with Sufi saints no longer of this world.

Experienced spiritual beings often have an aura about them that is sometimes palpable, especially to other mystics. Sufis opened my heart to the power of God's love like nothing I had ever experienced before. They left my mind and my body physically transformed.

Our last evening back in Istanbul, I begged Ismael to tell me his life story. He refused. But he did offer to use his story to teach me the Sufi practice of soul-sharing heart-to-heart, if I would also use my story to open my heart to him. We had the next day free, so after breakfast, we began telling our tales.

The youngest of four brothers, Ismael was born blind, in extreme poverty, in a village forty miles north of Istanbul. His parents doted on him, but his mother died when he was five years old, and his father died when he was six. He and his three brothers—now ten, eleven, and thirteen years old—were now orphans.

His brothers didn't want to care for their blind younger brother, so Ismael ran away. But being blind and not knowing his way, he didn't get far. Ismael devoted the next year to doing small errands for people in his village, carefully saving the tips they paid him. By the age of seven, he had saved enough to buy a bus ticket to Istanbul, where he became a street urchin.

To survive, he needed to earn money from tourists, most of whom spoke only English. Over the next two years, Ismael learned rudimentary English and lived on Istanbul's streets under the roughest of conditions. The spiritual resilience he developed from such survival would serve him well.

But by the age of ten, Ismael had developed a hashish habit. He was smoking one day in his favorite shop when some men paid his outstanding bill. It turned out they were Sufis.

The Sufi master offered to provide Ismael with food and a bed if he would give up his hashish and memorize the Qur'an over the next two years. When Ismael agreed, his teacher planted the Ka'ba of love in his heart. Ismael swore off intoxicating substances, learned Arabic, and memorized the Qur'an a page at a time. Without the distraction of sight, Ismael can recite any page of text word for word if someone reads it to him four times—a feat he once displayed for me during the pilgrimage.

Ismael spent his days as an English-speaking tour guide and his nights reciting the Qur'an in Arabic. His teacher also introduced him to the Sufi musical scale and instruments to teach him how to chant and sing the Sufi hymns to the Beloved. As one of a few English-speaking Sufis in Istanbul in the 1970s, Ismael became a popular religious tour guide.

"But how could you be a blind tour guide?" I asked him.

He laughed at me. "I guided them to what was significant, but I wasn't driving the bus!" he replied.

This way of guiding and teaching without ever taking the lead was Ismael's way. He was a Sufi with astounding spiritual audacity. And that spiritual audacity opened the world to him. Spiritual audacity, fervently pursued, opens the world to all sincere seekers of divine mystery.

By the age of thirty, Ismael had found his place in God's work: reciting and chanting the Qur'an; leading religious tours; and having a large and growing circle of friends, a ready laugh, and financial security. Then the Beloved disrupted his life again when a beautiful woman came on one of his tours.

"Ismael, you're blind," I interjected. "How did you know she was beautiful?"

"All the men said so," he answered. "But even if they hadn't, I knew it when I first heard her voice."

By the end of the week, he was in love. As he wooed her, she in return fell in love with this audacious, blind Sufi. She agreed to marry him, but only if he would relocate to Brazil, where she lived with her two young sons from her first marriage.

What could Ismael do for work? What would he do for money? How could he survive with this new wife and family in a strange land?

She laughed at his worries. She knew mystics in Brazil would flock to his voice. Besides, she was a senior vice president of J. P. Morgan, earning enough for both of them.

Ismael moved to Brazil, learned Portuguese, created a Brazilian Sufi community, and helped raise two sons while his wife traveled for work. As Ismael said, "When the Beloved invites you to tango, it is unwise and impolite to answer that you only know how to dance to rock and roll. Just dance with divine mystery! That is all that is required of any of us."

When he was fifty, Ismael's wife was offered a senior role at J. P. Morgan in New York City. They toured Sufi communities in Manhattan, but local teachers seemed to find Ismael's spirituality threatening. So, Ismael and his wife bought a house forty-five minutes north of NYC by train and created a new Sufi community.

Ismael and his wife now travel the world, leading Sufi meditations in Russia, India, Istanbul, Brasilia, and London. And he always manages to make his way back to Konya for Şeb-i Arus, the anniversary of Rumi's death and union with the divine.

Ismael then insisted I tell him the story of my spiritual journey as well. Even though my story isn't much compared to his, he drew out from me a tale as full of wonder and surprising serendipity as the one he had just told me. I knew the love of God in my heart. I could dance with the Beloved. I could rest within the peace that surpasses all understanding.

As our time together came to a close, after sharing soul to soul, Ismael made me promise to visit him and his wife at their home upon my return to Boston.

God as Beloved

On the winter solstice, which was a Wednesday, I flew home with God as my Beloved. Then, one cold January Saturday a few weeks later, I found myself driving to upstate New York. Upon arrival at Ismael's modest suburban home, I was greeted by his beautiful wife.

Ismael invited me into his study to once again practice soul-sharing. I explained my growing understanding of the illusion of the individual self. He shared with me an ancient Sufi teaching about the seven selves we are born to transcend. Most people only develop two or three of these selves—and often not fully. But a mystic's quest is to search the world, to come to deeply know and develop all seven selves. Mastering the ego-self makes way for the Beloved.

That is the secret of Ismael's journey. And since the Sufis had planted the Ka'ba of love in my heart during my time among them, he said that was the secret of my spiritual journey as well. He said my many years as an entrepreneur had brought me into the furnace to become soft and malleable, like hot lava. But the business world did not know how to mold me into a superior spiritual being. Now, in the second half of my life, my spirit would shine forth the love of the Beloved. As Unitarian Universalist minister and mystic Om Prakash Gilmore exclaims in his poem "The Stars Are Dancing":

The stars are dancing tonight,
while the moon sits in her golden hammock,
swaying back and forth to the rhythm of celestial voices.

The Beloved is full of rapture,
dancing worlds and stars into being,
drunk with the wine of passion
and filling the heavens with song.

Do not sit alone in the dark
while creation sings three-part harmony.
Dance, my friends.

Dance wildly,
sing joyfully,
fill your heart with the beauty of the Beloved
as the Beloved turns your soul to light.

My spirit was set free. Ismael's teaching brought new meaning to my favorite pilgrimage song in the Unitarian Universalist hymnal *Singing the Living Tradition.* The hymn is adapted from Rumi: "Come, come, whoever you are, wanderer, worshiper, lover of leaving. Ours is no caravan of despair. Come, yet again, come." We dwell in the Beloved as the Beloved dwells in us.

It took mystics, with the Ka'ba of love, to shape me into a mirror of the likeness of the Beloved. I still awaken some mornings to a red oval over my heart, and the sacred stories Ismael shared with me still break me open with renewed joy.

Our spiritual lives are meant to be full of risk and audacity. The Holy Spirit moves through the decades of our lives. This is meant to bring us immense joy, if we would only join the dance. Just dance, no matter how awkwardly. Just dance.

Befriending Ismael was like discovering the wise, spiritual elder brother I never had. He broke my heart open, invoking the fierce power of love to transform my soul. Through traveling with Ismael, I discovered a great secret: the longing of my own soul. I learned how to quench that longing through direct experience of the love of God. This was an awakening for me.

Sufis attune themselves to the Beloved. Mystic whirling dervishes dance with the divine. I never thought I danced well. But I found a reassuring poem by Hafiz:

> *You have not danced so badly, my dear, trying to hold*
> *   hands with the Beloved.*
> *You have waltzed with great style, my sweet crushed*
> *   angel,*
> *to have ever neared God's heart at all.*
> *The divine mystery is notoriously hard to follow.*

Even with no sense of rhythm, we can still dance with God with enormous joy in our hearts.

When God seems distant or uninterested in us, Hafiz advises:

> *So what if the price of admission to the Divine is out of*
> *reach tonight?*
> *So what, my dear, if you do not have the ante to gamble*
> *for God's love?*
> *Have patience, for God will not be able to resist your*
> *longing for long.*
> *You have not danced so badly, my dear, trying to kiss*
> *the Divine.*
> *You have actually waltzed with tremendous style, my*
> *sweet, sweet crushed angel.*

This is why I traveled with Sufis. To attain union with the Beloved. Rumi, my teacher, wrote:

> *Dance, when you're broken open.*
> *Dance, when you've torn the bandage off.*
> *Dance in the middle of fighting. Dance in your blood . . .*
> *When we depart this life at last, we'll carry only what*
> *weighs nothing.*
> *The sweetness and torments of love become tender with*
> *time.*
> *Those ego gains you pursue today become worthless, but*
> *love grows in worth . . .*
> *Each of us chooses every day a life with or without love.*

May we always choose dancing in union with the Beloved! May each of us choose every day a life centered on love, sharing our hearts with one another and bringing us into intimate communion with the divine mystery.

Islamic Mystics
BOOK GROUP DISCUSSION GUIDE

Author's Comment

The paths into ecstatic union with the divine are as many and diverse within Islam as they are within Christianity. I have been fortunate to be guided by the Mevlevi Sufis, who have a joyous, heartfelt connection to God.

Questions to Encourage Conversation

1. Is it possible that human spiritual journeys within the world's major religions might be drawing from the same living waters— the same spiritual techniques that precede modern religions and their practices?

2. Would you seek Sufis to teach you to whirl and dance with the divine? Why or why not?

3. How does the name Beloved fit with your notion of God?

4. Have you ever experienced a spiritual epiphany?

5. When religious hierarchy melds itself to worldly power, the purpose and process of faith often shifts markedly. How did this happen in Islam?

6. How does the trauma of Rumi's early life inform his spirituality?

7. What role did Shams of Tabriz play in cracking Rumi's heart open?

8. Does it seem likely that dancing dhikr can incite a state of divine ecstasy? Why or why not?

9. How does Ismael's story compare to the author's? To yours?

Reflection

As a group, reflect upon the importance of praying, singing, and dancing to physically embody union with God.

CHINESE MYSTICS

The Tao never does anything, yet through it all things are done. If powerful men and women could center themselves in it, the whole world would be transformed by itself, in its natural rhythms. People would be content with their simple, everyday lives, in harmony, and free of desire. When there is no desire, all things are at peace.

—Tao Te Ching, chapter 37 (Stephen Mitchell translation)

Tao Fong Shan

Six weeks after traveling with Ismael, I found myself on a mountaintop in the Chinese New Territories above Hong Kong at a Taoist Christian retreat center called Tao Fong Shan, where intellectuals openly and freely discuss emergent Chinese philosophical thought. Tao Fong Shan means "Way of the Spirit Mountain."

Because my wife, Loretta, is the American-born daughter of highly educated Chinese immigrants, Taoism would help me better understand her view of reality, even while transforming my own. This would be a month full of mystery and magic.

The Tao Fong Shan Chinese Christian Retreat Center is itself a magical, mystical place. The center's website suggests traveling from Hong Kong International Airport via the subway system, transferring to a train for the Chinese New Territories, crossing the Chinese border, and disembarking at Sha Tin New Town. Then it suggests making one's way on foot steadily uphill for about a half mile until the path arrives at the gate of the retreat center, on a mountain it shares with a Lutheran seminary, a Buddhist monastery, and other spiritual communities. Yet speaking no Chinese, I was very hesitant as a confirmed rationalist to risk following such a way alone.

Fortunately, the executive director of the center agreed to meet me at the Hong Kong International Airport upon arrival from my fifteen-hour flight. When we finally came to the mountain, he brought me to their guest house for pilgrims called Ching Fung Tai (meaning "relax into illuminated consciousness"). That first day he allowed me to settle in to deal with the vagaries of jet lag and shifting across thirteen time zones.

The guest house had a gorgeous view of the mountains across a skyscraper-filled valley. This was modern China—urban development encircled by mystic mountains. These mountains were the steep, pointy peaks of Chinese tourist brochures. Misty clouds clung to them like those often seen in Chinese landscape paintings. It was all surreal. Yet it was *real*. Watching those clouds languidly drift across the mountain ranges opposite my house became one of my most cherished memories of my time spent at this retreat center.

The next morning, we breakfasted together in Pilgrim Hall, where most of my meals were served during my stay. I then went to the director's office to go over my program, for which we had made preliminary arrangements via email for nearly six months. Wanting to make the most of this sabbatical time, I would study Taoism during my stay, and I had agreed to also teach some Chinese executives as an entrepreneurial visiting scholar. In addition, I planned to spend part of a week traveling on the mainland with Loretta and our son. The president of Andover Newton Theological School (ANTS) had suggested several people, particularly Chinese Christian ministers, for me to meet during my visit. It would be a busy month. I needed a plan if I was to fit everything in.

The executive director, a Chinese Christian minister and scholar, would become my spiritual guide in Chinese ways of knowing and being. I came to think of him as Changzu, a living embodiment of the ancient Taoist spiritual guide Chuang Tzu. He would help foster my becoming.

That first morning in his office, Changzu agreed to develop a plan for my transcendence. We talked for three hours, and he gave me a dozen books on Taoism in Chinese culture. He also agreed to make final arrangements for my program. It seems he needed to experience me in person, both my aura and my energy level, before he would commit to planning an appropriate program and schedule for the entire month of my visit.

That afternoon, Changzu took me down the mountain to introduce me to the shops in Sha Tin New Town, where I could purchase any extras I needed during my stay, such as shampoo, coffee, alcohol, or other food. It required a half-mile walk down the mountain, with the same walk back up the mountain while carrying my purchases.

Changzu was surprised how winded and slow I became in climbing back up the mountain. He said our physical wellbeing and spiritual wellbeing were two sides of the same coin, the yin-yang of being in dynamic interchange. He said both my physical and spiritual being would transform in my month living on the mountain. He would help make me whole.

The path was lined with monkeys in the trees. They chattered ceaselessly and seemed to follow me with their eyes. These monkeys were annoying, metaphysically and actually. Changzu said if I ignored the monkeys, they would not lead me astray. Otherwise, they would always be distracting me from my intention. I was often distracted, though—by monkeys and by my monkey mind.

Finally left to myself that evening, I settled in and began studying books on Taoism, having agreed to discuss them with Changzu on Friday. And so I began this pilgrim journey by studying the endless transformation of existence and how it manifests itself in transcendence.

By the next day, Changzu had already arranged six important visits for me over the next three weeks. He also arranged for me to lead three workshops and participate in two additional forums. And he had begun to make inquiries with Christian Taoists about my trip to the mainland.

Changzu suggested deepening my understanding of Chinese Christianity by joining the Christian monks for their Taizé prayer practice each day and by helping him lead a Sunday Chinese Christian worship service in Hong Kong. He also taught me more about the Chinese concept of six religions: Taoism, Confucianism, Buddhism, Protestantism, Catholicism, and Islam. In the Chinese mystic's worldview, each religion offered a different perspective on the divine mountains. I had many adventures and misadventures on those mountains.

Confucius

Confucianism cast a long shadow over the Chinese understanding of each of these world religions, so now I set out to understand the ancient wisdom teacher Confucius. Confucius, or Master Kong, lived from about 551 to 479 BCE, during what is known in China as the tumultuous Spring and Autumn period. The word *China* is from a later period, derived from the Sanskrit or Persian name of the Qin dynasty. But Confucius called his civilization Huaxia, meaning the "illustrious blossoming of human and humane civilization."

Confucius might well be the most influential teacher in human history, based upon the billions of people who have tried to follow his teachings about how to live as a human being. Living during a period of tremendous social upheaval and constant warring between small kingdoms, Confucius was deeply reverent toward the past while teaching that human flourishing could be the result of living in harmonious balance. His teachings would greatly influence human flourishing on the planet Earth, even among those people who have never even heard of him.

Confucius taught that we express our unique being through our relationships with our relatives (parents, siblings, spouses, and children) as well as our friends and neighbors. The foundation of being a good person always begins with being a good son or daughter. No matter what our parents are like, we owe them a duty of love and care simply for their giving us the gift of life. Our debt to them is beyond measure and can never be fully repaid. This is how I have always sought to relate to my large extended family.

Confucius's father, Shuliang He, was an old man when he married a teenage girl from the Yan family. She conceived and gave birth to Confucius. Shuliang He died three years later, leaving Confucius and his widowed mother in great financial hardship. Confucius grew up in the working class. He did menial work yet strove through a diligent education, studying history, philosophy, poetry, music, and religious rituals to cultivate a life of human flourishing.

Confucius married at the age of eighteen and with his wife raised two children, a boy and a girl. He spent most of his life working as a minor bureaucrat and political advisor to a few state governments. He was not particularly successful in any worldly sense. Yet he opens his teachings in the *Analects* with this description of human flourishing: "Having studied, and applied what you have learned, is this not a source of pleasure? To have many friends from distant places, is this not a source of enjoyment? To go unacknowledged by others without getting frustrated, is this not the mark of an exemplary person?" He led an exemplary life.

As an old man, he looked back over his life:

> *At fifteen, I set my heart on learning. At thirty, I*
> *created balance in my life through balancing*
> *yin and yang. At forty, I finally ceased to doubt*
> *myself. At fifty, I understood my life's purpose*
> *and what Heaven intended me to do. At sixty,*
> *I finally trusted my intuition. At seventy, I*
> *followed my heart's desire with bliss without*
> *overstepping the lines of propriety.*

Mountains beyond Mountains

Friday morning, we met in Changzu's office again, but he said I would learn more about Taoism by hiking than by talking. So we agreed to hike the nearby mountains together the next morning. Changzu estimated it would take about three hours ascending and descending.

I arrived the next morning in a sweatshirt, jeans, and sneakers, uncertain about what the morning might hold. We began by walking uphill on a trail crossing from our mountain to another, higher mountain behind us. The upward path gave way to a rather steep series of steps. I quickly became winded and unsure of whether I could safely make this ascent.

I must have looked skeptical, because Changzu said not to worry—there were only a little over two thousand steps on this part of the path. He had counted them as part of his morning meditation hike. He said a brief prayer on every step. Changzu said we could stop to take breaks as needed.

We had ascended well above our mountain retreat, and I was already quite out of breath. The blood drained from my face, turning me a whiter shade of pale. Changzu suggested focusing on my breathing as a way to calm my body and quiet my mind. But instead of becoming more grounded, I found myself focusing on how difficult it was to regulate my breathing.

Changzu next suggested I no longer focus upon my breath. Instead, I should focus just on putting one foot in front of the other. He taught me to take smaller steps and to walk more slowly and deliberately, which was a faster and surer way to cover the mountain. Many small steps covered more ground with less strain than my lunging forward could. As my fears began to calm, my body somewhat relaxed and the blood returned to my face.

Finally, we reached a flat area, which felt like the top of this mountain range. Changzu applauded my efforts, mentioning that we were now a quarter of the way up our hike to Needle Hill (which was, in fact, the hilly peak of a mountain range). After resting, we went on.

My mantra became "Step by step, inch by inch, with mental focus, climbing a mountain is a cinch." As silly as it sounded, this simple mantra worked for me. By transcending mind, I was able to change what was possible. Through concentration and simple walking meditation, my body was able to do the seemingly impossible.

The next stage of the hike included a discussion about Taoism, or finding the Way of Integrity. I had to regulate my breathing in order to talk while climbing higher. Every so often, whenever I felt unable to continue upward, Changzu would encouragingly say it wasn't much farther—perhaps a few hundred more steps. My calves ached, my heart pounded, yet I settled into simply enduring the wretched muscle tightness and pain.

We climbed, we talked, and eventually we came to the end of the two thousand steps up the mountain. It was then that I discovered this had brought us into a mountain hiking park. This was a thing of beauty. However, we would need to hike a good distance farther down this trail before we could even see, much less climb, to the top of Needle Hill. Thankfully, hiking in the park was not nearly so strenuous. Our conversation became more philosophical, and I began to relax and enjoy myself.

Before too long, we found ourselves at the foot of a steeper series of steps leading up to the top of Needle Hill. Our view of surrounding mountains and valleys was breathtaking. Very reassuringly, Changzu said it was only seven hundred steps—perhaps more—to the top of Needle Hill.

As we climbed, my heart began to pound ever more tightly, forcing me to stop for another break about halfway up. At this point, Changzu said I had gone farther without a break than he had expected. On his own first climb of the mountain, he too had needed to rest about halfway up.

Although I appreciated this consolation, I still was in deep pain—yet I was beginning to learn how to achieve equanimity even under pain and stress. Changzu said we could turn back if my heart couldn't take it. He didn't want me to die on the mountain. I asked him how much farther it would be. He said perhaps several hundred steps—perhaps more—but we were close to the top now.

I pushed on, determined to bring my body to the top of the mountain. The spiritual point of this climb was for me to transcend my mind and realize my body was not limited to what my mind imagined it was capable of. This was wu wei in nonaction. I changed my mind rather than my physical circumstances, and that made all the difference to my perception of reality.

Finally, we reached the marker at the top of Needle Hill after nearly two hours. I was ecstatic! We were literally on top of the world and could see for miles, looking out over the beautifully varied Chinese landscape, which looked just like a painting to me.

Changzu pointed out that our pace was faster when we walked deliberately and in tune with the mountain rather than when we attacked the mountain at a higher speed, which required frequent stops along the way. The mountain had more yang energy than either of us ever would, so attacking it was fruitless and tiring. But yin energy allowed us to flow with the mountain in harmony. As Changzu said, it is difficult to conquer a mountain, far easier to let the mountain carry you step by step upward. You begin to become one with the mountain and surrounding environment.

Indeed, I experienced a deep sense of peace. By climbing Needle Hill, I came to embody wu wei, or effortless accomplishment. It is a core teaching of Taoism. When nothing is done, nothing is left undone. This was the truth the rogue Taoism teacher Alan Watts taught me decades before: "Wu Wei is . . . not simply intellectual [understanding]; it is also the *unconscious* intelligence of the whole organism and, in particular, the innate wisdom with taking the line of least resistance in all one's actions." I was learning how to embody the Tao, to join in its flow of being, with the least effort necessary.

On our hike back down, we came across an elderly fellow taking pictures of a flowering bush on his Apple iPhone. Changzu greeted him and told me he was the head gardener at the monastery on this mountain. This Chinese gardener loaded this picture into his wildflower app and was able to confirm immediately it was a rare flower never before documented this close to Hong Kong. Juxtaposing old and new, all is beauty.

Taoism

During our mountain hike, I could feel my chi, or life force, growing stronger and responding to these Taoist spiritual exercises. Taoism, a complementary but distinct philosophical tradition from Confucianism, grew out of the same yin-and-yang period of Chinese culture. Taoism always held a great fascination for me, especially after Loretta and I were married and I discovered her father's worldview was Confucian and Taoist, though of the Dongba variety of the rural Naxi people.

Taoism emphasizes compassion, spontaneity, simplicity, frugality, humility, and naturalness. It attempts to maintain a dynamic balance between human nature and the earthly nature that surrounds us. Taoism's central text is the Tao Te Ching, otherwise anglicized as Dao De Jing. It emerged during the early part of the Chinese Warring States period (475–221 BCE), when internecine warfare between the contending states did much to destroy physical, mental, and spiritual wellbeing. Taoism arose in response to aggression and human striving.

We are born, we experience life, and we die within a network of relationships and events that encompass the entire field of human experience. The Tao is a focused and sustained approach to human life that draws upon these events and relationships to make the most of our unique life experiences. What Confucius meant by *tian*, or heaven, Taoists refer to simply as the Tao, or the Way. Following the Tao makes my life significant.

As the philosophy professors Roger Ames and David Hall describe in the introduction to their Dao De Jing translation, "The reality of time, novelty, and change; the persistence of particularity; the intrinsic, constitutive nature of relationships; the perspectival nature of experience—taken together, these several presuppositions that ground the Daoist worldview and provide Daoism with its interpretive context set the terms for optimizing our experience." The Tao Te Ching is a user's guide to the ultimate and ineffable nature of the divine mystery. It teaches how to live life with grace and joy, both actively involved and not taking things too seriously.

We can never understand the Tao through mere study—we must actually experience it. The Tao Te Ching, in its opening lines, plunges us directly into the mystery:

> *The Tao that can be spoken is not the eternal Tao.*
> *The name that can be named is not the eternal*
> *name. The nameless is the origin of heaven and*
> *earth. The named is the creator of myriad things.*
> *Thus constantly without desire, one observes its*
> *essence. Constantly with desire, one observes its*
> *manifestations. These two emerge together but*
> *differ in name. The unity is said to be the mystery.*

Unlike Confucians, many of whom made their living by serving the state, Taoists were more likely to be hermits or recluses. The Tao Te Ching is attributed to Lao Tzu, which simply means "the old man"—a humble appellation for a religious founder or wise sage. He is said to have written it in a day, to summarize all his teachings so he could leave this state behind and return to a life of contemplation and ecstasy in harmony with the natural universe.

My favorite expositor of Taoism as a coherent spiritual philosophy and the ontological process of becoming has always been Chuang Tzu, or Zhuangzi. He lived from about 369 to 286 BCE, or the latter part of the Warring States period.

Chuang Tzu writes with happy ambiguity and ease about the constantly emerging and transforming web of all being, of which human beings partake. Everyday living is both our curse and the source of our transcendence. To rightly understand our role in the universe is to attain spiritual realization.

As I walked the Chinese mountains and meditated on these ancient teachings, Chuang Tzu traveled with me. He taught that words are merely symbols to capture an idea; once captured, the words are unnecessary. Chuang Tzu said, "The point of a fish trap is the fish: once you've got the fish, you can forget the trap. The point of the rabbit snare is the rabbit: once you've got the rabbit, you can forget the snare. And the point of a word is the idea: once you've got the idea, you can forget the word." I got the idea beyond the words.

Chuang Tzu was famously skeptical of all dialectical argumentation. Using the concept of "three in the morning," he discussed how we can wear ourselves out trying to articulate the unity of all things without actually realizing they're just the same:

> *There was a monkey trainer who fed monkeys three bananas in the morning and four bananas at night. The monkeys got very angry. So he fed them four in the morning and three at night. At this, the monkeys were happy again. Nothing was lost in either name or reality, but they were angry one way and pleased the other.*

This is how it is with scholars who insist upon "three in the morning." They mistake words for reality, their mere thoughts for what is ultimate, and miss what is real.

My favorite Chuang Tzu teaching asks, what is the underlying nature of reality, and what is merely dream?

> *Long ago, a certain Chuang Tzu dreamt he was a butterfly—a butterfly fluttering here and there on a whim, happy and carefree, knowing nothing of Chuang Tzu. Then all of a sudden, he woke to find that he was, beyond all doubt, Chuang Tzu. Who knows if it was Chuang Tzu dreaming a butterfly, or a butterfly dreaming Chuang Tzu?*

I began to pay particular attention to the butterflies on these Chinese mountains. They had lessons to teach about the nature of being and becoming. The caterpillar turns into a loathsome moth or a beautiful butterfly, depending upon its inherent nature. Both serve the purposes of emergent life on this planet. I awoke to a resilient Way of human flourishing.

Wu wei is sometimes illustrated through a traditional story about Chuang Tzu. One sunny day, his disciples found him sitting happily and peacefully in the sun in front of his house. His freshly washed, uncut hair tumbled down around him. They asked him if this was a form of meditation. He said, "I am drying my hair in the warm sun." They asked how they might join in meditation. He said, "I am drying my hair and resting in the origin of all being."

On warm sunny days at Tao Fong Shan, I would bathe early and sit in front of my pilgrim house looking over the valley below. I would watch the morning star fade in the gathering light and thrill to the morning birds beginning to sing. I would observe Sha Tin New Town springing to life with all its urban noises. I would dry my hair in the warm sun, resting in the origin of all being.

Through the practice of transcending the mind, modern Chinese Taoism certainly has something to teach those who wish to follow a mystical path into the divine mystery. Over the course of the month, my studies taught me to climb mountains because mountains are sacred. Climbing them brings us closer to *tian*. It increases the flow of chi energy through our bodies. This spiritual mountain climbing is one of the hardest things I've ever done. I climbed Needle Hill four more times during my month on retreat.

Embodied Taoism draws on the essence at the core of reality—what is ultimate—to balance our yin and yang life forces, each spilling dynamically over into the other in harmony. I now had the spiritual force to climb metaphorical mountains beyond mountains with true joy. This is the art of living as a mature and awakened person of authentic integrity. This is the art of living the Way of the Tao.

Taoism and Confucianism grew together, first one and then the other claiming precedence. They shared many of the same terms and concepts as they flowered forth together in what would come to be known to the West as Cathay, or China.

Several hundreds of years later, yet another Way emerged in China when Buddhist teachers brought Gautama's teachings and scriptures. Buddhism was initially seen as quite foreign to Chinese thought. That is, until Buddhist scriptures were translated into Chinese, employing Taoist concepts and categories. The result was Ch'an Buddhism, which became very popular in China and later would be the basis of Japanese Zen Buddhism.

Chinese Buddhism

Now, well ahead of my reading schedule on Confucianism and Taoism, I decided to explore Chinese Buddhism. To do so, I made my way down to the Ten Thousand Buddhas monastery, a magical place rising above Sha Tin New Town. This had been a prominent Chinese Buddhist monastery before the Chinese government closed it and sent the Buddhist monks away. It had recently reopened as a Buddhist tourist destination, but this morning I had it largely to myself.

I ascended from a neighborhood just behind the Sha Tin train station. I had ten thousand thoughts running through my mind. *Ten thousand* is a traditional Chinese phrase meaning "too many to count." What Taoists call ten thousand things, we might call overwhelming numbers or perhaps even infinity. I was engaging with the cosmos in an effortless fashion.

As I began my ascent up this mountain, continuous rows of golden buddha statues lined both sides of my path. Most were middle-aged or of indeterminate age, but a few were ancient, and some were quite young-looking, including some who looked like children. Most were male, but a few were female. Most looked Chinese, but some looked east Asian (from India), a few looked Western, and one or two even as if they came from Africa. Most were quite bald, but some had abundant hair, often including beards or mustaches. Ch'an Buddhism and Taoism often universalize divine mystery as a radiant gift for all humanity.

Most of the statues were standing or sitting alone, but some were clearly buddies. Most looked well-fed, though a few looked emaciated, and others looked positively rotund. Many of the statues representing men from India had the traditional third eye of an enlightened buddha in their forehead, as well as the Aryan cross, or swastika, on their chest. This is a symbol that has ceased to be acceptable in the West, after the Nazis imagined they were descended from Aryans and chose the swastika as their symbol during WWII. Farther up the mountain, symbols became more Chinese and less Buddhist. This was an enlightening interreligious dialogue set in stone.

The eight Chinese immortals figured prominently. The sixty enlightened figures of the Chinese zodiac were there in their places. Buddha statues were shown riding horses, dragons, deer, fish, and any manner of different creatures. Buddhahood is not restricted to humans. Whole rows of statues of Buddha's mother, the mother of God, recognizable by her buddha crown, greeted my journey. At one of the uppermost pagodas was what looked like an Aramaic long-haired, bearded buddha, recognizing and honoring Jesus's Buddha nature.

Then I came upon what looked to be an unfinished side court. Here was Budai, the Laughing Buddha, in all his smiling, rotund glory! Yet I also noticed there were other open spaces for yet more statues, perhaps for buddhas yet to be born, or perhaps those who hadn't yet realized their buddha nature. Chinese Buddhism creates an audacious, synergetic faith that welcomes all.

Awakened to this reality, living between two worlds, I found my way back down the mountain to further explore Chinese Christianity. We are one and all will be one.

Chinese Christianity

For the month I lived on the mountain, many evenings were spent sitting on floor cushions doing Taizé prayer with the Christian monks. Most Sundays were spent participating in or helping to lead Christian worship services either at the seminary on the mountain or in Hong

Kong. Much of it was familiar, but even with a translator by my side, much was lost on me.

Through ANTS introductions, I met several leaders of large Christian churches authorized by the Chinese government. We talked about the difficulties of being a minority religion under a godless Communist regime and the constant threat of persecution. I also met Chinese college professors who were secret pastors of Christian underground churches. They seemed to have a more mystical sense of the divine than the formally recognized congregation—and a real fear of being persecuted if discovered. Yet they also feared that if they registered with the Chinese government, whether as Christians or even as Taoists, they would be vulnerable to future changes in government policies concerning religious organizations.

When Christianity arrived in China, it followed a similar pattern as Buddhism, which arrived many hundreds of years earlier. Initially, it made very little headway because its theology was so foreign to established Chinese thought. However, after many decades, the Bible was translated into Chinese, employing Taoist and Confucian concepts and categories. Jesus seemed to use the words *heaven* and *God* interchangeably, as in the *kingdom of heaven* or *kingdom of God*. Both were translated as *tian di*, what we might call "heaven and earth" or "ultimate reality," which was readily understandable and acceptable to the Chinese. This *was* heaven and earth, intimately interconnected and interpermeable, as two sides of the yin and yang of harmonious relationship.

For Confucians, *tian* meant "heaven" in the sense of both a supreme being who could and would care about us and the ultimate impersonal divine state of being. And *di*, "earth," is both the ground we walk upon and the ground of being. So *tian di* is the dynamic yin-yang interplay of these states of being. We were born out of a natural process of the earth's becoming holy, and we return to it in death. Following the Tao, or Way of Heaven, gives our existence its ultimate purpose and becomes the source of our deepest joy. Thus, following the Tao becomes the path to becoming fully human.

But for Christianity, this requires a new understanding of the nature and idea of God. In John 14:5–6, doubting Thomas asks, "How can we know the way?" Jesus replies, "I AM the Way, and the Truth, and the Life. No one comes to the Father [God] except through me." Using Taoist and Confucian categories of thought, this conversation becomes: "How can we know the Tao?" Thomas asks. Jesus replies, "I AM the Tao, and the Tao, and the Tao. No one comes to *tian* except through the Tao." This act of imaginative translation between cultures enables deeper interreligious spiritual experiences and yields new insights into divine mystery.

Following the Tao is central to Chinese thought. It's a dynamic process, which changes based on the nature of our various relationships. Within a Chinese worldview, I am not the same person as I was at my baptism at age thirteen, nor the same person as the young entrepreneur taking companies public, nor even the same person I was in relation to my marriage or my ministry. I am a mature spiritual mystic, yet I remain in intimate relationship with all those different selves. They are part of the composite being I call me. Our sense of self is mediated by our relationships. We become fully human only within the context of our relationships.

But like most Americans, I had always thought of myself as essentially the same person. As Roger Ames, a leading Western scholar of Chinese philosophy, writes: "Essentialism is virtually built into English—indeed into all Indo-European languages—by the way things, essences, and substances do something or have something else attributed to them." English tends to focus on independent objects and Chinese on relationships. As a Christian mystic, Chinese Christianity would ultimately help transform my faith and my relationship to the divine mystery.

Chinese Christianity, especially in the ubiquitous illicit Chinese house churches, is deeply Taoist and Confucian in nature. I had been approaching the divine mystery in awe and fear, as a good Christian should. But engaging with divine mystery was now translated for me using Confucius's *Analects* as "Fearful, fearful; as if treading on thin ice, as if peering into an abyss." The Tao is dynamic, requiring both persistence (continuity) and transformation (change). We are both the continuity and the change. The Western notion of objective reality doesn't work in such a context, but we can grow spiritually through embracing both continuity and change.

Confucians measure success in becoming flourishing human beings by our depth of self-understanding and personal refinement, independent of our life circumstances or public personas. A worthy person is self-differentiated and truly knows themselves. Such a person grows in compassion and wisdom, eventually reaching that stage of wellbeing Confucians and Taoists call a living sage. There are no shortcuts to becoming such a sage—Confucius said few achieve this state before the age of sixty. It lifts us above our prior state of being into transcendent bliss. Such people are distinguished by their *ren,* which can be translated as "humaneness" or "human kindness." I have always believed human kindness is the surest recognition of our shared humanity and spiritual maturity.

Studying with Confucians and Taoists encouraged me to become such a sage through developing spiritual maturity. Mystics had once again transformed my journey. My trust in serendipity and highly improbable synchronicities soared as a result of these experiences. My sense of the awesomeness and dynamic transformation of the divine mystery was changed. Serendipitous creativity—which some call God, others call love or grace—transforms our being.

Yet I pondered how to interpolate ancient Chinese philosophers into my twenty-first-century Western thought. Much of what is written in English about these Chinese philosophical concepts is wrong or at least inadequate.

One of my teachers at the retreat center invited me to meet the only two known Unitarian Universalists in Kowloon. How would Unitarian Universalism translate into Chinese? Sufis, shamans, Buddhists, Bahá'í, UUs, and Taoists all universalize the divine mystery with spiritual practices that can bring all people into oneness with the divine, creating authentic human beings.

Arriving for my meeting a few minutes early, I ducked into an English-language bookstore and discovered *The Tao of Joy* by Derek Lin, a Taiwanese Taoist living in California and writing for people like me. The very first passage I read said, "The Tao is often compared to a river. When we talk about going with the flow, we are describing the Tao as having a definite direction, just like a river flowing in a certain way. . . . Moving with the Tao is like swimming downstream. It requires little effort, and you can go a long way in a short time." I was again in the flow!

Lin describes the Tao as the Way of all existence. He says, "We observe the world and see creation happens continuously. In every moment, babies are born, ideas are conceived, inventions are crafted and songs are written. Thus, the way of existence seems to be this process of constant and never-ending creation." The spirit of life is continual emergence.

Lin also affirms, "If there is one concept that encapsulates life, the universe and everything, it must be dynamic exchange. No matter where you look, every part of the world is engaged in a continuous, nonstop exchange of energy, molecules and information. A tree that seems perfectly still is actively exchanging oxygen for carbon dioxide; a cup of coffee is actively radiating heat energy. . . . Dynamic exchange is happening everywhere all the time." This is life!

Lin says the Tao expresses itself through synchronicities: "If they are happening frequently, it can mean you are on the right path and there is something you are meant to learn from them. Keep doing what you are doing, and enjoy them as wondrous gifts." This is why traveling with mystics had so dramatically increased my awareness of serendipity in life.

Mystics say that when the student is ready a teacher always appears, so I kept my mind and heart open to synchronicities. But our teacher often presents itself in a form or person we may not recognize, so we must encounter every experience as our possible teacher.

As it turned out, I learned next to nothing from the Kowloon UUs at that meeting. Yet a Taiwanese Taoist living in California had the message I needed in Hong Kong. Derek Lin finally helped me understand part of my wife's spirituality. Blessed be.

In the entire month I spent at the mountain retreat in China, it never rained during the daytime. It sometimes rained late at night, and often there was misty fog on the mountains at dawn. But the day I finally left the retreat, it poured great sheets of water, drenching the mountain. One of my teachers said I should feel beloved when even the mountains cried to see me depart.

The Naxi People

From the mountains above Hong Kong, we journeyed to mainland China to trace the roots of Loretta's family. Loretta's father was a descendent of the Naxi people and a Dongba universalist. He grew up in the tiny village of Baisha in Yunnan province, in the foothills of the Himalayas, the mystical Chinese Shangri-la. By the late twentieth century there were only a few hundred thousand Naxi people living in Yunnan province, mostly poor and oppressed. They tended to all be related one to another in a close-knit series of family bonds and relationships.

This would be our third attempt to visit her father's village. We first tried in 1983, shortly after his death. But the government discouraged us, there was no local airport, it was too remote an area, and it required too long a train ride while traveling with a toddler.

By 1996, Yunnan province had a newly opened airport in Lijiang, so that year, we traveled with Loretta's mother and two of her sisters to explore my father-in-law's early life. We were greeted at the Lijiang airport, ten miles south of Baisha, by the entire regional high school's brass band! But our China Travel Service guide required her own local guide, who could speak both Mandarin and Naxi, to find our way. We were able to see my father-in-law's childhood home—a dirt-floor house with the animals living right outside— but much of what was said was not translated for us.

But this time in 2012, we had the help of my Chinese Taoist teachers. They told me that upon my checking in to the only American hotel in Lijiang, the head of guest services would approach me with an offer to do anything necessary to make my stay more productive and comfortable. It was in that moment that I should make my most audacious request. Loretta and our son, Robert, would then join me later that afternoon.

Sure enough, as I checked in, a young Chinese woman, speaking excellent English, approached me with just this expression of helpfulness. I explained who my wife and her father were and the purpose of our visit. I asked for a Naxi guide who could make this possible for us. She paused, then said this would be most difficult, but I did not relent. She was able to find us a Naxi translator, fluent in English and Mandarin, born after the Cultural Revolution, who was willing to drop everything else and be with us twelve hours a day during our stay in Yunnan. I trusted serendipity and wu wei on our spiritual journey.

The most famous relics of Baisha's and Lijiang's many-centuries-long role on the old Silk Road of commerce are the Baisha frescoes. The original frescoes were once distributed among more than fifteen Buddhist and Taoist monasteries and palaces in the area. They reflect a remarkable blend of Dongba, Bön, Taoist, and Buddhist influences. Once numbering in the hundreds, there are still fifty-three frescoes preserved in the ruins of the old Dabaoji Palace in the tiny village of Baisha. Our interpreter and guide took us to see them our second afternoon.

As we walked and talked together, we asked about the scholarships Loretta's mother had given in her husband's name after his death to help young Naxi people get an education. We learned how those scholarships had helped many local students over the last twenty years. Our guide and the retired provincial governor took us to see the entire wing of the Baisha elementary school, which was rebuilt with donations from Loretta's mother following an earthquake. Then we visited the Hall of Ancestors at her father's high school in Lijiang and saw that he was commemorated there as one of the fourteen most important graduates of the school. I felt so proud of Loretta's father. His sacrifices in immigrating to America and choosing to raise his family there helped his Naxi people in powerful but unexpected ways.

We met Loretta's second and third cousins and learned how they survived the Cultural Revolution. One of Loretta's cousins graduated high school after the Cultural Revolution and had a college education. He was now head of tourism for the entire province and managed the Chinese Himalayan resort located on Jade Dragon Snow Mountain. He had his driver take us past all the waiting lines of Chinese tourists to ride the Swiss-made gondola up onto the glacier. Our guide pointed out how much the glacier had receded over the last decade due to global climate change. We saw Tibetan farmers plowing fields in mountain valleys that used to be permafrost. Loretta's cousin also hosted us for lunch in a restaurant called in English the "Very Important Person Restaurant."

These experiences in China went way beyond what we could have possibly imagined. Suddenly the Naxi world view came into focus, helped by practicing wu wei and transcending my mental limitations. This was a spiritual and family pilgrimage to one of the most remote parts of China.

The Naxi people are indigenous to Yunnan, genetically related to the Burmese and Tibetan people, and first enter the historical record as nomads living in the grasslands of what is now northeastern Tibet. They were mountain herders of sheep and yaks. According to Pedro Ceinos Arcones in *Sons of Heaven, Brothers of Nature: The Naxi of Southwest China,* they trace their Dongba religious beginnings to one Aming Shiluo, who evidently lived around 1050 CE. Dongba shares many concepts with ancient forms of the Bön religion and Tibetan Buddhism. Donga is deeply steeped in Taoist ideas as well.

However, what is particularly distinctive about Dongba is its focus on heaven (represented by mountains) and earth (represented as the universal mother). In this sense, it retains a deeply shamanic relationship to the divine mystery. We are of the earth and have heaven in our hearts, so we aspire to the heights of mountains, as sons and daughters of heaven and brothers and sisters of nature.

The shamanic Dongba use rhythmic music and dance to enter a trance state. Altered states of consciousness are common during long religious ceremonies, not unlike the practices of the Sufis I had traveled with in Turkey. They are the indigenous *tian di* mystics of southwest China.

The Naxi were an independent mountainous kingdom and a crossroads along the east-to-west Silk Road until Kublai Khan's army swept across the Yangtze River in 1253, on his way to conquering much of China. The Naxi king allied with the Great Khan, paying tribute and sending troops to help the Mongols defeat Beijing, and so maintained his people's independence. When Mandarin rebels overthrew the Yuan dynasty in 1368, these mountain tribes of northwest Yunnan were too remote to administer from Beijing. So they simply changed to whom they sent their tribute and remained independent for another several hundred years.

By the late eighteenth century, transportation of armies and administrators became much easier. The Mandarins began to treat this formerly independent kingdom as a rural province to be ruled by Chinese magistrates on behalf of the emperor. Finally, with the founding of the Republic of China in 1912, the last vestiges of a Naxi monarchy and independent kingdom were destroyed. In the eyes of Beijing, these regions remained a backwater, yet also an important source of supplies and commerce when needed, as they were along the Silk Road over the Himalayas.

Lijiang would enjoy its greatest and last moment of prosperity and importance to republican China during the 1937 Japanese occupation. It became a center of resistance and commercial enterprise. The American volunteer group the Flying Tigers built their airport at Baisha to fly critical supplies, military and otherwise, across the trans-Himalayan trade routes. This claim to fame for helping the Chinese republican army, however, meant the Naxi were particularly despised when the Han Chinese Communists came into power, leaving these backwoods farmers to starve in their fields. They suffered mightily for their support of previous governments.

For the Naxi people, the rich agricultural plains around Baisha and Lijiang–situated as they are in the shadows of the Himalayas– represent the axis mundi of their world. Jade Dragon Snow Mountain is their sacred mountain, with its imposing snowy peaks dominating the horizon above both Baisha and Lijiang. It provides myriad streams for their fields and living water to most Lijiang and Baisha homes. It is their holy fountain of life.

As Arcones writes, "Villages are usually sited alongside a stream or a spring, following a plan which reflects a radial division of space. A village usually consists of a cluster of 10 to 30 family compounds, each comprised of two or more buildings facing onto a central courtyard." He also writes, "The main residential building contains the kitchen, larder, living area and sleeping quarters; it is the focus of the family and the place for entertaining guests. Directly opposite is the stable, which provides shelter for some combination of horses, mules, sheep, goats, and cattle."

When we revisited Loretta's ancestral home and met her closest Yunnan relatives, the residential complex followed the pattern Arcones describes. Perhaps the only thing that had changed from our first brief visit in 1996 was that the household floors were now concrete. This represented a marvelous juxtaposition of East meets West. On this, our third attempt, we discovered a deeper sense of where Loretta's father came from and how he grew up than we had ever imagined possible.

On our last day, we wandered a bit in Baisha with our Naxi translator. Some of the locals were surprised and excited to meet a hometown hero's daughter, who had come all the way from America to visit their village. We met a man in his nineties who remembered Loretta's father fondly. He told us wondrous stories of Loretta's father as a child and a youth, some of which our translator said might even be true.

We reconnected with a whole generation of Loretta's relatives and explored primitive shamanistic Taoism unaffected by Christianity or Western thought. These rural farmers had joy in the midst of suffering, equanimity in the face of poverty, and a deep sense of connection with their American relatives, whom they had never previously met. Our hearts swelled with joy.

Taoists taught me to focus my mind and transcend modern categories of meaning in order to embrace my own direct experiences of the divine. Taoists introduced me to a deeply humanist understanding of divine mystery—neither theist nor atheist but simply the essence that underlies all realities.

They taught me wu wei: being clear about our intentionality and then acting without attachment to bring about harmonious results with effortless effectiveness. Wu wei makes the improbable possible. Nonattachment frees us from the burden of anxiety and regret while opening us to new ways of being in the world. Not only did wu wei give me the focused attention to finish a dozen philosophical books in rapid succession and even read some a second and third time—it also allowed my mind to effortlessly make sense of complex esoteric materials with comfort and joy.

Returning from China, I completed the 181-page first draft of my doctoral dissertation at twice the pace of my previously unfocused fashion. Without attachment to outcomes, effort became effortless. Wu wei focused my productivity and dramatically increased my sense of accomplishment. I learned mastery of myself.

I left China with a deeper and richer spiritual life and a greater desire to experience even more mystical religious traditions. I had learned how to focus and control my mental abilities. I had learned a deeper appreciation of family relations and ancestors. I had discovered the shamanic roots that lie behind each of the major world religions. And I had experienced the breathtaking beauty of these rural and rare parts of the earth. I sought even more experiences.

I returned from sabbatical to lead my small UU congregation again, yet it all felt different somehow—perhaps too tame, too predictable. My soul yearned for something more. Global climate change was an increasing part of my concern for the planet and for humanity's future, so I began to consider which shamanic realities spoke most directly to how we as humans need to fundamentally change our relationship to Mother Earth in order to live in greater harmony with nature.

I discovered that in the ancient Mayan tradition, Pachamama is the term for the earth goddess Gaia, whom I had already encountered and who encompasses all that is worthy of love. I began looking into South American indigenous vision quests and shamanic ways of encountering the divine.

Each step on my journey—from ancient Christian mystics, to entrepreneurial pilgrimages, to Unitarian Universalist vision quests, to whirling with Sufis, to climbing mountains with Taoists—was taking me further from my small-town New England comfort zone. Yet the Way was calling me forward.

Chinese Mystics
BOOK GROUP DISCUSSION GUIDE

Author's Comment

Sometimes our philosophical reflections and our family histories intersect. And when they do, remarkably serendipitous events may occur. We must stay awake to such a possibility in order to embrace serendipity when it comes.

Questions to Encourage Conversation

1. Does the Chinese concept of balancing yin and yang speak to you? How?

2. Do you, like Confucius, make human relationships the core of your spirituality? Why or why not?

3. How does the Way expressed in Taoism deeply shape Taoists' spiritual journeys?

4. Could you wander at ease in the universe, like Chuang Tzu? Why or why not?

5. How would you approach a month-long stay at somewhere like Tao Fong Shan?

6. How might you describe the universalizing nature of the Ten Thousand Buddhas temple?

7. How does Chinese Christianity relate to American or European Christianity? How does it differ?

8. What strikes you as most important about the Naxi people?

9. Do you have interreligious perspectives in your family of birth? Are you eager to go forth and explore them?

Reflection

As a group, reflect upon the aspects of family history that might inform or impact an individual's spiritual journey.

SHAMANIC MYSTICS

I am the wind that breathes upon the sea. I am the wave on the ocean.
I am the murmur of leaves rustling. I am the rays of the sun.
I am the beam of the moon and stars. I am the power of trees growing.
I am the bud breaking into blossom. I am the movement
of the salmon swimming... I am the thoughts of all people
who praise my beauty and grace.

—*Black Book of Camarthen*

Early Human Mystics

Since humans attained consciousness, there have always been some in-
dividuals thought to possess magic or superpowers when, in truth, they
were simply more in touch with divine mystery than most. Over millennia, these people developed techniques for obtaining spiritual ecstasy,
a trancelike state often described as a mystical journey, a magical flight,
or an ascent into heaven. These techniques were passed down from
teacher to student, from generation to generation, and varied from one
cultural tradition to another around the primitive world.

Always there have been shamanistic techniques for encountering
and experiencing—albeit with fear and trembling—the awesome power
of divine mystery. Whether gained through use of psychotropic substances and sorcery or through deep and long meditative disciplines,

spiritual ecstasy is still considered an important stage on the journey toward enlightenment.

I first encountered shamanistic spirituality in Mircea Eliade's magisterial book *Shamanism: Archaic Techniques of Ecstasy* when I was twenty-two years old. This dense book describes how to become a shaman, including methods of selection, initiation ceremonies, magical powers, and the varieties of ancient shamanism found in the Himalayas, the Far East, Southeast Asia, Australia, northern Europe, Africa, North America, and South America.

Writing in the mid-twentieth century, he begins his study with these words:

> *Since the beginning of the century, ethnologists have fallen into the habit of using the terms shaman, medicine man, sorcerer, and magician interchangeably to designate certain individuals possessing magico-religious powers and found in all primitive societies.*
> *... We consider it advantageous to restrict the use of the words shaman and shamanism precisely to avoid misunderstandings and to cast a clearer light on the history of magic and sorcery. For of course the shaman is also a magician and medicine man; he is believed to cure, like all doctors, and to perform miracles ... like all magicians, whether primitive or modern.*

Until about 600 BCE, all religion was essentially shamanism. Then Pythagoras began to systematize Greek thought, while Confucius was doing the same in China, and Zoroaster was doing the same for what became the roots of the Abrahamic faiths.

Even as modern religion took shape, however, the ancient ways of shamanism were sometimes acknowledged. In the Gathas, the Zoroastrian sacred scriptures, Zoroaster refers to his own shamanic experiences and states of ecstasy. The Bible's Zoroastrian Magi (the three wise men) seem to be a continuation of such shamanic spirituality. But these mystical connections with divine mystery were often denigrated and discouraged in Judaism and later would be discouraged in Christianity and Islam as well.

Growing up Protestant in a small New England town, I knew that ancient Christianity and its predecessor, Second Temple Judaism, viewed primitive shamanism, witches, and sorcerers as evil. New England had its own history of hysterical fear of witches and mediums, leading to the Salem witch trials. Yet there remained something exotic, interesting, and deeply intriguing about shamanistic spirituality for me, despite how the Bible sharply distinguishes earth-based nature mysticism from text-based institutionalized religion.

When the book of Exodus sets forth its social and religious laws, it places its command "You shall not permit a female sorcerer to live" squarely between its verses on dealing with rape and those dealing with people who sodomize animals. The writers wish to ensure that any magicians, wizards, or sorcerers are anathema to the people.

In Leviticus, the ancient priests' manual, a passage immediately following instructions to not make your daughter a prostitute and to keep the Sabbath contains the instruction: "Do not turn to mediums or wizards; do not seek them out to be defiled by them: I am the LORD your God." It would seem that following traditional shamanic practices was deemed a most heinous crime against God to be avoided at all costs.

In the following chapter, Leviticus returns to this subject, saying, "If any turn to mediums and wizards, prostituting themselves to them, I will set my face against them, and will cut them off from the people." And also, "A man or a woman who is a medium or a wizard shall be put to death; they shall be stoned to death, their blood is upon them."

Nonetheless, redacted versions of ancient shamanic mystical experiences can still be seen in modern religion. This includes Ezekiel's cosmic vision, Jesus Christ's Transfiguration, the apostle Paul's claim to have ascended to the third heaven, and Muhammad's own spiritual night journey. These extraordinary shamanic experiences by foundational religious figures are preserved in the sacred texts—even though the evolving faith traditions have ceased to recognize or support such experiences for current spiritual seekers.

To understand shamanism, many people look outside the Abrahamic traditions, turning instead to native North American spirituality. Growing up, I had some knowledge of these traditions, though much of it was either grossly distorted or simply wrong. Then, during the 1970s, books by Native Americans such as *Black Elk Speaks* helped this amateur scholar and mystic make some sense of their deep and rich tradition.

Ellen from the Blessing Wood retreat center in the mountains of Vermont was a Unitarian Universalist shaman trained in the Native American and Celtic shamanic traditions. She aided our spiritual journeys during the six UU vision quests I experienced with my men's group. Ellen was the first Unitarian Universalist interreligious mystic I met. She drew upon the teachings of Dhyani Ywahoo, a twenty-seventh-generation female shaman of the Eastern Tsalagi (Cherokee) people.

We humans live our lives within the larger circle of life. As Ywahoo teaches, "All creatures walking about the circle experience birth, pain, old age, death; no one is above or below [these experiences]. When it comes to dying time, all go alone without the comforts of wealth or friends. Birth of any form has its attendant struggle. All beings seek peace and the comforts of a secure home and healthy family. All young and aged beings require care and support. Here arise patterns of relationship giving order to what could be chaotic." The mystic enters this spiraling dance to learn how to maintain harmony and balance.

In our vision quests, we used the creative principle of affirmations and sacred practice to actualize into reality that which we wished to manifest. This mostly meant bringing our hearts and our minds to a state of stability, grounded upon thankfulness for our lives, prayer, and deep meditation.

As Ywahoo taught, "Sitting easily, spine erect, breathing in, breathing out, allow your thoughts to slow down, your mind to become quiet. Visualize yourself surrounded in light, receiving heaven's light through the crown of your head, earth's energy through the base of

your spine. Maintain the inner motion as you sit. Attune to the primordial force of life, will to be, and cause of your living in this time."
In deep ecstatic meditation, we connected heaven and earth through our own bodies.

Shamanic practices are also linked to the ancient spiritual traditions of northern Europe. While living in Germany in the early 1980s, I had been introduced to Nordic and Germanic mysticism, with their ecstatic meditation trances that could allow a shaman to manifest Odin, the almighty sovereign of heaven and hell, to perform sympathetic magic. The ecstatic journey with Odin often included tales of shape-shifting, where the shaman transformed into various animals, as well as ravens and crows serving as helping spirits on our spiritual quest. Echoes of this magic remain in popular culture and German folk tales, but their source in shamanic meditation and trance states is often forgotten.

These northern European cultures also have a memory of drug-induced warriors—the so-called berserkers, who were fearless, ferocious, and superhuman in terms of fighting capabilities. This shamanic tradition is at least partly responsible for the savageness and success of the Norse raiders over a thousand years. It is also said to have been critical to the surprising Nazi blitzkrieg that demolished French forces so easily at the beginning of World War II.

Drugs play such a twisted role in human consciousness—always have and perhaps always will. However, in many shamanic traditions throughout the world, neuroactive drugs interact with prayer, meditation, and fasting to produce spiritual ecstasy. In our travels to India and the countries of the Himalayas, we were introduced to the transformative power of sacred fire and Soma, a hallucinogenic drink in the ancient Vedas. In both the Middle East and the Far East, hashish and opium still often serve such a role. Whether aided by drugs or meditation, African and Asian shamans are said to fly, withstand cold, do sympathetic magic, and sometimes control life and death.

During the axial age, religions based more upon reading and reason arose. For a time, they coexisted alongside spirit-filled shamanism. Over the last two thousand years, though, reading-and-reason religions have increasingly persecuted or marginalized shamanism and faiths based on magic.

But now we appear to be entering a new era for the world. As we recognize the explicit limits of reason, we can increasingly embrace an archaic consciousness and shamanic traditions that have survived two millennia of marginalization and persecution.

Living between Two Worlds

On family vacations in the late 1990s and early 2000s, I discovered that shamanism still holds sway in many parts of the world. Traveling in Africa on safari with our children, we visited a rural Masai tribe one afternoon. We learned that the tribe's leader holds his position by virtue of his knowledge, psychic insight, mystical experiences, age, and personal authority. He is the consummate teacher, healer, and leader of the tribe. He is the tribe's shaman and spiritual protector. All yielded to his wisdom and experience.

A few years later, while traveling in the Australian outback, we encountered Aboriginal men of high degree. For many Aboriginal peoples, both men and women, life is a dance of ritual ceremony and daily living. Its mysterious origin is in what they call the dreamtime of the universal eternal now. The shaman's work is to awaken in the dreamtime. Then he employs his mystical experiences for his tribe's salvation.

In *Voices of the First Day*, Robert Lawlor says, "The Australian Aborigines, and indeed the indigenous tribal peoples all over the world, believe that the spirit of their consciousness and way of life exists like a seed buried in the earth. The waves of European colonialism that destroyed the civilizations of North America, South America, and Australia began a five-hundred-year dormancy period of the *archaic consciousness*." That period is coming to an end. Now the budding seed is again beginning to bear fruit.

In explaining the Aboriginal vision of dreamtime, he writes: "[Mother Gaia] Earth holds an infinite profusion of seeds. [These]

seeds contain forms and worlds yet to germinate. . . . The seed's capacity to engender new life seems to derive from the imprint of patterns carried through the ages."

This concept seems consistent with Carl Jung's idea of the col-
lective unconscious. All that humanity needs for a healthier, more enlightened future lies already in dormant seeds. Humanity, collectively,
must simply find the courage and audacity to awaken to our potential.

One of the last major shamanic traditions to make contact with
the developing world appears to be that of the indigenous tribes of
the South American rain forest. Some of these tribes resisted contact
with so-called civilized societies until well into the 1970s and beyond. In *The Shaman and Ayahuasca* Don Jose Campos says, "That
their secret knowledge and technologies are emerging into the modern world during this time of global peril is a blessing of inestimable
proportion to humanity. With widespread environmental devastation, staggering economic disparities, unceasing violent conflict
throughout the world, and frightening arsenals of conventional and
nuclear weaponry, the human race, along with all the species on the
earth, stand on the brink of annihilation." Now is the time to tap
those ancient seeds of potentiality.

These ancient South American peoples speak variations of the
Quechua language, which has embedded in its structure "the realization and appreciation that all life is both finite and eternal." They
call themselves people of the forest. Their home is the Amazonian
rain forest that includes large parts of Ecuador and Peru. It is an area
as large as Portugal yet sparsely populated by these forest people.
Their history seldom goes back beyond childhood memories, and
even then, tribal history is frequently replaced by mythology about
the world they inhabit.

The most remote tribes include the Jivaro people, who live hundreds of miles deep within the forest below the southeastern foothills of the Andes. The Jivaro are divided into four main tribes: the
Shuar, the Achuar, the Aguaruna, and the Huambisa. Only the first
two have regular contact with outsiders.

The Achuar have developed a trusting relationship with an Ecuadorian-American group called the Pachamama Alliance in order to bring fellow travelers and much-needed resources into their forest abode. They have a deep relationship with the plants of the rain forest and a willingness to share their ayahuasca ceremony with spiritual pilgrims.

I met representatives of the Pachamama Alliance in 2010, when they presented at First Parish in Concord, where Loretta and I have been members over thirty years. They were looking for friends and fellow travelers for their journey. So when my spiritual pilgrimages finally drew me to them again, serendipity assured they could take me to the Achuar people for the next stage of my spiritual journey. We agreed I would head to Ecuador with them the following summer.

Pachamama Alliance

After flying to Quito, we began our quest in the Andes village of San Clemente, where the Karanqui-Quichua, a small, indigenous tribe, lives on the side of an extinct volcano near the border of Columbia. The lunar cycles balance dualities here in the mountains. Father Sun and Mother Moon shine down upon Imbabura and Pukyu Pamba, which are known respectively as Papa Volcano and his mate, Mama Volcano.

The cosmic serpent, often taking the form of a double helix, was everywhere around us. Later, in deep meditation trances, I would come to trust the serpent, the jaguar, and the condor as spirit guides.

My purpose in this remote mountain village was not tourism, the study of Mayan culture, nor even enlightenment. It was simply responding to the call of the spirit. I would have many spiritual adventures: here and now on an Andean mountain, later on a vision quest in the Andean high sierra desert, and still later on my trips into the rain forest with the indigenous tribes. I felt called into these pilgrimages of the spirit with shamanic teachers as my guides.

I shared a one-room cabin on the side of the mountain just below the head chief's house. My morning meditation included the three worlds of Mayan culture: *below the earth, upon the earth,* and *above the earth.* I began by climbing the mountain for blessings from the ancestors. Then I ritually walked the labyrinth to take myself inward—so surprising to find a labyrinth on this volcanic mountaintop. Finally, I ended by meditating in a cave beneath the earth.

Daniel, our Ecuadorian guide, explained that the three levels of spirit correspond to the condor for the sky, the jaguar for the earth, and the serpent for the subterranean. Each spirit animal encompasses powerful spiritual forces.

The mountain shaman instructed me to stand naked while he purified my body using sage smoke, stinging nettles, alcohol, and rosewater. The process stung slightly. Daniel said the shaman was cleansing away negative power and refilling my depleted self with positive energy. When we enter into the spirit, it enters into us.

This would be the first of my several shamanic initiations into divine mystery. They were often bizarre and seldom fun, but they enabled a deepening of spiritual understanding that would otherwise not be possible. These were trials and tests set by Pachamama herself to guide me into the deeper mystery. This was learning not through reading or reason but through a deepening of the spirit by experience.

I was instructed to nap after the cleansing ceremony, to let my subconscious process this initiation, as this first ritual was primarily to embody my spiritual intentions. I dreamed of a talking python wisdom teacher who had much wisdom to teach me as I slept.

Later that night as I sat in the dark cave, I discovered my perception of the light and sounds from the valley below were greatly magnified. Joyous sounds of a festival rose up from the valley. I perceived sounds of nature much more clearly. Even though it was the dry season, it began to rain heavily. As the rain fell harder, I meditated louder and chanted "O Pachamama, O Pachamama," repeatedly. I seemed to give off sweet incense smoke with every breath. It was not nearly cold enough to see my breath, yet I was exhaling incense.

It was thick and plentiful and maybe something magical. The cosmic serpent became the ground of my being.

The rain finally stopped, so I headed to bed. The silhouette of the volcano demarcated the night sky. Frogs began to serenade. I surrendered to the gods of the mountain. My soul was at peace.

I have always been drawn to mountain spirituality. I once again walked the mountaintop agricultural calendar and labyrinth the next morning and felt this mountain had adopted me. It was an old volcano—a very wise one, having observed wars, pestilence, peace, and much lovemaking. I came to know and be known by the mountain.

The next day, our group took a five-hour bus trip, descending more than ten thousand feet down from the Andes to the rain forest. We overnighted at El Jardin hotel with a hot shower, a hot tub, and a relatively gourmet meal. We waited for hours for the rain to stop so we could fly by bush plane into the rain forest to visit the Achuar.

When we finally got clearance to fly, I began to realize my oversized body was too big for this part of the world—my legs were too long to fit into this tiny nine-passenger plane. So I flew for an hour on a bumpy flight with my knees up in the air, my legs pressed against the seat in front of me, and my feet a good ten inches above the floor.

For grown men of the indigenous tribes, the average height is about four feet ten inches, and the average weight is under 120 pounds. At six feet one inch tall and weighing a massive 255 pounds, I was a monstrosity, a giant among them. This sense of being oversized and clumsy would stay with me the entire trip. Beds, doorframes, and structural supports were often inappropriately sized for me. Sometimes I learned to adapt, and other times I just struggled through, being too big for the world I now inhabited.

The long plane ride not only made me feel like a giant but also left my knees painfully inflamed. After twenty years of playing volleyball, my knees were in horrible shape. They had lost any ability to absorb shocks. My doctor said they were raw bone on bone, so they became inflamed, puffy, and painful if I played for even a few hours. An orthopedic surgeon said even surgery might not help, so I had reluctantly given up volleyball, losing one source of joy in my life.

Needless to say, having my knees propped up against the seat in front of me for an hour was quite painful. The view flying just above the treetops was awesome, but I was stiff and cranky by the time we landed on a muddy airstrip in the dense forest.

We were met and greeted by the entire village. Passenger planes don't land there very often. We enjoyed a delicious box lunch of sandwiches before heading on our way.

With everything covered in slippery mud, the local guides handed out boots for everyone in our group. Realizing what a giant I was in this land, I was certain no boots would fit me. But Daniel had notified the guides about my big feet, so they proudly presented me with brand-new size 12 men's mud boots from Texas.

Daniel and our local guides were looking out for me. I had boots that fit, and I did not die in our perilous flight into the rain forest, no matter how painful it had been. I was grateful for life itself.

But even in size 12 boots, I still felt titanic as I made my way over this foreign terrain. During the afternoon hike through the jungle to get to the river, I twice sunk knee-deep into mud, requiring two native guides working together to pull me out. I also completely lost my balance over a muddy stream, resulting in my falling headlong into the mud. I was a mess.

Daniel later told me that when he first saw my size and my slow, cumbersome gait, he feared I would never survive the rain forest. It seems an obese, 255-pound person sinks much deeper and more quickly into mud than do 120-pound-or-less native guides.

We finally reached the river. I stumbled, filthy and exhausted, into a motorized dugout canoe, which was also rather small for my length and girth. We traveled another hour and a half downriver to the Achuar village, where we would spend the next three days.

Arriving ashore involved another half hour of hiking to reach our campsite. This time, we hiked uphill in slippery mud, testing the limits of my physical endurance. I began to use my Taoist training of mindful intention to see me through: *Step by step, inch by inch, even climbing in mud is a cinch.*

Our forest encampment spread out over three large, interconnected wooden platforms about four feet above the forest floor. There were hammocks with mosquito netting and a small outhouse in the back, about fifty feet into the forest. There was very little privacy for the fourteen of us men and women, but it roughly replicated the living conditions of the indigenous people we were visiting. I was so tired that I fell quickly into a deep sleep.

I'd been told for years that I snore loudly in my sleep. I was worried I would disturb the others, but I was assured that at least two other larger men—one Australian, the other Ecuadorian—also snored. Vicky, our American guide, told me she had dreamed that night of three friendly, snoring jaguars guarding our camp through the night, and it had given her a sense of peace.

I too dreamt many dreams that night. In the first, Madonna visited me (not the rock star but rather the Mother of God). She exuded a blue radiance. I was sitting in the cave on the Andean mountain, and she just smiled at me. My heart cracked open. I too now radiated light.

In another vision, I was working as a minister and spiritual leader just as I usually do—entering into relationships and simply trying to help people, though with little thought as to how those people related to my journey. Yet this way of being suddenly felt hollow and empty. I felt useful, but I wasn't making real relationships or connecting on a deeper spiritual level. The dream taught me to focus on what life calls me to do, rather than on what I choose for myself. There can be no true joy without ego surrender.

Ayahuasca

The next day began with a long hike into the rain forest, which included crossing an *Indiana Jones*-style, wobbly, old bridge across a stream. The guide had everyone else cross first in case my weight broke the bridge. But moving slowly, with Taoist intentionality, I crossed safely. I was delighted to again survive the rain forest. Later we kayaked on a lagoon filled with piranha.

We spent the afternoon with the Achuar people, exchanging greetings, having a late lunch, playing music, demonstrating arts, playing volleyball, shooting blow darts, and buying crafts. Finally, we hiked back to our camp, exhausted. I watched the glorious sunset from my hammock as we waited for the food to be prepared. I was too tired to even move.

The following day, we endured a cleansing ceremony, then fasted all day. It was all in preparation for the ayahuasca ceremony we would engage in that evening.

Humans have coevolved with the rain forest for thousands of years. Indigenous people use medicinal plants for many purposes, and some of these plants have come to help humans remember we are one with the forest and the universe. All are one. The plant medicine would transform me.

We met the shaman. Like most shamans, he was chosen for his trustworthiness, compassion, self-assurance, peacefulness, and humility. He was a short, squat old man who exuded equanimity. He seemed very serious, very calm, very focused on the dangers involved in tonight's ritual.

No one present spoke both English and this Quechua dialect well, but all the South Americans spoke Spanish fluently. Everything required two translations, passing through Spanish on its way to my understanding.

The guide explained that the shaman concocted this plant medicine today, meditating upon each of our journeys. The dosage depended upon body mass and spiritual understanding. The shaman poured into my cup a large quantity of a bitter brew from the ayahuasca plant. Then he looked deeply into my eyes and poured in yet more.

I drank the bitter potion down directly and then used water to rinse the taste from my mouth. The local guide said I had received the largest portion because I was so big and spiritually advanced. I grinned.

I went to the far side of our sleeping platform, at the forest's edge, to wait for the drink to take effect. After about forty-five minutes, the forest became louder, as if I could hear for miles, and its colors became deeper, so many different shades of green and darkness. Then I noticed a single star coming out from behind the overcast sky. I had never seen anything so bright, so beautiful. I was thoroughly stunned and overwhelmed.

I was already in ecstasy, though now somewhat worried about the size of my dose. All my senses became extenuated, open, amplified. I suddenly could see, hear, smell, feel, and breathe the rain forest better. I could hear, or at least imagine, the activities of the plants and animals coexisting with me in the forest. It felt as if my brain's synapses, the components of my entire mental operating system, were being reprogrammed in real time. I was tapping directly into the power of the universe. This was awesome, far beyond my wildest imaginings.

I moved to the center of the sleeping platform, where no trees obstructed my view. The sky opened up above me, showing more stars than I had ever seen, like in a planetarium. When I focused on individual stars, it was as if I could telescope my vision into the night sky. I moved my gaze across the Milky Way, watching entire solar systems with their planets revolving around them, even seeing stars being born. When a cloud crossed between me and the sky, I could see right through it to the stars.

This experience of oneness with the universe brought tremendous joy and overwhelming awe. We are literally stardust, the universe is our rightful home, and I now knew this in my bones. It was time to claim our birthright.

But then I became quite ill, with vomiting, diarrhea, and so much nausea that I could not sleep, no matter how tired and exhausted I was. Over the next several hours, I was so sick that I never wanted to experience this again, despite the glorious visions. I finally did manage to sleep, though fitfully. I had many dreams, some quite wonderful and others quite terrifying.

In the morning, the shaman debriefed the six of us from the night before. As the others recounted their experiences, he had little good to say. Then I told him my experiences through our two interpreters.

"It is rare to find someone from the North so spiritually mature," he said.

Again, I grinned, and I thanked him.

But I was still feeling nauseous, so I went to the edge of our four-foot-high platform to vomit. Suddenly, I collapsed and fell head over heels onto the muddy ground. I lost consciousness.

When I reopened my eyes, I was dazed, completely disoriented, with no sense of where I was in space or time, or why. I had no memory of falling or landing in the mud. All I had was a strong sense of disorientation and pain—pain from head to toe.

I initially could not recognize the scared and concerned people standing around me. For a moment, some had thought I was dead—or in need of an ambulance, which could be worse than being dead so deep in the forest. The nearest hospital facilities were a day away by dugout canoe and bush plane.

But I awoke and reassuringly bounced back up onto the platform in good spirits. I apologized for disrupting my conversations with the shaman, a holy man.

Daniel told me my fainting protected me from more serious injury and perhaps saved my life. By going completely slack as I fell, my body better dissipated the energy upon impact than if I had tensed.

It was a resurrection experience. I knew from my many pilgrimages that death and resurrection are often parts of the spiritual journey. I felt redeemed. I was sore, bruised, and battered, but also filled with deep equanimity and eagerness to continue my journey.

To help my massive headache and the inflamed muscles in my back, our American guide took up a collection of everyone's pain pills—mostly Advil and Excedrin. While greatly appreciated, none of them helped very much. My body was in deep distress, and I needed magical, spiritual help in order to heal.

The shaman mixed another plant medicine, a nasty brew. My guide told me it could sometimes activate the body's anti-inflammatory response, but unfortunately took several days to work. Sure enough, a few days later, the pain was mostly gone, as was the inflammation—not only in my back but also in my knees. It allowed me to walk better in the rain forest. And when I returned home, I even began playing volleyball again. From every bad circumstance, some good can come.

Daniel later told me nothing happens by accident. My fall and the subsequent healing were all part of my spiritual encounter with the rain forest and its wisdom. Pain and death are not to be feared. They can lead to peace beyond understanding. Equanimity. We are cocreators of a sacred play that leaves us transformed.

A scientist traveling with us said science could not adequately explain my sublime visions or even my miraculous healing, except by accepting the inherently mysterious nature of life in the universe and coming to better understand quantum biology as the basis of life. I have so much more to learn. It seems quantum biology can disrupt the space-time continuum, allowing for seemingly miraculous enhancements of sight, sound, and perception and perhaps even altering our neural synapses and connections to the entire universe. If so, this is a form of serendipity and grace.

I had looked divine mystery full in the face, or at least encountered God's backside. And that memory of divine power cannot be erased. Scary! Awesome! Terrifying! Wondrous! My experience with the divine mystery and my experience with near-death came so close together, and I had no control over either. What does it mean to carry on in the face of the miraculous? How will we live once we have been transfigured?

We spent several more days in the deep forest and visited yet another tribe. The night skies were brilliantly clear and full of stars. My heightened awareness faded even as my pain did. On the day we planned to fly home, it poured down rain as if the forest did not want us to go—the heavy rain of departing and returning to a more normal reality. Our small planes could not fly in such weather, so we waited and waited. As we waited, Daniel told me he knew another shaman who he thought could take me further on my next pilgrimage without using ayahuasca.

I flew home the next day, returning to Boston a changed person. But I also sensed there was so much more to learn. I made plans to travel with Daniel into the Ecuadorean high sierra desert the following January. If this was the Way I was called to walk, then I might as well audaciously walk it with enthusiasm and joy and make the most of every experience.

High Sierra Shaman

Six months later, I flew to Guayaquil, Ecuador, to meet Daniel. We first traveled southwest to his home in the small city of Cuenca. From there, we drove his truck through the high sierra desert to the tiny village of Susudel. There we left the paved road and traveled over deeply rutted paths and muddy trails hugging the side of the cliffs, with sheer drops just off the road.

After another ten miles, we arrived at the home of this shaman. This house was in a remote mountain valley that once grew sugarcane and then barley, but with climate change was now too dry to grow anything commercially. Much of the valley was covered with acacia trees, reminding me of the African savanna. It had a certain unnamable, austere beauty.

The shaman grew up on this land, leaving home to attend university and become a pharmaceutical salesman. But at midlife, during a vision quest on this same mountain, he had a vision commanding him to move back here and adopt the ways of his ancestors. His uncle trained him as a shaman. He seldom accepted guests or tourists, but Daniel had assured him mine was an authentic spiritual pilgrimage.

I was ready for another spiritual initiation. I grounded myself in this reality. Three juvenile condors circled overhead, catching the wind currents to stay aloft.

Daniel suggested I go to bed early, for the sweat lodge ceremony would begin at three in the morning. Through Daniel as translator, the shaman suggested that I should first write twenty-nine prayers to express my intention for my vision quest, and should pray them repeatedly throughout the quest. This spiritual pilgrimage would occur within divine mystery. And so I prayed for the following:

Humility to face my limitations
Optimism in the face of loss
Openness to everything
Willingness to make it happen
Integrity at all costs
Authenticity to my truest self
Thankfulness for whatever comes
Courage to affirm my truth
Confidence to pursue it
Curiosity about reality
Patience in the face of failure
Steadfastness to see it through
Enthusiasm to lift all up to God
Ambition for meaning-making
Hunger for experience
Gratitude for failure
Eagerness to always show kindness toward strangers
A constant love of life
A vision of what is possible
The strength of character to pursue the ineffable
Willingness to cooperate
An ability to see God however manifested
To love with an unrestrained heart
To think beyond self-limiting categories
To believe beyond boundaries
To feel beyond pain
To follow my intuition
To accept what is
And to accept everything

These were my twenty-nine prayers for this vision quest. I fell into deep sleep.

I anxiously awoke well before 3:00 a.m. They finally came to get me closer to 6:00. We had again left ordinary time behind. I had been fasting since the night before and would continue to fast the next four days.

The sweat lodge was a large, womb-shaped igloo of bricks with a tiny doorway covered by a heavy tarp that, when closed, plunged us into total darkness. Thirty-nine rocks had been absorbing heat for three hours in the middle of a small bonfire. The first thirteen were placed in the middle of the sweat lodge in a central stone pit built for that purpose. The whole setting was one of gathering gloom in the early-morning light.

We circled the lodge once, then ducked down through the small doorway to enter in a clockwise fashion. We sat in a circle around the central pit. Since my vision quest was commencing, I was seated in the spiritually auspicious place directly opposite the shaman.

Fasting, meditation, and sweat lodge combined form perhaps the oldest systematic human spiritual experience. It was sort of like taking a sauna—in complete darkness, with drugs, drumming, chanting, blessings, singing, and the small room filling with smoke and steam whenever the shaman threw water on hot rocks. This was, I think, intentionally disorienting.

The shaman fed me small balls of grainy-tasting paste. Daniel told me it was a form of peyote, from the outer skin of a certain cactus. It would alter my state of reality.

Just when the smoke and heat finally became completely intolerable and I was choking and ready to bolt, the shaman shouted to have the heavy flap over the door lifted, bringing light into this dark, smoky space. Greatly relieved, I began to deeply breathe the fresh air—but then it became clear they were merely bringing in more hot rocks. Our meditation would continue in complete darkness.

Rocks, water, and music filled my consciousness. They chanted and sang in Quechua, and I rocked with the rhythm. Yet as the sweat lodge filled with acrid smoke, I again found myself choking and gasping for breath. The medicine I had been consuming made me both nauseous and hyperaware. I slipped in and out of normal reality.

The ceremony lasted about two hours, with two more rounds of hot rocks. It left me less than completely coherent. I was glad when it finally ended and we made our way back out into the air. I was already anxious that we planned to do it all again in four days' time. However, I focused on the moment and prepared to go forth on my quest.

The shaman and Daniel escorted me to my vision quest site. It was less than a mile away, under a brittle, dry acacia tree on a stony hillside overlooking a desert valley. We planted sticks in the four directions to mark out an eight-foot-by-eight-foot site delineated by string. This was to be my home in the wilderness for the next four days.

I tried to construct a small shelter with only my sleeping bag and a small tarp, but the branches of the acacia were brittle, with sharp, six-inch-long needles, and broke under the weight of my tarp. I finally gave up and simply sat on my tarp on the ground with no sun or rain cover.

The high sierra winds seemed to blow much of the time, lifting the heat from the valley below and desiccating the soil and the scraggly trees clinging to this desert hillside. Within hours, I too began to feel desiccated and windblown. My patch of earth seemed to be home to at least three different species of biting ants. My legs and torso were soon covered with bites. It was pure torture.

I sat there, part of nature, the breeze blowing through the trees. Nature made sounds, and I responded with sound in return. Acknowledging reality without judgment had always been hard for me, as had been not caring about the ill-formed judgments of others. Now I simply communed on my own. This was a gateway I had previously failed to embrace. I welcomed it now and entered an alternate reality.

The ants began to devour me one bite at a time. I would die from a thousand small bites. I had no food, no insect repellent, no means to protect myself, so I began squishing as many ants as I could kill. The feeling of being grossly titanic returned to me. After many hours of this, hundreds of their tiny carcasses covered my tarp. Eventually they stopped coming—perhaps they smelled death. I could finally lie down with a sense of relief. Life and death, large and small.

I dozed, and awoke to the sound of a dove descending—the Holy Spirit descending. I heard cooing and the fluttering of wings, but I could not see the bird. Wasps buzzed near me, attracted to the blossoms of the acacia tree. I was deeply present to all that was.

Watching fog slowly drift across the ridge, seemingly in slow motion, gave me a new appreciation for how clouds operate in the mountains. Like my earliest spiritual teacher, Alan Watts, I was now covered in cloud, whereabouts unknown.

The condors returned with the setting sun, gently floating below low-hanging cloud cover, drifting upward on the air currents. Condors are the spiritual masters of the desert high sierras. A little red bird, and then two more, came to roost in my tree. A bullfrog called in the dusk. A cow gently mooed as it returned home. Some sheep bleated far down the valley. Surrounded by nature, I was never truly alone. I became part of the local ecosystem.

With darkness came swarms of mosquitos, but I had no deet. Constantly slapping at them, I was unable to sleep. The idea of being their sustenance so they could reproduce held no appeal for me. Then, when I finally dozed off, two large animals pounced on me, scaring me nearly to death. They were only black dogs from the shaman's place, but I screamed at them in such terror they quickly decided to run off home.

Later in the night, I heard a predator chasing a hoofed creature. I wished to be neither predator nor prey. *Just let me be.*

This was a time of fear and night terrors. My imagination ran amuck, populating the night with sounds and strange creatures. With my augmented perceptions, I could hear the myriad nightlife, but things were mostly beyond my sight. My eyes adjusted to the dark, but never to the sounds. This was an entirely different form of the dark night of the soul. Fortunately, the creatures didn't sound as if they were coming my way. At least for now.

Sometime later, a small, black mammal came down the trail toward me but merely growled as it passed by. In the early-morning light, a red fox passed by, but it looked away as it trotted by my site.

My early-morning meditations were disrupted by a foraging bumble-bee, which sounded as loud as an outboard motor.

My senses were heightened beyond belief. I experienced profound meaning and an incredible lightness of being. There is so much life to be lived; I vowed to live it deeply.

Halfway through my quest, Daniel returned with the shaman to see how I was doing. The shaman repurified my space by chanting while blowing tobacco smoke over me. I was dehydrated and out of water, so they gave me more. The shaman also fed me hallucinogenic medicine to aid my meditation, provided a salve for my painful sunburn, and gave me some aloe cut from a nearby plant for my various bites and bruises. I was in an altered human state within an altered sense of space and time. This was a bizarre vision quest, yet I welcomed it.

The shaman said the first half of the quest was for wisdom and the second half was to express gratitude. *Gratitude. Thank God for this amazing day; for the friends along the way; for Pachamama, the fruits of the earth; for the sun, whose light fills the earth; for the moon that rules the night; for the spirit that fills everyone; for the will that helps it all get done; for the losses that teach humility; for the strength that builds integrity; and for the light that keeps me on the Way. Gratitude for life and for this day. From processing pain can come understanding.*

This is a special place upon the earth. Thank you, spirit of this mountain valley. I sensed that over the eons, there were many vision quests between these surrounding hills. Perhaps that had helped my meditation go so far so fast.

The medicine seemed to increase the acuity of my long-distance vision, depth of color, fullness of sound, and overall perception. I heard drumming and chanting around a spirit circle, in what sounded like the local Quechua dialect, just over the next ridge. For several moments, I was tempted to leave my site and walk over the ridge to see if it were real.

However, what would that accomplish? If this were a form of psychosis—the materializing of chanting indigenous people out of space and time—might it only deepen my crisis? And if this were not psychosis, why would I break my trance state?

Finally, my vision quest came to an end. When Daniel finally returned, we recompiled the four poles, releasing my twenty-nine prayers and the spiritual energy accumulated in my meditation site. I was in a weakened state. We walked slowly back to the house.

The evening brought food, company, and a return to normalcy as the skies opened up and began to rain heavily. But now I had returned to warmth and shelter. With a meal in my stomach, a roof protecting me from rain, and no bugs to contend with, I slept a deep and peaceful sleep through the entire night.

We repeated the sweat lodge ceremony the next morning. This time, the shaman's girlfriend, an American from Florida, joined us. Now I had an ally to explain it all to me. She taught me some secrets of the sweat lodge ceremony, including how to avoid inhaling deeply, how to duck below the billowing smoke and lean back against the outer wall to avoid the hottest smoke, and how to enter a trance state of equanimity. It all went so much better this time.

The shaman confirmed that the indigenous ceremony I had overheard was real, but not of this space and time nor of this reality. He also said the red fox was probably a shaman; hence, it averted its gaze so as to not intrude on my spiritual space.

Later that day, despite the muddiness of the roads, we drove slowly back to Cuenca. From there, I flew back to America to resume my parish ministry. But my journey on the shamanic path was not over. Ayahuasca had more to teach me.

Seven months later, I would continue my pilgrimage with Robin, a young shaman in Peru. Now in his early thirties, he had been one of my daughter's classmates in Concord, before being trained for seven years as an ayahuascan in Peru.

Peruvian Ayahuasca

It was August 2015, and I was standing outside the tiny airport in Puerto Maldonado, Peru, waiting for Robin, this young shaman, to arrive. I couldn't help but wonder what I was doing there, in oppressive heat, in a strange country where I didn't speak the language, feeling quite lost and vulnerable.

Robin came roaring up on his motorcycle, and we headed off. The next morning, we drove forty minutes over unpaved roads, past neighborhoods of squatters, a military installation, and slash-and-burn farming. To catch our boat, we were told we needed to arrive on the banks of the Rio Madre de Dios by ten in the morning. As it turned out, perhaps predictably, our boat was running late, but we were stepping outside normal time, giving up control, again.

A little over an hour later, our boat arrived, and we began the three-hour trip upriver. The river was seasonally low and barely navigable. We encountered many sandbars we needed to make our way around or else run aground. The outboard motor banged against large rocks thrusting up from the bottom.

We made it to Robin's conservation farm by late afternoon. He had allocated me a hard bed in the corner of the main building, with a 180-degree panoramic view of the farm, a mild cross breeze, and mosquito netting. The netting was also to protect me from vampire bats. I had been starting to relax until he told me that.

From a hammock near my bed, I had a gorgeous view of a magenta-colored flowering tree and the green forest amid the constant chirping of birds. This was a transcendent, Amazonian rain-forest paradise. The nature of reality here seemed so vibrant and full of life.

Robin walked the cultivated grounds with me, explaining what everything was. Then we walked down to the muddy river for a predinner wash, making sure we splashed about loudly enough to scare away any caimans or anacondas. In the rain forest, we shared our reality with scary animals.

The next day, we began our rain forest hikes, spotting wild pigs, a large snake, and macaws along the way. This subtropical jungle includes greater species diversity and larger animals than the Ecuadorean rain forest I'd visited the previous summer. It perhaps represents greater ecological diversity than anywhere else on earth. The river brings sandstone and minerals from the Andean highlands a hundred miles north, so this land is richer and more fertile. Everything here grows so fast and so big. This is an equatorial paradise of fecund existence.

I picked up seed pods along the trail, and Robin got quite excited. This particular tree, a Peruvian balsam, hadn't dropped its seed pods for two years, yet now, this very week, it had dropped enough to double the 200 balsam trees Robin had already planted on his 250 acres. We returned in the afternoon with his crew to find other ripe balsam trees and gather their seeds as well. We spent all afternoon gathering seeds. It felt great to be part of this cycle of nature, to help do my small part to restore the despoiled rain forest

We also found some brown seed pods from another Peruvian hardwood tree, only to discover wild pigs had broken open and eaten most of them. As I was gathering seed pods beneath the one tree that appeared still healthy and untouched, I suddenly found myself face-to-face with a large wild sow.

I stared at her. She stared at me. Finally, she grunted and left those seeds to me. She was followed by four smaller pigs that had also been hoping to feast upon them.

Back at Robin's farm for the evening, thoughts of vampire bats, anacondas, caimans, and wild pigs were enough to keep me under my mosquito netting from dark of night until nearly dawn.

Later in the week, we hiked along a section of the river contiguous with Robin's conservation land. The damage from people illegally harvesting the forest was heartbreaking. Robin suggested these forty acres could be purchased from its absentee land owner. I saw an opportunity to help heal the planet. Robin agreed restoring this riverfront property would be a great way to largely offset the effect of my family's carbon-rich American lifestyle.

I offered to donate money from our family's charitable gift fund to his conservation trust, Camino Verde, the Green Way, to buy the land and a boat. He suggested we call the restored area the Sherblom Family Forest.

The world is becoming a better place, at least in parts, and I played my own small role in making it so. Camino Verde would create an aerial map and inventory of the trees, restoring and replanting wherever possible, to bring the forest back to its wild fecundity.

During the remaining days of this pilgrimage, we trekked conservation and ecotourism trails created by a growing network of concerned local environmentalists. Yet I had come to Peru looking for what ayahuasca still had to teach me.

Robin explained he was not currently in a spiritual state to lead such a ceremony. But he agreed to be my spiritual companion for the ceremony and reached out to a shaman friend to actually lead me through it.

Our final day, we hiked four hours through virgin rain forest to make our way to the nearest road, where Robin had a car and driver waiting to take us back to Puerto Maldonado.

Late afternoon found us driving past Peruvian whorehouses on our way to a sustainable rain forest agricultural venture, where Alice, the ayahuascan shaman, would lead the ceremony. Robin served as my translator and guide.

The others began to arrive. Gina, a young mother, returned for her fifth ayahuasca journey, and Philippe, a Chilean ecological guide, returned for his seventh time, while I was only on my second journey. They were all friends and, unlike me, fluent in Spanish, allowing me to drift upon the sounds and colors without need for translating. They were a young and friendly group of expats who had taken this journey before.

The vibe of this gathering was a world apart from my experiences with the Ecuadorian indigenous shaman. Alice and Gina had small children with them. We fasted all day, drinking tea and chatting about nothing until the children go to bed. Then, at about eight in the evening, we gathered in our designated places in a large circle. Alice gave us detailed instructions, which Robin translated. I could already tell my ayahuasca dosage would be more manageable with Alice.

"To avoid nausea, sit up straight," she said. "Don't drink too much water. To get through the hardest parts, just focus on my singing."

We were sitting in a covered, raised platform open to the forest on two sides. Our bedrooms lined the third wall, with a small kitchen and bathroom completing the fourth wall. Our space was lit only by a single small candle.

Not far from the edge of the shelter, I positioned myself sitting against a wall to support my back, to see the stars come out, and to more easily vomit over the edge. I wanted all the joy with less of the wretchedness. I had a wide view of the surrounding dark forest. The darkness deepened into night.

Alice gave us each our portion of ayahuasca after praying and blowing tobacco smoke over it, and then she took a large portion for herself as well. The friendly warmth amongst the five of us was deeply reassuring. I relaxed into the experience as my anxiety subsided. I opened myself to getting the most out of my coming together again with the ayahuasca plant medicine.

Alice suggested the ayahuasca would begin to take effect in about thirty minutes and would run its course through our bodies over three to four hours. She asked us to stay upright in our loose circle until she felt the energy level in the group had depleted enough to suggest it was time for bed.

We sat in silence. After about half an hour, I noticed my enhanced sight, seeing farther into the forest, through the dark, with many more shades of darkness apparent. It was happening again!

I now could hear the regular breathing of Gina's sleeping baby in her bedroom in a way I couldn't earlier. As my senses expanded, the night noises of the forest blended with the newly audible music coming from the whorehouses in the far distance.

Alice began to sing ayahuasca songs. Gina and then Robin joined in, bringing warmth and depth to the chanting. Philippe began to play softly on his guitar. The night was heavily overcast, with slight precipitation, so I was thankful for our warm, dry setting. I decided to just focus deeply on the experience.

What looked like stars beginning to twinkle in the night turned into fireflies. They flew through my awareness. One firefly settled on a nearby beam to be my companion through the evening.

Ayahuasca once again expanded my sense of being, of consciousness in tune with the universe and the forest. I had this growing sense of bliss, of resting in the bosom of God, rocking in the cradle of the universe with creative serendipity.

I closed my eyes and was drawn inward. There were vast galaxies behind my eyelids. On opening my eyes, they disappeared. I experienced dynamic phantasmagoric images in my mind's eye—some beautiful and some horrific—but each stopped when my eyes opened. For the next few hours, I would journey through the universes in my head. It was scary and also awesome.

Alice's singing provided a positive context in which to explore the colors of my mind. The singing brought me to a peace beyond understanding. My brain's synapses felt as if they were firing randomly and repeatedly. This quest was an inner journey entirely in my head.

Nausea came up regularly. Although sitting up straighter helped me manage it, the sounds of Alice, Gina, and Philippe vomiting made throwing up feel like a viable option. Instead, I rested in the dark, trying not to fall asleep, simply one with all.

After a couple of hours, the diarrhea began, though with lesser urgency than the last time. I found it manageable to get to the toilet as needed. My eyes had adjusted to the dark, so I could find my way easily, even in a moonless night lit by a single candle. I was at peace.

In many ways, this inward journey felt reciprocal to last summer's outwardly soaring ayahuasca journey. The warmth of feeling in the group—with them making small jokes and comments among themselves in Spanish and randomly joining in together to sing ayahuasca songs—brought a charm to the whole experience.

As the medicine began to metabolize in my system, my visions disappeared. I struggled to remain upright and awake now that nothing important remained to be experienced. I was exhausted. But it had already been a glorious night!

Gina appeared to be struggling with difficult visions, so Alice held her fast and rocked her. Philippe had spent what seemed like an hour lying at the edge of our platform, vomiting over the side, but now he got up and played his guitar softly.

Alice resumed meditating and singing in the center of the circle to keep our focus and balance. Finally, well after midnight, she suggested I go to bed when ready. I headed off to sleep as the others continued to sing and talk in Spanish into the night. For the next several hours, I had the most vivid dreams.

My whole life I had been a striver in one form or another, seeking to please others or to exceed my own unrealistic goals. But the next stage of my life would go beyond striving to simply being in the eternal now. This may have been the central meaning of this quest. I contain universes. I am enough. All the accomplishments and failures of my nearly sixty years mean nothing next to this. I need only please God, Loretta, and myself—and not necessarily in that order. Joy will inevitably emerge.

I awoke early as the morning birds, my favorite harbingers of hope, began to sing. I used the toilet and took a long, cold shower. I still had an unsettled feeling in my stomach and intestines. Otherwise, though, I felt good, content, and pleased with the work of the night.

Gina was the only other person awake. She told me she hadn't slept at all, but she seemed happy with her experience. A little later, I heard her taking a cold shower and saw her running naked back to her bedroom. Living is bliss.

I had the entire day to begin to heal and integrate my experiences in this lovely ecological setting. I still had two days to explore Puerto Maldonado before flying home. Human life is good and worth the living.

I returned home to see through the completion of my Unitarian Universalist parish ministry, to finish another stage of my life, and to become a full-time spiritual seeker, wisdom teacher, and author of spiritual nonfiction books. I was turning sixty years old. I had done well in my decades as a husband and a father, employee and employer, student and teacher. I had much to show for my efforts, but now it was time to be an authentic person of no fixed position and to follow in the footsteps of my many teachers of divine mystery.

Buddhism was a path that had strongly called to me since my trip around the world in my twenties. Now serendipity called me forth again. My favorite comparative religion professor at Harvard, who had strong ties to both Hinduism and Buddhism in India, announced she would lead a spiritual pilgrimage from Kolkata up the Ganges to walk in the Buddha's footsteps. It seemed the universe had decided I was ready, so a teacher once again appeared.

From reading as a college student in Yale's Sterling library, to traveling the world as a young adult, to meditating at midlife with Unitarian Universalist mystics in the mountains of Vermont, to whirling with Sufis, to practicing mental shifts of reality with Taoists, to experiencing psychotropic medicine with shamans, I would now return to India to explore Hinduism and Buddhism as part of my interreligious spiritual pilgrimages toward awakening.

Shamanic Mystics
BOOK GROUP DISCUSSION GUIDE

Author's Comment

To enter into the world of shamanic mystics, I had to let go of everything I had learned growing up about shamanism, witches, and mediums. Their plant medicine has power for spiritual understanding and
healing, depending upon how and when it is used and by whom.

Questions to Encourage Conversation

1. What do you know about shamanism, witches, and mediums?

2. Have you ever consciously employed affirmations to actualize
   your intentions?

3. What do you know about shamanistic use of drugs to enhance
   spiritual performance?

4. When Australian Aborigines slip over into dreamtime, where
   do you think they have gone?

5. How would you make sense of ayahuasca's impact on the
   author?

6. Can you experience the author's horrible fall and subsequent
   healing as a blessing?

7. Have you ever experienced a sweat lodge ceremony or a vision
   quest?

8. Can you feel the difference between the first and second ayahuasca experiences?

Reflection

As a group, reflect upon the shamanistic Way and whether it speaks to
you. Why or why not?

BUDDHIST AND HINDU MYSTICS

*The Buddha said: "Life can be found only in the present moment, but
our minds seldom dwell in the present moment. Instead we chase after
the past or long for the future. We think we are being ourselves, but in
fact we almost never are in real contact with ourselves. Our minds are
too busy chasing after yesterday's memories or tomorrow's dreams.
The only way to be in touch with life is to return to the present moment.
Once you know how to return to the present moment, you will become
awakened, and at that moment, you will find your true self."*

—Thich Nhat Hanh in *Old Path White Clouds*

Awakening

The term *Hinduism* was created by Western scholars to encompass the
ancient religions from the Hindu Kush mountain range through the Indian subcontinent. Buddhism formed and developed within this same
geographical and cultural context.

Making a holy pilgrimage to an ancient monastery or sacred site
can lead to spiritual awakening. However, as a twenty-seven-year-old
spiritual seeker, I was overwhelmed by the poverty and despair that in-
fuse India's Buddhism and Hinduism. Now, as a sixty-year-old, mature
spiritual seeker, I was returning—first to India and then to Southeast

Asia—to practice spiritual disciplines and walk more mindfully in the footsteps of the Buddha.

Jet-lagged and disoriented, but meditating mindfully and full of hope, I arrived in Kolkata (formerly Calcutta) on New Year's Eve 2015 and joined our small group of pilgrims. That evening, our Harvard professor described Rabindranath Tagore, one of India's greatest transcendentalists, who led the Bengal Renaissance with the Upanishads at its center. Rabindranath Tagore is someone many Unitarian Universalists know well. There are seven selections from Tagore's writings in our Unitarian Universalist hymnal, one more than even Ralph Waldo Emerson. My favorite is called "The Stream of Life":

> *The same stream of life that runs through my veins night and day*
> *runs through the world and dances rhythmic measures.*

> *It is the same life that shoots in joy through the dust of the earth in numberless*
> *blades of grass and breaks into tumultuous waves of leaves and flowers.*

> *It is the same life that is rocked in the ocean cradle of birth and death,*
> *in ebb and in flow.*

> *I feel my limbs are made glorious by the touch of this world of life.*

> *And my pride is from the life throb of ages dancing in my blood this moment.*

When I first encountered the stream of life in India during our round-the-world pilgrimage in 1983, it seemed beyond human control, requiring the spiritual seeker to learn how to dance with chaos. Life is lived in the eternal now, in the borderlands between order and chaos.

Indian mystics navigate these borders through meditation focused upon breathing. The ancient Vedas and Upanishads create small, temporary islands of order in the midst of the swirling streams of chaos. Hinduism and Buddhism developed mindfulness meditations to calm our monkey mind and produce order from chaos, if only transiently. So breathe with focused awareness, and awaken to divine mystery.

A story is sometimes told to illustrate the monkey mind: Apparently, once the English had colonized the country and established their businesses, they decided to build a golf course in Kolkata. But golf in Kolkata presented a unique obstacle. Monkeys dropped out of the trees, scurried across the course, and seized golf balls. The monkeys played with the balls, tossing them here and there.

At first, the golfers tried to control the monkeys. Their first strategy was to build high fences around the fairways and greens. This approach initially held much promise, but it was abandoned when the golfers discovered that a fence is no challenge to an ambitious monkey.

Next, the golfers tried luring the monkeys away from the course with bananas. But the monkeys found nothing as tempting and amusing as watching humans go wild whenever their little white balls were disturbed. In desperation, the British began trapping the monkeys. But for every monkey they carted off, another would appear.

Finally, the golfers gave in to the reality of their situation and developed a rather novel ground rule: play the ball where the monkey drops it. As you can imagine, playing this way could be maddening. A beautiful drive down the center of the fairway might be picked up by a monkey and then dropped in the rough. Or the opposite could happen—a hook or slice that had produced a miserable lie might be flung onto the fairway.

It did not take long for the golfers to realize that playing this particular course was an apt metaphor for our experience of life. There are good breaks, and there are bad breaks. We cannot control the outcome of the game, but our play can flow along with the stream of life.

It's this principle of the nonduality of the life force that draws me again and again to the Upanishads. Every living thing, including human beings, arises as a manifestation of the emergence of life. As the wisdom teacher Yajnavalkya says in the Brihadaranyaka Upanishad:

> *A wife loves her husband not for his own sake but*
> *because the Self lives in him.*
> *A husband loves his wife not for her own sake but*
> *because the Self lives in her.*
> *Children are not loved for their own sake but*
> *because the Self lives in them...*
> *The universe is loved not for its own sake but*
> *because the Self lives in it...*
> *Everything is loved not for its own sake but because*
> *the Self lives in it.*
> *This Self has to be realized. Hear about this Self and*
> *meditate upon Him.*

In speaking of the importance of living life as a spiritual pilgrim, Tagore said: "The great morning which is for all appears in the East. Let its light reveal us to each other who walk on the same path on pilgrimage." I had come to the East to awaken to my higher Self on pilgrimage.

My first morning in Kolkata, I awoke early to find a large raven perched at my window and squawking at me. It was sitting among the flowers in a large window box. It was soon joined by two more. I recognized their presence as potential spirit guides on my Way. I could use the help.

Looking further afield in the growing light, I discerned dozens of large, hairy bats hanging from trees in a nearby park. Even as I watched, a few late ones ended their nighttime feeding and came to hang upside down on tree branches, joining the others to sleep the day away. This was New Year's Day 2016.

Our professor continued her lecture on how Kolkata—once known as Kalikata, meaning "the field of the goddess Kali"—came to be purchased by the British East India Company at the end of the seventeenth century and militarized. For nearly two hundred years, Calcutta was the British capital of India. Signs of its imperial past were everywhere.

After touring the city, we transferred to the *Bengal Ganga* riverboat. For the next ten days, I would sleep in a single stateroom on the port side of this recreated river steamer. I never slept better.

We set out upriver. Most of India is still remarkably rural and remarkably poor. We soon passed the temple town of Kalna, with its richly ornamented terra-cotta buildings. Then we passed a Hindu temple at the village of Mayapur, where life seems to revolve around the river. In rural India, we saw cows, goats, water buffalo, and tiny villages separated by large fields. I began to understand and appreciate how everything, even poverty and hardship, can be holy.

The next day, we visited a brass-making village named Matiari, where I purchased some lovely brass figurines. The following day, we walked the town of Murshidabad, visiting palaces and mosques built by Islamic rulers in the eighteenth and nineteenth centuries. We embraced the rural countryside. In Baranagar, we saw the great epics depicted in terra-cotta in a large Hindu temple complex, and we passed through the locks near Bangladesh as we entered into the Ganges River proper. The holy and mundane were constantly intermingling on our way.

We traveled slowly across space and time, guided by the gods on this holy pilgrimage on India's holiest river. A small statue of Ganesh sat on my desk projecting prosperity on my pilgrimage. Krishna guided our pilgrim journey. We were manifesting in the eternal now. As Krishna says to Arjuna in the Bhagavad Gita concerning self-realization:

> *There has never been a time when you and I and the kings*
>   *gathered here*
> *have not existed nor will there be a time when we will cease*
>   *to exist.*
> *As the same person inhabits the body through childhood,*
>   *youth, and old age,*
> *so too at the time of death he attains another body . . .*

The impermanent has no reality; reality lies in the
eternal . . .

Even if you believe the Self to be subject to birth and
death, you should not grieve.
Death is inevitable for the living; birth is inevitable for
the dead.
Since these are unavoidable, you should not sorrow.
Every creature is not manifested at first and then attains
manifestation.

We visited the Raj Mahal, a historic Muslim town with a royal palace at its center. Like the more-famous Taj Mahal, it was built by the Mughal Islamic emperor Akbar in the sixteenth century. These ancient Islamic spiritual warriors brought architecture and culture to a poor and desperate land. In the eighteenth century, the British turned it into a center for indigo-dyeing cotton cloth. Now most of the town's residents are Hindu. So many layers of culture.

We continued to enjoy scholarly lectures as we cruised. Our boat was equipped with a filtration system that sucked in the Ganges water and purified it overnight so we could shower and bathe in the Ganges as part of our morning ablutions. We were being physically and metaphysically cleansed on this journey following the Buddha.

We visited the ruins of the Vikramshila university at Bateshwar Asthan, where Buddhism flourished during the eighth and ninth centuries. From here, teachers were sent forth throughout Southeast Asia. It is still an awesome sight a millennium later. That day, I decided I should also explore Buddhism in Southeast Asia if I ever hoped to fully understand and embrace Buddha's equanimity as expressed in Vietnamese and Cambodian culture.

The mixing of religious cultures over the millennia was nearly as extreme in India as it was in China during most of its recorded history. The Euro-American notion of national religious homogeneity is a foreign concept here. Here, all is interreligious dialogue

across space and time, across philosophies and experiences—all constantly intermixing.

This section of the Ganges was shallow, with frequently shifting
currents creating sandbars where once there was open channel. Our
riverboat's draft was fairly shallow, yet we frequently ran aground on
these unseen sandbars. Freeing ourselves often required the crew to
push us off with long poles, or to reverse the engine and rock the boat
forward and aft. The crew once even hired a tugboat to tow us back into
the mainstream. This too had metaphorical significance. None of us is
self-sufficient or in control. However, we can do together what we can't
do alone.

Migratory birds and river dolphins followed our boat along the river. They frolicked around us and set the tone for our journey. We held
reality lightly and enjoyed what we discovered.

What we discovered in Sultanganj was images of Hindu gods and
goddesses as well as the Buddha carved into the granite bluffs along the
river. In Munger, we visited a Mughal fort and a school of yoga.

Yoga is so much more than the series of positions, stretches, and
exercises that have become popular in the West in recent years. In India, *yoga* refers to any spiritual disciplines for awakening, practices for
controlling the body and mind, or systems of philosophy for attaining
ultimate union with divine mystery. The spiritual disciplines I described
in my first book, *Spiritual Audacity*, are a form of yoga. Each mystic tradition I have traveled with has invited me into its own particular yoga.

We arrived in Bihar, perhaps the poorest part of rural India, where
the Buddha spent most of his life. This is a part of the country that seldom sees white foreigners. For our entire stay in Bihar, we were joined
by armed police guards to protect us from bandits.

We investigated the archeological site of the Nalanda university,
once a center of Buddhist teaching for the world. Then we visited Ra-
jgir, where the Buddha taught his early followers. We were traveling
in Buddha's footsteps on this Ganges pilgrimage, and through lectures
and learning, he was traveling with us.

Finally, we left the river and boarded buses surrounded by local villagers taking pictures of us on their smartphones. We traveled to Bodh Gaya, where Siddhartha Gautama attained enlightenment under the Bodhi tree. The Mahabodhi Temple attracts monks on pilgrimage from around the world.

Outside the temple, our local Buddhist guide suggested I exchange a thousand-rupee note (about fifteen dollars) for a stack of one hundred ten-rupee notes. I was also to purchase a bouquet of blue lotus flowers for fifty rupees as a gift to the Buddha. I then made my way into the giant temple complex with thousands of Buddhist monks from Tibet, Mongolia, China, Korea, Japan, Thailand, and Sri Lanka. Following Tagore's teaching, we embraced the mystery to "reveal us to each other who walk on the same path of pilgrimage."

We circumambulated three concentric rings around the central temple building that houses a giant Buddha statue under a gigantic Bodhi tree. Our guide said this tree is a descendent of the original Bodhi tree, grown from a seed brought back from Sri Lanka.

As we approached the temple of the Buddha, I left my lotus flower offering on a small altar, then walked beneath the Bodhi tree, Buddhist prayer beads in hand. A monk with a strong spiritual aura stood up and offered me his spot on a stone bench directly beneath the Bodhi tree's outstretched branches. I sat and meditated upon my prayer beads for about fifteen minutes, the world passing me while I prayed. I was at peace. Then an ancient monk walked beneath the tree. I offered him my spot on the bench and moved on with my walking meditation. Blessings abound. All is a blessing.

Several abbots and monks consecrated my head with oil or asked me to bless them. I was in ecstasy to be recognized and accepted as a spiritual being. My prayer beads were blessed by dozens of Buddhist monks and their teachers. I gave each a ten-rupee note in exchange. One Indian monk offered me the gift of a leaf he had picked up from the Bodhi tree, so it would always be with me. I later saved it in my spiritual journal. This was bliss.

I understood ever more concretely what the American Buddhist mystic Jack Kornfield says in his book *After the Ecstasy, the Laundry:* "Enlightenment does exist. It is possible to awaken. Unbounded freedom and joy, oneness with the divine, awakening into a state of timeless grace—these experiences are more common than you know, and not far away." I manifested this awakening in my life.

On the way back to the bus, I purchased a consecrated Buddha-head statue to add to my growing eclectic altar of divine mystery. Finally, I understood awakening. Having sat and meditated under the Bodhi tree, I knew this sense of awakening would never leave me.

In a small bookstore outside the temple complex, I purchased Thich Nhat Hanh's *Old Path White Clouds: Walking in the Footsteps of the Buddha,* a spiritual guide and biography of the Buddha drawn from twenty-four ancient Pali, Sanskrit, and Chinese sources. Buddha taught that any living being only sees and hears a small part of reality. No matter how much we know or experience, we ought to be humble and open-hearted. We ought to acknowledge that our understanding is incomplete and practice nonattachment toward what we believe is true. Buddha showed how to live and practice the Way in order to create peace, joy, and happiness for all beings. Buddha named five powers necessary to nourish the fruits of enlightenment: confidence, energy, mindfulness, concentration, and understanding. I consider these aspects of spiritual audacity.

Later that day, we visited the Deer Park of Isipatana, where the Buddha gave his first sermon on the four noble truths. I bought some tender leaves and lovingly fed the deer.

We spent a few more days in Varanasi, but now I longed for home. I had taken refuge in the Buddha, and it transformed me. I could never have anticipated where the spirit was leading me. Now I would wait to discover what new spiritual callings might emerge in my life.

Vietnam

The next year, I was offered the chance to travel up a holy river to explore Mahayana and Theravada Buddhism, especially in relation to Hinduism—only this time, I would experience these religions as they are practiced in Southeast Asia. We would travel by riverboat up the Mekong River in Vietnam and Cambodia. Vietnam remains one of the most Chinese and most Buddhist countries in Southeast Asia. Confucianism, ancestor worship, and Buddhism (Mahayana, Ch'an, and Theravada) run deep in its culture.

My last pilgrimage had been organized by Harvard; this one would be with a group of scholars and alumni from Yale. Most of my fellow travelers were intellectual tourists, but I was a spiritual pilgrim. Mindful intent makes all the difference as to what we experience.

Because of flight delays, I arrived in Ho Chi Minh City (formerly Saigon) shortly before midnight local time. I was immediately struck by the kindness and compassion of the Vietnamese people to Americans. They appeared to bear Americans no ill will for the death and destruction our government inflicted on them fifty years ago.

I came to Vietnam and Cambodia in pursuit of Buddha's equanimity. If the first noble truth is that all is *dukkha*, or suffering, as is taught in India, then why does Buddha smile? And if achieving spiritual equanimity brings satisfaction and contentment, why don't all awakened beings have such glorious smiles? These were the metaphysical questions that would inspire my pilgrimage up the Mekong River to the ruins of Angkor Wat in Cambodia.

But first, I had to recover from the jet lag of crossing thirteen time zones in a day. I was physically exhausted! The late-night city was remarkably alive and awake as I made my way to my hotel. It would be a short night.

The next morning, following a substantial breakfast with generous amounts of black coffee, we headed out with our guide to explore the Cu Chi tunnel complex. This is where Vietnamese revolutionaries brought their resistance to the very suburbs of Saigon.

Here by the side of the Saigon River, the Vietcong built a massive, interconnected system of secret tunnels that could move soldiers and weapons right to the edge of Saigon under the very noses of the American occupation troops. These tunnels show why America's demoralized young soldiers were never able to kill and destroy the Vietnamese, who were defending their homes and ancestors. Ancestor worship tied these people to this land in a way Americans often failed to understand. These Vietnamese soldiers chose poverty and death before dishonor and would fight to their last breath for freedom and their ancestors.

As a titanic American male, I quickly discovered I couldn't even fit into many of their secret tunnel entrances, which were often hidden under fallen leaves and brush. Yet our Vietnamese guide climbed down into them quite easily. The local guide eventually found me a larger entrance through their underground hospital or medical facility. Even there, I had to duck down to enter in a crouched position, my shoulders scraping both sides of the tunnel. I was left feeling extremely vulnerable. I needed to slow my progress to a defenseless crawl every time the tunnel turned or changed elevation. I'd have been dead long before I saw it coming.

This 250-kilometer tunnel system—with distributed places for eating, sleeping, living, meeting, and fighting—provided safety for the Vietcong but was a death trap for American soldiers. This complex of tunnels was the Communist Party's headquarters for their attacks upon Saigon, only kilometers away. The rebels could easily attack under the cover of darkness and then disappear into their tunnels before daylight. Most of the tunnel network was deep enough to be safe from overhead bombings. American soldiers routinely walked, unaware, directly by their hidden entrances. This was a war we never could have, nor should have, won.

That afternoon, we visited the War Remnants Museum, which carefully documents the war crimes and atrocities committed by the American government against the Vietnamese people. The massive American carpet-bombing of civilians and widespread use of the toxic defoliant Agent Orange against villages in both the north and the south verged on genocide. Yet unlike the French troops during World War II or our 1960s American draftees, the Vietnamese, with their Ch'an Buddhism and ancestor worship, would always fight to the death.

The next day, we departed our hotel and boarded the *Mekong Princess* to embark upon the more spiritual aspects of this pilgrimage. We spent the rest of our time in Vietnam along rural waterways.

Our first scholarly lecture focused on the complex history of Indochina, the large land area southeast of India and China that includes the countries of Myanmar, Thailand, Laos, Vietnam, Cambodia, Malaysia, and Indonesia. Indochina was once many independent kingdoms, seemingly perpetually warring among themselves and with their larger imperial neighbors to the north. Ancient Chinese records talk of commercial trading and fighting with the Mon (predecessors of the Thai or Siamese), Funan (predecessors of Vietnamese), and Chenla (predecessors of Khmer) kingdoms.

Each kingdom seemed to have, however briefly, its own period of dominance and expansion within this relatively small land area. As the result of nineteenth-century Western imperialism, these various competing tribes and kingdoms were resolved into the countries we know today.

That evening, dinner was preceded by a classical Chinese-inspired Vietnamese opera, but I could barely keep my eyes open. I skipped dinner and went to bed as our boat made its way along canals toward the Mekong.

I awoke before the sun, having slept over nine hours. I went up on deck to watch the day awaken. In the early-morning light, we passed tugboats leading barges piled high with timber or soil. A few night fishermen were returning with their catches. I listened to the putt-putt-putting music of their motors as the sky tinged pink against the gray rain-laden clouds.

Daylight gradually emerged as the fog of night lifted. A red pagoda appeared on the shore in the brightening day, followed by radio antennae, electrical lines, and office buildings in the distance. Morning fishing boats passed us, trailing nets. The river began to awaken to life. The early-morning breeze brought cooling comfort while keeping bugs and mosquitos away. The sun emerged from behind a bank of clouds, casting its beams across the water. I was awakened!

Later that morning, we boarded sampans to visit some small villages in a mangrove swamp. These were people living a simple life, largely self-sustained, far from the urban environment. Subsisting on the swampy land, they produced traditional products from water hyacinth for their own use and even some for export.

Our visit to the Phuoc Hau pagoda and monastery in the rural village of Tra On was my first deeply spiritual experience within a traditional religious setting for this pilgrimage. The pagoda has dozens of Chinese Buddha statues and portraits within the main sanctuary. It is clear many local families have earned spiritual merit over many years through contributing such statues and portraits. It is a place of peace, calmness, and equanimity. I flourish in such places.

The surrounding monastery and grounds have a run-down and unattended feeling about them, but they still exude a certain shabby spirituality that is easy to embrace. The mostly older monks wandering about their tasks also exude this same sense of equanimity and wellbeing in a distinctly shabby sort of setting. Nothing matters—there is no one to impress. They simply get on about this matter of enlightenment in a very muggy, rural setting. Buddha smiles.

The monastery tombs and gardens have hundreds of sutra verses, many drawn from the *Dhammapada*, which is often called Buddha's last sermon. These verses are inscribed in Vietnamese on large granite tablets to aid in walking meditation. This helps keep the dharma, the teachings of the Buddha, ever present in the sight and minds of the monks, while also helping to educate the local Buddhist population. Our local guide translated some of these sayings:

> *To follow the dharma revealed by awakened ones is to live in joy with a serene mind.*

> *Our life is shaped by our mind; we become what we think. Suffering follows evil thought as the wheels of a cart follow the oxen that draw it.*

Our life is shaped by our mind; we become what we think. Joy follows a pure thought like a shadow that never leaves.

Do not give attention to what others do or fail to do; give it to what you do or fail to do.

One who conquers herself is greater than another who conquers a thousand men on the battlefield. Be victorious over yourself and not over others.

Wake up! Don't be lazy. Follow the right path; avoid the wrong.

Hasten to do good; refrain from evil. If you neglect the good, evil can enter your mind.

Learn what is right, then teach others, as the wise do.

We gained our understanding of the rural parts of Vietnam by visiting many side canals and tributaries of the Mekong. We were invited into many small villages and private homes, and we enjoyed tastings in fruit orchards and local markets. The rural people seemed to experience life less intellectually and more sensually. Most of them seemed at peace, happy with their lot, and content with their lives. Perhaps it was just social affect, but it felt real—and important.

How they practiced their Buddhism appeared to matter. The most common form of Buddhism in these parts of Vietnam seemed to be Mahayana Buddhism. But there was also a strong cultural emphasis on family and community obligations. So Ch'an Buddhism, which draws as deeply on Taoism as it does on traditional Mahayana Buddhism, also seemed well represented among the monks and monasteries.

Further along the Mekong, toward Cambodia, Theravada Buddhism seemed to become more prominent. New and syncretistic forms of religion, such as the Cao Dai or Hoa Hao religion, also have their millions of followers. Doctrine doesn't seem to matter so much as depth of feeling in religion. These people live an interreligious dialog with equanimity.

As we made our way along the Mekong delta, we experienced a mash-up of cultures and religions, perhaps best exemplified by the Vinh Trang Temple near My Tho. Here on the banks of the Bao Dinh canal is a pagoda first built in the Angkor Wat architectural style in the mid-eighteenth century. Its many carvings are truly ancient and incredibly diverse.

After these southern Vietnam provinces were ceded to the French colonial forces in the late nineteenth century, the temple was largely rebuilt and expanded in a French architectural style. A tropical storm ravaged the main temple building early in the twentieth century. It was rebuilt with additional renovations in classical Vietnamese style. Each new tradition preserved the best of what came before, even as it added its own distinctive touches.

Vinh Trang has over sixty statues from different Buddhist traditions. As a Cambodian-style Theravada Buddhist shrine, it gives pride of place to Gautama but makes space for local bodhisattvas, or Theravada saints. With its strong ties to Vietnamese Mahayana Buddhism, it has prominent statues for many of the various manifestations of Buddhahood beyond Gautama. Given its strong Chinese influence, it includes statues of Chinese immortals such as the Jade Emperor and Budai as well. There are also graves for the many Buddhist priests who cared for the monastery over time.

I relish my own satisfaction with Budai. Also called Hotei, he is traditionally depicted as a joyful, fat monk with a big belly. As a good and loving character, he is always shown smiling or laughing, so his nickname in Chinese is the Laughing Buddha. He is a Buddhist manifestation of equanimity. He teaches contentment, generosity, wisdom, and openheartedness. He mischievously plays with children and brings prosperity to the poor. He is a model for being spiritually fat and happy, rather than serious or dour. He exudes silly joy and laughter.

In Mahayana Buddhism, Budai is identified as an incarnation of the future Buddha, Maitreya. In folk tradition, people rub his big, fat belly for good luck and future prosperity. At Vinh Trang, his large, smiling statue is prominently seated immediately behind the standing statue of Gautama. This mixing of traditions, with its deep emphasis on human flourishing, greatly attracted me to this form of nondoctrinal, universalizing Buddhism. I took refuge in this mixing.

The next evening, we arrived in Can Tho, the epicenter of the Mekong delta and the region's largest city. After days exploring the rural backwaters, the bright lights of the big city reminded me of Hong Kong, especially with its neon-lit restaurants and floating markets. Following dinner, we walked along the waterfront, enjoying the myriad sights and sounds. Much to our local guide's amusement, I sampled large quantities of the local scorpion brandy and river-snake wine. They were potent and delicious!

We dived into, even for just a small time, this Vietnamese urban environment. But the energy, activity, and noise soon felt exhausting. This highly stimulating environment tends to encourage late nights and wild living. I found this urban setting spiritually draining.

Fortunately, we traveled on the very next day. Back on the river once again, I fell into a daily pattern of enjoying an extended dinner with pleasant conversations before turning in for the night relatively early so that I would awaken naturally in the predawn light to greet the new day. This became a form of meditation: listening to the earth gradually awaking, the activity beginning to pick up along the river, and the day taking on its hustle and bustle once again. Life is abundant on the river and its banks.

The sun rose slowly above the trees; once it had risen, the breeze picked up. We were visited one morning by hundreds of small swallows with bright red and yellow colors beneath their wings, playing on the air currents, rising up against the air resistance, and enjoying the new day! This was the joy of abandoning city hotels for the quieter equanimity of river travel.

Our final day in Vietnam, we visited an island village with its own sedate pace and commercialism. The village had a small Theravada Buddhist temple, where they happily allowed us to meditate for a while. There was also a small textile manufacturer who used forty-year-old American equipment to make multipurpose scarves for export across the border into Cambodia.

Cambodia

That afternoon, we crossed the border into Cambodia to experience a different land and people. The country is also known as Kampuchea, which literally means "the Golden Land." The Mekong River seethes with life at its borders.

We began with a scholarly briefing on Cambodia's language, people, and history, dating back to the Khmer Empire. Most people in Cambodia belong to the Khmer ethnic group. In addition, Khmer is the official language of Cambodia. The ancient Khmer rulers had their greatest period of wealth and dominance in this region between the ninth and fourteenth centuries, and Angkor was their religious and governmental center.

We also heard our first lecture on the "Gods of Angkor," the ancient capital of the empire. In a few days, we would arrive at the Angkor Wat temple. Their religion was initially a form of Hinduism, reflecting their strong ties to India, though Mahayana Buddhism had a growing influence over time. Here was an interreligious confluence that grew into its own unique form of human spirituality and flourishing.

That evening, we docked in the Cambodian riverside capital of Phnom Penh. This modern commercial city belies the horrors and atrocities of the Khmer Rouge, which still haunt it.

On April 17, 1975, the Communist Khmer Rouge regime defeated the American-backed president Lon Nol and the corrupt democratic government. Pol Pot, the leader of the Khmer Rouge, sought to radically remake Cambodian society on a Communist peasant model. He began by destroying the imperialists' city of Phnom Penh.

He wanted to obliterate Cambodia's imperialist past and so tortured or killed anyone in anyway connected to it. He began a genocide in which the Khmer Rouge attempted to reeducate or exterminate all capitalists, intellectuals, urban dwellers, educated elite, and those with ties to Western imperialists.

It was nearly four years before the Vietnamese government, who themselves had just recently expelled the American occupation of Vietnam, were strong enough to mount an invasion in January 1979. But by then, the Khmer Rouge had killed 1.7 million people—nearly a third of the Cambodian population—through starvation, forced labor, torture, and mass executions.

This was all a revelation to me. Even though I was in college when it happened, I knew nothing about it. Now, nearly forty years after its Vietnamese liberation from devastation and destruction, we would explore the restored capital. Our touring began with a cyclo ride. Peddled by a driver, a cyclo is a bicycle taxi with an oversize basket in the front to comfortably seat a single passenger. It was a great and inexpensive way to see this tropical city and discover its vibrancy. At the restored palace of the king, we saw some of the Khmer Empire's ancient glories.

At the National Museum of Cambodia, I bought a translation of the Cambodian best seller *First They Killed My Father*. The memoir tells this sordid tale through the eyes of Loung Ung, the daughter of a Lon Nol–appointed police commander living in Phnom Penh. She was only five years old when her family was forced to resettle in the rural areas. It is a story of paradise lost and eventually, painfully, regained. She tells of the paradise that she experienced growing up in Phnom Penh, the purgatory of the poor rural villages and forced labor camps, and the hell of the death and destruction of her father, her mother, and two of her sisters under tragic circumstances. It also tells of the trials and tribulations that finally led to new lives for her, her three older brothers, and her older sister.

That afternoon, we visited the Choeung Ek Killing Field outside Phnom Penh, where hundreds of bodies were buried in mass graves.

Many victims had their heads severed from their bodies. The Khmer Rouge had so many people to execute that they didn't have enough bullets to shoot them all. Often, they simply had people kneel graveside as they cut their heads off, one after another.

Then we returned to Phnom Penh to visit the Tuol Sleng Museum of Genocide at S-21 Prison. The Khmer Rouge had turned this former private school into a prison and the main interrogation and torture center in Phnom Penh. At the site, we walked through holding cells and torture chambers. We got a chance to meet and talk with Chum Mey, a former prisoner in this place. He had been tortured simply for having been a car mechanic working for the Lon Nol government. I was reminded that too often empires are built upon other people's suffering.

The next day, we sailed back out of the Tonle Sap River and into the upper Mekong River. It was great to be back on the river. The floating fishing villages were a remarkable sight. Even though rural poverty stretched nearly to the border of Phnom Penh's urban capital prosperity, the land was peaceful and the people thrived.

All of life was juxtaposed in this confluence of three rivers—not unlike the confluence of Mahayana, Theravada, and Ch'an Buddhism in Cambodia. Religion here is synchronistic. Life is balanced between despair and equanimity. Many of the older, generous, joyful Cambodian people we met were survivors of this horrible holocaust.

At Phnom Udong we visited our first Cambodian Theravada Buddhist monastery, with its spacious and grand assembly hall and its dozens of Buddha statues. Five Buddhist monks blessed us in a complicated ceremony.

Because this compound included a Buddhist school and monastery, dozens of Buddhist novitiates—young boys, some appearing only eight or nine years old—followed us with their eyes. They had seldom seen white Westerners before.

I proceeded to play with the children and give donations to the poor. Our lecturer on Buddhism came along and saw my smile of equanimity as I played with the children. She called me a manifestation of Budai. I was content. I wanted to always passionately engage with life itself.

The setting of the temple—with its grand assembly hall, many housing units, and myriad classrooms—bespoke a place of prosperity and respect in the surrounding community. We were told that under Pol Pot, this monastery was destroyed and all the Buddhist monks killed. But this place had seen a remarkable resurgence in the years since that time of horror and destruction. From that horrible past a place of peace, love, and contentment had emerged. All was well.

We walked through the village, seeing houses raised on stilts against the river flooding. Each family owned one, two, or even five Brahman cows, showing the wealth of these farmers. Our local guide explained that in this largely cashless society, farmers store and grow their wealth in the value of their cows: hundreds of US dollars per calf, thousands of dollars per full-grown cow, and tens of thousands of dollars for really good stud bulls. Our guide explained that his family had to sell a small cow to pay for his first year of college, as did the families of many intelligent and ambitious children growing up in rural Cambodian communities. But now, with his good income as an English-speaking guide, he was paying to send his two youngest siblings to college. His parents didn't need to sell any further cows. This was a different economy.

The elementary students in this rural village attend classes for reading, writing, and arithmetic in Khmer from seven thirty in the morning to two thirty in the afternoon each day. Then the ambitious ones also attend English classes from three to five each afternoon.

We sat in on one such English class. Each American adult sat surrounded by three or four Cambodian children as we let them experience our diverse accents and ways of talking. An eight-year-old happily pointed out to me the English nouns in her picture books. They all giggled when I asked them to name the English words for my eyes, nose, mouth, hair, arms, and elbows. Their eyes positively twinkled as they showed they knew the correct words. These kids were very sweet and eager to please. This may have been one of the highest points of the trip for me. We talked about colorful butterflies emerging from the transformations of caterpillars.

But I could not reconcile the 1970s genocide in this land with the giggling of the schoolchildren. This genocide happened so recently and involved some of the people I was meeting every day. How could the kindest people I had ever met, with their easy smiles and good nature, have killed each other so brutally?

As I continued to read *First They Killed My Father,* the intimate details of this horrid story began to disrupt my sleep. So many killed for so little purpose. But I had to finish it, so I limited my reading to the early-morning hours.

The next morning, I rose with the unseen sun. Here on the river, in the early-morning light, the swirling and sweeping of birds and dragonflies encompassed a rich flora and fauna. But the overcast nature of the day meant the rising sun was obscured by cloud cover. I could not see the sun, yet I knew with certainty it was there. It would be discerned only with the brightening of the day.

Perhaps that is an adequate metaphor for human goodness and wellbeing in the midst of such horror and destruction. Atrocities blur our vision of human goodness, yet we know with certainty that goodness remains and will shine forth again another day.

Temples of Power

Finally, we departed the *Mekong Princess.* We rode for five hours by bus to reach our destination of Siem Reap, the gateway to the Khmer temples of power. At the height of the Khmer Empire, Angkor was a paradise on earth, a pantheon of the spirit, and an engineering marvel that exceeded anything in Europe during this period. Some ancient civilizations achieved human flourishing we haven't yet exceeded.

In the Angkor National Museum, there are over one thousand Buddha statues reflecting the nature of Cambodian Buddhism, which give particular emphasis to Buddha's smile along with his distinct postures and dynamic gestures. My favorite was the full-length reclining Buddha with its beatific smile.

One of the earliest surviving Khmer temple mountains is Bakong at Roluos, built in the late ninth century as the state temple of the capital city. Dedicated to Shiva, whose sacred dance brings about both creation and destruction, this temple consists of a five-story step pyramid surrounded by three concentric enclosures and two moats presenting a stylized representation of the mythical Hindu Mount Meru.

It is oriented toward the cardinal directions, so it is particularly appealing in the early-morning and late-afternoon light. The four entrances to the central tower each features Nandi, Shiva's bull, patiently awaiting its master. The stairways are protected by Chinese-style lion guardians. Though the buildings are much eroded, and much statuary is broken or missing, it still is awe inspiring.

On this holy temple mountain, I prayed a traditional Hindu prayer translated for UU's by Abhi Janamanchi, a south-Asian Hindu Unitarian Universalist minister:

May good befall all.
May there be peace for all.
May all be fit for excellence.
May all experience the holy.
May all be happy.
May all be healthy.
May all experience what is good.
May no one suffer.

Next, we visited Phnom Bakheng. Our local guide told us this early-tenth-century temple mountain was the state temple overlooking Yaśovarman I's new capital, a four-kilometer-square palace surrounded by an earthen bank. Phnom Bakheng looks much like Bakong, but it is dedicated to Yasodharesvara, "the one who brings glory."

Like Bakong, Phnom Bakheng is oriented to the cardinal directions. To the northeast and southwest are holy mountains; to the west, a great reservoir making this land fertile; to the north, the dark forests; and to the southeast, the massive structures of Angkor Wat. So we rose at four in the morning to climb to Phnom Bakheng in order to watch the sunrise over Angkor Wat.

We arrived at the base of the mountain about an hour before sunrise. The ascent in the dark was surprisingly steep. To save time, we went up a steeply inclined footpath rather than the wider, more gradual ceremonial elephant path. We reached the ramparts of the Phnom Bakheng temple just as the first cock crowed. The waning, nearly full moon beamed down upon us. The morning star was the only star still visible in the sky.

Slowly the sky lightened in the east. The details of geography took on a more definite form as the world emerged into the light of day. The first birds began to sing in the predawn light. My heart soared! Life constantly renews itself. I was awakened.

It was nearly the winter solstice, so the rising sun lined up directly through the sacred portals. The Buddha sitting in the central tower was bathed in morning light. I sat in a sacred portal, bathed in morning light, aligned with the universe and all that is. All is one, and I was glad to be alive.

We hired a guide and driver to travel twenty kilometers north of Angkor to the foothills of the Phnom Kulen mountain to visit Banteay Srei. As "the citadel of beauty," Banteay Srei is reputed to be the most beautiful of the temple mountains.

Though it wasn't rediscovered until well into the twentieth century, Banteay Srei was built in the second half of the tenth century by Yajnavaraha, the guru to the future king Jayavarman V. This temple celebrates spiritual power rather than military power. It is not a royal temple; it doesn't exude state power. There is nothing massive here. Even the beautiful stone carvings feel delicate. Located in a peaceful, isolated, semi-wooded area, it was consecrated through the prayers of holy monks and pilgrims. A feeling of deep peace and equanimity permeated the entire area for this pilgrim.

The temple exudes an almost feminine quality of spirituality. Appropriately, sometimes its name is translated as "the citadel of women."

Nearly every surface is decorated, and even the side galleries contain important motifs—spiritual yin energy to balance perhaps the king's yang energy. The site follows the three-level concentric enclosure pattern of the earlier temple mountains, yet this one feels spiritually quite different. It is a place of peace. The carved details are works of art. My blood pressure and existential angst were significantly lowered just from being in this space.

The carvings of the central sanctuary depict brutal battles and violence from the poem *Ramayana*: Ravana abducting Sita, wife of Rama; Vali and Sugriva, two monkey brothers, battling for the crown; Krishna killing demons; Vishnu in the form of a wild boar. Yet these depictions were carved so artfully that the spiritual seeker is inclined to take this violence in stride, as part of life, as something the equanimity of enlightenment allows awakened ones to transcend. Ever since the Bhagavad Gita, awakening comes through inner struggles.

Now that we were staying in Siem Reap, Cambodia's tourist destination, I began to experience its nightlife. After wandering through the night market, I found a small bar called the Nest, where I sat alone and talked to the bartender. I was Budai and content.

Throughout our travels, young Cambodian men—merchants, clerks, *tuk tuk* drivers, bartenders, and wait staff—sought to strike up conversations with me to pass the time, improve their English, and perhaps learn more of the world. Like many of these young men, this bartender was born in a rural village, but studied and learned English so he could work in the hospitality trade.

For these poor but ambitious young men, tourism was a path to a better life and to one day being able to support a wife and family. How a poor boy from a poor family makes a life varies tremendously around the world, but those with resilience and discipline rise with spirit.

Angkor Wat

We spent the better part of the next day exploring the main Angkor Wat temple. King Suryavarman II had the temple built in the early twelfth century, largely by slaves captured in wars, especially from the Cham kingdom of present-day central Vietnam.

Unlike Banteay Srei, the Angkor Wat complex exudes enormous power, with its massive, thick, heavy blocks of stone and its depictions of military might. This was a place built to impress and intimidate foreign powers into accepting the might of the Khmer over them. Let there be no mistake: this was intended to be the domain of the supreme king of the world. King Suryavarman II's subjects literally saw him as a living manifestation of the Hindu god Vishnu.

The massive temple complex covers almost five hundred acres and represents a model of paradise. Five towers represent the five peaks of Mount Meru. At the center is a stepped-terrace pyramid, creating a sense of encompassing the Hindu world. The complex is surrounded by a broad moat representing the ocean of chaos from which life emerges. The temple mountain is built on three distinct levels as we traverse from lowest sentience to the highest enlightenment.

The outer temple walls once depicted at least two thousand *apsaras*, angelic, celestial dancers moving with the divine in *Ramayana* fashion, bringing sensual rewards to kings and heroes who died bravely in pursuit of their Hindu life calling. The interior walls at the ground level are covered by bas-relief carvings depicting Hindu themes, mainly the *Ramayana* and *Mahabharata* epics. They also include the coronation procession of Suryavarman II and Hindu depictions of multiple heavens and hells.

But the most fascinating for me was the classic depiction of creation through the churning of the cosmic ocean, as told in the *Mahabharata*. It depicts gods and demons in a tug-of-war over control of the universe, with the body of Naga, the serpent god, serving as the rope stretched between them. The demons pull the serpent's head while the gods pull the tail. Vishnu oversees the battle. So in the end, goodness always wins—but never without completely risking failure. Every entrance to Angkor Wat includes the head or tail and the long body of Naga to hold back chaos.

In the fourteenth century, the Khmer kings more formally adopted Theravada Buddhism as their core accepted form of Buddhism. And so they added the Gallery of a Thousand Buddhas on the second level of the Angkor Wat temple, making this an important Theravada Buddhist pilgrimage site.

The second level also includes four pools capturing rainwater for ritualized purification rites. This remained an important center for religious ritual for many centuries. It was initially used for Hindu rites in honor of Vishnu and Shiva, and later it was used for Theravada Buddhist rites. The doctrines may have changed over time, but the spiritual power of this place remained quite intact. All is change; thus, there is continuity in change.

It is believed that Siem Reap and Angkor Wat were captured by a Cham army in the twelfth century, causing the Khmer king to flee, perhaps to southern China. Four years later, Jayavarman VII led a large Khmer army and navy—perhaps with the help of Chinese mercenaries—to reconquer his kingdom. They drove the Cham army back across the Mekong River to Vietnam.

In celebration of his victory, he built the new imperial city of Angkor Thom, which means "great city," just north of Angkor Wat. This new and far more impressive city incorporated and enveloped the earlier capital city of Angkor. The expanded result became one of the largest cities in the twelfth-century world. It probably remained the imperial capital well into the seventeenth century.

The Angkor Thom site covers nine hundred hectares within its city walls, surrounded by a three-kilometer moat on every side. Entering by the south gate and crossing the moat, we again encountered statues of gods and demons in a tug-of-war pulling on the serpent god Naga. The gods are ever on the verge of utter failure, yet they grasp order out of chaos, thus linking the world of men with the mysterious spirit world.

This Way brought us to my favorite state temple in Angkor Wat: Jayavarman VII's Bayon (which means "holy leader") temple, at the very center of his imperial city. Jayavarman VII as well as his successors wanted to be seen as both worldly kings and religious manifestations of the divine. This was the final temple built at Angkor, and it includes Mahayana, Theravada, and Hindu elements. It was a pantheon for all the gods, a sanctified site for Hindu worship, and a center for Buddhist study and meditation. The temple evidently began with a typical three-level design. But due to extensive additions and reconstructions over the centuries, the design is both crowded and complex, with diverse levels and side chapels throughout and meditating Buddhas in odd corners. Here, Shiva's fertile lingam will be juxtaposed with Buddha's calm serenity, both overseen by small ancient deities. Dead kings are venerated in shrines alongside demons and mythical beasts.

After the claustrophobic lower terraces, one enters a different world in the uppermost terrace, where an atmosphere of peace and equanimity takes over. Its defining features are the thirty-seven smiling buddha faces on the freestanding towers that greet you at every turn.

Each one is a work of art; they are slightly different, yet each evokes calm, serenity, and equanimity. In the central chamber, a classical three-and-a-half-meter Mahayana Buddha once sat on Naga, mindfully meditating and contemplating the world into existence, but it was destroyed as part of purging foreign influences from their kingdom. What remains there with equanimity, however, is the Bayon, the holy leader, and his endlessly multiplying smiling face of contentment, which scholars claim bears a strong resemblance to Jayavarman VII.

There in the upper terrace, I found a quiet corner to meditate with smiling Bayons in every direction. I was content. My spiritual journey had brought me beyond striving, beyond clinging, beyond success or failure; it had brought me to simply being content to smile.

What remains is the Laughing Buddha. Having awakened to enlightenment, everything can be faced with equanimity. There is no failure or success, no hardship worth worrying about, no luxury worth pursuing. Spiritual maturity and awakening transcend earthly riches and power. Life is suffering, yet a mature, spiritual being responds with equanimity and a smile. That is all there is, all there need be, and all there ever will be. Blessed be that it is ever thus.

Equanimity Found

I had found what I had come to find. It was the end of my pilgrimage and time for me to leave. My last night, I offered to take our Cambodian guide, Tek, and his nine- and six-year-old daughters out to dinner at any restaurant of their choice. The girls, Regina and Reginie, chose their favorite place for french fries and pizza.

The girls attend Khmer public school weekdays from seven thirty in the morning to one thirty in the afternoon. After going home for lunch, they then attend an English-language class from two thirty to five thirty. As a result, Regina speaks remarkable English and was eager to practice with me. We spoke of many things, particularly similarities and differences between growing up in Cambodia versus America. In many ways, she seemed to be living in a paradise regained.

Twenty-first-century Cambodia is an extraordinary place, especially at Christmastime. Despite the Khmer Rouge genocide, they are a gentle, happy people. Being a deeply religious Theravada Buddhist country, they welcome any reason to celebrate life. Despite having no evergreen trees, snow, or Christian traditions, they celebrate Christmas in joyous fashion—so much so that middle-class Chinese tourists travel to Siem Reap to celebrate Christmas there. The big tourist hotels are decked out in Christmas lights, Santa and his reindeer, fake evergreen trees, and displays that make it look as if it were snowing in this tropical country.

A big Christmas display was visible across the street from our restaurant. The girls sang me Christmas songs they learned in school, none of which were religious, and they talked about presents they hoped to receive. For them, Christmas is a joyous, family-centered international holiday with lots of presents. It doesn't conflict with their Theravada Buddhist family traditions. Santa appears to

them as a silly, happy, Laughing Buddha–type figure; a jolly manifestation of divine mystery. They seemed to be willing to also accept me as
such. I was deep in equanimity.

Regina finally asked me an important question: "If snow is made
from frozen water, doesn't it hurt you when it falls from the sky?"

I explained to her how ice crystals form in the clouds, resulting in
the airy fluffiness of snowflakes, and how children catch snowflakes on
their tongues.

"Can you eat snow?" she pensively asked me.

And then I explained about snow with flavored syrup, skiing, snow
fights, and snowmen.

The girls were enchanted by snow. But now it was time for them to
go home to bed, with dreams of snow and Santa in their heads.

In the morning, Tek took me to the airport for my flight to Hong
Kong, where I had a planned four-hour layover before flying on to Boston. My son, Robert, had upgraded me to first class for my fourteen-
hour flight to Boston, so I got to enjoy the Cathay Pacific first-class
lounge while I waited.

The first-class lounge had a large plate-glass window that provided
a panoramic view westward from the airport. This was my first time in
Hong Kong since my month-long retreat with the Taoists years before.
As I settled myself down with a cognac and a good book, the glorious afternoon sun peeked through a cloud layer offset by the silhouetted mountains of the Chinese New Territories above Hong Kong, the mountains
where I learned Taoist mountain climbing. Their beauty again astonished
me. I had come so far in the five years since my sabbatical.

The airline announced over the intercom that my flight had been
delayed due to incoming aircraft. I felt no anxiety or angst. No stress.
No worries. Equanimity. I no longer cherished any illusion of control. I
watched the beautiful sunset over the Chinese mountains and ordered
another cognac. All manner of things will be well.

In six months, I would renew my travels, this time with Christian
mystics. But for now, I simply savored the cognac and life itself. I was
awake. I was content. Who could ask for more than that?

Buddhist Mystics
BOOK GROUP DISCUSSION GUIDE

Author's Comment

Each of the major world religions, including Christianity, Islam, and Buddhism, contains as much theological and geographical diversity within its faith as between it and other faiths. Traveling the world on pilgrimage, I encountered very different and meaningful expressions of Buddhism.

Questions to Encourage Conversation

1. Have you ever read the Vedas or Upanishads as a guide to divine mystery?

2. How does experiencing India from the Ganges transform the author's pilgrimage?

3. Which rituals does the author practice in Bodh Gaya to achieve awakening?

4. How would you explain the Vietnamese and Cambodian peoples' equanimity?

5. How does following the Mekong River transform the author's pilgrimage?

6. Have you ever read and pondered the Buddha's *Dhammapada*?

7. What might it have been like when the Khmer Empire was the most powerful on earth?

8. Can you imagine a temple with nothing but smiling faces of spiritual enlightenment?

Reflection

As a group, reflect upon the parts of these Hindu and Buddhist practices that resonate for your spiritual journey.

CHRISTIAN MYSTICS

*In the beginning, it is always necessary to be faithful, both in actions
and in the renouncing of self. But, after that, there is only indescribable
joy. If difficulties arise, simply turn to Jesus Christ and pray for his
grace, with which everything will become easy . . . All that is necessary is a heart dedicated entirely and solely to Him out of love for Him
above all others.*

—Brother Lawrence

In Jesus's Footsteps

The Word became flesh and dwelt among us. But long before the birth
of Jesus, spiritual disciplines that would later become associated with
Christian mysticism were being practiced in Antioch, Alexandria, and
Jerusalem. Antioch, in what is now Syria, drew upon ancient traditions of Zoroastrianism and brought those rituals and traditions into
Christianity. In developing its form of Christian mysticism, Alexandria drew upon the ancient mystery cults of Egypt and their hidden
gnostic teachings, some of which pass down to us in the teachings of
the Desert Fathers.

This is yet another example of what I learned from mystics in multiple religious traditions: The forest of faith often looks like many separate and individual trees, spreading their branches to soak up the sun

in competition with each other. But in fact, the roots beneath the earth are deeply intertwined, and all draw deeply from the same living waters.

My spiritual tap root, the center and core of my interreligious faith, remains deeply within Christianity. Resonances abound across traditions, from the smiling Shiva Nataraja dancing the cosmic dance that both creates and destroys the universe, to Jesus Christ becoming beloved as the Lord of the Dance. Creation and destruction, death and resurrection are together part of the divine mystery. God's Word and God's breath incarnate accompany me on my spiritual journey.

And so I would travel first to Israel and Palestine, the Holy Land, and then to Spain, the site of the Camino de Santiago. On these pilgrimages, I would seek to better understand this dancing with divine mystery and to deepen my relationship to God as a mature Christian mystic.

Having traveled on spiritual pilgrimages with my family, my books, Unitarian Universalists, Sufis, Taoists, shamans, and Buddhists, it was finally time for me to travel with Christian mystics to make better sense of my relationship to gnostic Christianity. Now was my chance to see with my own eyes and feel within my own heart the love that surpasses understanding at the foundation of my faith. I would walk in the footsteps of Jesus.

My faith journey began in the Baptist Sunday school classes of the 1960s, but as a teenager, I became estranged from the Jesus Christ of my youth. I repudiated the Nicene Creed. Instead, I learned to experience the divine mystery as working in me and through me.

As I made my Way down my mystic path, the archangel Michael—pronounced "me-kale" in ancient Christian teachings—came to me as the countenance of Christ. Unitarian Universalists often call it simply the Spirit of Life. Then, during my August 1999 UU vision quest, Jesus Christ came to me directly himself.

Now, on this gnostic Christian pilgrimage, Jesus would be my companion and my guide. As he promised, "I will be with you always." I took refuge in that promise. I became part of the mystic body of Christ.

Jesus of Nazareth's earliest followers were simply called followers of the Way. Jesus is the Christian Way for ascending from the world of the senses into the supersensible wilds of divine mystery, living between two worlds. With Jesus Christ, everything becomes transformed, regardless of whatever Way calls to you, yet human beings and the spiritual journey remain essentially the same.

Jesus had brothers and sisters. He laughed, told stories, walked nearly everywhere he went, slept when he was tired. He cared for his mother, cherished small children, paid his taxes, experienced temptations, and wept over a friend's death.

Jesus was a man with friends and, potentially, lovers. He had moods, certainly feelings, and attitudes. He acted with compassion, enjoyed good food and wine, and hung out with inappropriate people. He was human. Profoundly human.

But being human did not separate Jesus from God. He had a particularly intimate understanding of and relationship with divine mystery. He taught how to manifest the kingdom of God, or heaven, in our daily lives. On this pilgrimage, I wished to recover and redeem my own Christian upbringing in order to live my life largely in heaven on earth.

Progressive biblical scholars often draw a distinction between the Jesus of history and the Christ of Christian tradition. They contend that we see only some of Jesus as man and only some of Christ as God in the orthodox Christian scriptures. I am content with Jesus as my spiritual teacher and Christ as my Savior. I wished to deeply engage them both.

But what, then, of the Jewish messiah? What is Jesus's relationship to the ancient prophecies? Christ is the answer to the hopes and prayers of a religious tradition that has elevated him to a singular role of being *the* savior, judge, comforter, and redeemer—the resurrection and the life.

The Jewish claim to being God's chosen people is based upon Yahweh's promise to Abraham in the Torah. God supposedly promised all of Canaan to Abraham's descendants. But this claim is complicated for non-Jews. Scholars cannot document, at least outside of sacred texts, many Jewish origin myths. This includes the Exodus, the fall of Jericho, or any combined kingdom that ever ruled all of what would one day become the kingdoms of Israel and Judaea.

And how do we reconcile the many nations and faith traditions that reportedly descend from this same promise God made this man Abraham? Muslims claim that God's promise to Abraham descends to them through his eldest son, Ishmael. They believe they are the inheritors of this promised land for all time. Both religious traditions, as well as other local traditions, rely upon their own traditions and sacred texts to validate their claims from this God of Abraham.

Like any long-populated area, Palestine has many layers of human history, with different tribes and peoples having both built upon and obliterated the remains of previous civilizations. Abraham was the father of many nations. The ancient desert tribes of Midianites, Edomites, Moabites, and Canaanites gave way to the conquering tribes of Phoenicians, Philistines, Israelites, and Judaeans. In turn, they were conquered and partially repopulated by Egyptian, Assyrian, Babylonian, Greek, and Roman armies. Racial, ethnic, cultural, and religious mixing was the norm for millennia.

The Phoenicia, Gaulanitis, Galilee, Decapolis, Peraea, Samaria, Judaea, Philistine, and Idumea that Jesus knew were quite distinct districts in a very small geographic area under Roman occupation. They were populated with a mix of Semitic and non-Semitic tribal descendants. Jesus was a Galilean, not a Samaritan or Judaean, and this set him and his followers apart as religiously suspect. These important distinctions are often overlooked or ignored.

However, this history was not portrayed to me in my 1960s Baptist Sunday school. Rather, the entire region was described as simply the "land of the Jews." I would later learn that faith is generally more heterodox than often described and sacred claims often contested.

There are many religious and cultural contexts through which to view this land and its peoples. As I prepared for my pilgrimage, I realized that whichever context I chose would deeply shape my experience. I decided to travel with the Sovereign Military Order of the Temple of Jerusalem, known as the Modern Knights Templar. I would journey in the footsteps of my spiritual ancestors and of course walk with Jesus Christ, relying on millennia-old religious traditions and practices, and the Bible's Gospel ("good news") accounts to help me discern God's will in this conflicted land.

Samaria

We flew into Tel Aviv—the urban city that sprung from the ancient port of Jaffa—and made our way north along the Plain of Sharon to the Mediterranean seacoast town of Netanya to spend our first night. We had entered the ancient kingdom of Samaria, now a pleasant coastal resort area populated largely by relatively recent Jewish immigrants to the modern State of Israel. Only a few thousand ethnic Samaritans remain in what had once been their land.

I rose early to take a long walk along the shore and enjoy the pleasant breezes blowing off this end of the Mediterranean Sea. Sunrise lifted my spirits.

Sufi stories say Francis of Assisi was taught and enlightened in Palestine by Shams of Tabriz. In 1217, the Roman Catholic pope granted custody of the Province of the Holy Land to Francis of Assisi and his order of Franciscan monks. Since then, Christian pilgrims in Palestine have been under the special protection and guidance of the Franciscans. The Franciscan headquarters in Jerusalem since 1272 has been the Cenacle, the so-called Upper Room, believed to be the location of the Last Supper of Jesus with his disciples on the night he was betrayed.

Father Peter, the current Franciscan pilgrim master, would be our guide during our visit in the Holy Land. The Franciscan order and the Modern Knights Templar are deeply intertwined, with the Templars helping to fund important Christian Holy Land work.

Father Peter told us, "God has brought each of us on this pilgrimage in order to heal us, guide us, or touch our hearts." He instructed each of us to meditate and pray to discern God's intent for us on our journey. God appeared to have brought me here, to this place and with these people, for a reason. My pilgrimage would be deeply connected to communing with God through Jesus Christ.

Father Peter has led pilgrimages in the Holy Land for over thirty years, but I was the first Bible-carrying Unitarian Universalist minister he had ever encountered. I knew it would be interesting. While Father Peter did not appear to be a mystic himself, he did appear to have strong relationships with many local Christian institutions and mystics, allowing us access to places we otherwise could not have visited. This would be a very multilayered pilgrimage.

We traveled up the coast to the district originally settled by the Mediterranean peoples called Phoenicians. We stopped at the fortified Roman port city of Caesarea Maritima, which was a center of governance and commerce during the Roman occupation of Palestine.

Here, reputedly, the apostle Peter had visions concerning God's view of clean and unclean food practices. This was also where the apostle Paul was imprisoned for two years before being sent to be judged in Rome. Then it served as early Christianity's major theological library and repository. Finally, after recapturing the Holy Land for Christianity, Richard the Lionheart refortified this port city as his capital and base of operations. It became the most important commercial port in the world for a time during the Crusades. We were already encountering layers upon layers of religious meaning and discordance.

Next, we traveled farther north to Mount Carmel, where Elijah had his famous battle with the priests of Baal. Where Elijah had heard the still, small voice of God on this mystical mountain, the Carmelite monks later built their founding Stella Maris Monastery.

The Carmelites—officially, the Order of the Brothers of the Blessed Virgin Mary of Mount Carmel—are a Roman Catholic charismatic order that predates the Franciscans. They trace their roots back to pre-Christian hermits who lived on Mount Carmel and dedicated themselves to the prophet Elijah. They came under the protection of the Knights Templar during the Crusades. The order now draws inspiration from both Elijah and Madonna, the Blessed Virgin Mary. The Carmelites focus on a life of contemplation, prayer, community, and service. The male Carmelite friars are contemplatives actively engaged with the world, whereas the female Carmelite nuns are cloistered.

I felt the presence of God in this place. Near the traditional site of Elijah's tomb, the monastery includes a devotional chapel for the two most important Carmelite mystics: Saint Teresa of Ávila and her confessor, Saint John of the Cross. This journey brought me deep into the heart of Christian mysticism. I meditated and communed with saints, who guided me on my journey into intimate communion with God.

A little north of Mount Carmel are the important Crusader ports of Haifa and Acre, also known as Akko. The Crusader Fortress at Acre is one of the finest restored medieval castles I have ever seen. From the Hall of Pillars to Saint John's Church to the Knights' Halls to the refectory, prison, and latrines, there is a sense of a well-defended Crusader castle. The city also features a complex underground tunnel system designed by the Templars. The ancient Templars were well-armed fighting knights, trained religiously and grounded in their sense of God. Between this fortress defending the Mediterranean shore and Belvoir Fortress sitting atop the Jordan River valley, the Crusaders could defend access to Jerusalem from the north.

Beyond Acre are the famous ancient Syrophoenician cities of Tyre and Sidon. Sidon was a Canaanite and then Phoenician fishing village, and it became a center of Zoroastrian religious practice in this area. The Gospels tell us Jesus visited both Tyre and Sidon, placing him in the midst of the Zoroastrian religion, which perhaps influenced his teaching.

Weary and jet-lagged, we turned our eyes toward Galilee and the Crusader town of Tiberias. This town was in the midst of Jesus's travels and ministry, but he was most likely not allowed to visit under the Roman occupation. The Roman military occupation of Palestine greatly impacted Jesus's short ministry.

For the next few nights, we stayed at an off-season Israeli resort hotel in Tiberias. It had a panoramic view of the Sea of Galilee. I woke early to birds singing. I walked the shore by myself, though when Jesus Christ walked with me, I never felt alone.

Sea of Galilee

The Sea of Galilee, also called Lake Tiberias or the Kinneret, was the central feature of Jesus's early ministry. I felt his presence here from the very first day of my stay. The surrounding hills looked just as I'd pictured them as a boy. They brought me an overwhelming sense of peace and connection with Jesus. As the old Christian hymn affirms, "Jesus walks with me, and he talks with me, and he tells me I am his own; and the joy we share as we tarry there, none other has ever known."

We traveled south to Cana of Galilee, the biblical site where Jesus turned water into wine at a wedding. Several couples from our group renewed their wedding vows in the chapel. Then we moved onward to the tiny village of Nazareth, where Jesus is said to have grown up. Nazareth housed perhaps two hundred Galilean peasants in the time of Jesus. It was now completely built over, with five different levels of construction atop the supposed site of the Annunciation alone.

I found it easier to meditate with Jesus in the quiet places than in the crowded basilicas and consecrated holy places built on these traditional sites. I was always looking for the dark, quiet corners or the windswept, open areas. I tended to hear the still, small voice of divine mystery better when I was alone with my own thoughts and God.

An interesting exception was the small, austere synagogue the Templars had built in Nazareth in commemoration of Jesus's first reading of sacred text in the synagogue. Here, I was at peace. Here, I heard God's still, small voice.

That afternoon, we climbed Mount Tabor to visit the traditional site of Jesus's Transfiguration. I meditated with the southern portion of the Sea of Galilee spread out before me. This rocky, uncultivated land felt largely unchanged since the time of Jesus. The dual horns of an extinct volcano, known as the Horns of Hattin, loomed above us. This place is remembered both as where Jesus transformed in glory before his disciples and where, a thousand years later, the Muslim armies of Saladin defeated the Crusader forces, driving them out of the Holy Land. We returned to our seaside Tiberias hotel exhausted but feeling as if we had been accompanied on our Way.

The next day, we traveled a short distance to Magdala to board a Galilean fishing boat called the *Promised Land* to take us to the archaeological site for the tiny village of Capernaum, where Jesus taught and gathered his first disciples. He gathered to him the brothers Peter and Andrew, who had followed John the Baptist, and also the brothers John and James. These four became his closest male disciples.

Two thousand years ago, Capernaum was a Stone Age village of interconnected houses. A prominent house, near the center, is remembered as Saint Peter's house, and there are still the ruins of a large synagogue nearby.

Saint Peter began life as Simon. He is often remembered in Christian tradition as a gruff, unkempt, vulgar fisherman. But Jesus taught Simon and his closest friends the spiritual power of generosity and abundance. Through Jesus's teachings and subsequent death and resurrection, Simon was transformed into the preeminent Christian religious leader, especially following the fall of Jerusalem in 70 CE and the rise of Roman and Greek Christianity.

In Christian tradition, Jesus changed Simon's name to Petra (Peter) to reflect his desire to build a catholic, or universal, church upon Peter's rock-hard constancy. Of course, this was also the Peter who the Gospels say denied Jesus three times. But in the Roman Catholic and Eastern Orthodox faiths, apostolic succession traces itself, symbolically, back to Saint Peter. I meditated on this devious and hidden path into divine mystery in the rocky remains of Peter's house.

We walked and meditated along the shore where Jesus called his disciples to leave behind their material concerns to join him and where he reportedly saw them again following his resurrection. Jesus walked and taught along this shore. Here, he tested his first disciples' faithfulness.

This place offered my strongest feelings yet of connection with the actual footsteps of Jesus. I felt his presence in my heart in this place. I picked up a fist-sized piece of volcanic rock to remind me of my deep sense of connection with Jesus on this rocky shore. I am a spiritual pilgrim. My rabbi, my teacher—Jesus Christ—leads me along the Way.

This small village of Capernaum was located in the northern borderlands between Roman governor Herod Antipas's Galilee and Roman governor Philip's Gaulanitis, so it was less strictly controlled by Rome and more open to free thinkers and prophets. Jesus was a renegade religious teacher. He seems to have relocated his ministry here after being rejected in his hometown of Nazareth, farther south on the Sea of Galilee. Half of his male disciples came from this tiny village of no more than fifty adult males in total, making it the base for his ministry over the next two years. For lunch, we feasted on grilled Saint Peter's Fish with bread and were satisfied.

From the Sea of Galilee, we observed the Mount of Beatitudes, the presumed site of the Sermon on the Mount. This was where Jesus taught these declarations (my rendition):

> *Blessed are the selfless and humble, for theirs is the kingdom of God.*
>
> *Blessed are they who suffer and mourn, for they shall be comforted.*
>
> *Blessed are the gentle and kind, for they shall inherit the earth.*
>
> *Blessed are they who hunger for justice and righteousness, for they shall be satisfied.*
>
> *Blessed are those merciful to others, for they shall obtain mercy in their suffering.*
>
> *Blessed are the pure of heart, who transcend material cravings, for they shall see God.*
>
> *Blessed are the peacemakers, with true equanimity, for they are children of God.*
>
> *Blessed are those persecuted for their righteousness, for theirs is the kingdom of heaven.*

These represent core teachings of Jesus's ministry. To be faithful, one must feed the hungry, give drink to the thirsty, clothe the naked, shelter the homeless, comfort the imprisoned, visit the sick, bury the dead, and honor all beings. The world would be transformed if contemporary Christians heeded this message of humility, resilience, kindness, justice, mercy, and equanimity.

The next day, we visited Tabgha, the reputed site of the multiplication of the loaves and fishes. On the far shore are the Golan Heights. Once part of Syria, most of the Golan Heights has been Israeli-occupied territory since 1967, after Syrian artillery on the heights fired down upon the Israeli town of Tiberias. No wonder the Israelis won't give up their occupation of this territory, only twenty miles from the Syrian border, as long as they are surrounded by such hostile forces. But in many ways, modern Israel's military presence in Christian and Arab Palestine is not unlike that of the Roman occupying army in Jesus's time.

The prominent cliff on the heights is thought to be where Jesus performed an exorcism and drove evil spirits into a herd of swine, sending them plummeting over the cliff to their death. So many swine sacrificed to clear one man of his evil spirits. It's also where many of the Zealots hid from Rome in Jesus's time. Jesus grew up in a war-torn land. Many of his followers hoped he would overthrow the oppressors, using violence and military might as necessary to create God's just kingdom.

After visiting the village of Bethsaida, where Peter and Andrew were from, we made our way over the Golan Heights into Israeli-occupied territory to circumnavigate the Sea of Galilee on our return to Tiberias. Looking back over the Sea of Galilee, the setting sun from the Golan Heights was breathtaking. So much austere beauty in the midst of so much human suffering.

Mount Hermon borders the Golan Heights. Three streams from Mount Hermon feed the Sea of Galilee. The sea, in turn, flows into the Jordan River, providing most of the usable water flowing through this desert valley toward the Dead Sea. The Sea of Galilee provides much-needed, life-giving water in the midst of a desert land. Living waters flowing through the parched desert—so many of our spiritual metaphors are anchored in this sense of place.

Palestinian Christians

We finally headed south for Jerusalem through what was once the Roman Decapolis district, now largely part of the Israeli-occupied West Bank. We mostly saw Palestinian Muslim villages as we drove south. Increasingly, we also saw recently-imposed Jewish settlements as we made our way south through the Jordan valley toward Jericho, not far from where Jesus was tempted in the wilderness.

This seems to be a land of great complexity and many temptations. Based upon Muslim readings of the Qur'an and Palestinian Christian readings of the Gospels, many mystics feel they have a claim as great as, or greater than, the modern Jewish settlers believe they have.

As we made our way south into the Judean Hills, we began to see more bedouin encampments, remnants of the ancient Nabataean kingdom. These desert people are still largely agrarian and nomadic, though they are slowly dying away.

Our bus brought us at last to Belvoir Fortress, the last Crusader fortress to fall to Saladin because of its impregnable position overlooking the Jordan River valley. Rising 550 meters above the valley floor, the fortress has an unrestricted view across the entire Transjordan plain. Muslim historians of that period described it as "a nest of eagles and the dwelling place of the moon."

This was a place of great security and power—now in ruins. The inner fortress, outer fortress, and surrounding moat have all been restored, so we could see how the Knights Templar were able to resist Saladin's siege for another two years following the fall of Jerusalem.

The eventual fall of Belvoir Fortress ended the military protection of Palestinian Christians in the Holy Land. But Palestine has always been a crossroads between larger powers. There has been a continuous Christian presence here for two thousand years. The fortress itself overlooks the trade routes and crossroads that have always passed through this area.

Now we traveled into the Judaean wilderness, much of it still occupied by Palestinian Christians and Muslims. In the small town of Bethany, we visited an ancient tomb associated in Christian tradition with Jesus raising his friend Lazarus from the dead. The monastery church is devoted to the memory of Lazarus's sisters, Martha and Mary. I barely fit my 250-pound frame down the narrow stairway constructed to bring me to the reputed tomb of Lazarus.

We're told Jesus received a message that Lazarus was deathly ill; his sisters begged Jesus to save him. But when Jesus arrived in Bethany, Lazarus had been dead and buried for four days. Seeing the pain and suffering in Martha's and Mary's eyes, Jesus wept. As God's Son, Jesus appealed to God the Father to raise Lazarus from death. Lazarus arose, demonstrating Jesus's special relationship with the Father. Christian mystics say it was Lazarus's death and resurrection that led the Sanhedrin to arrest and torture Jesus, leading to Jesus's own death, resurrection, and eternal life.

These three siblings—Lazarus, Martha, and Mary—living just three miles east of Jerusalem, on the southeastern slope of the Mount of Olives, appear to have been Jesus's closest friends in Judaea. Judaea, much more than Samaria or Galilee, was under the direct religious authority of the Sanhedrin in the Jerusalem temple. It was dangerous territory for a Galilean religious renegade. The Gospels are replete with religious challenges set by the Sadducees and Pharisees to show Jesus as a heretic and apostate. The Gospels say that Jesus cleverly defeated them.

In Jerusalem, we stayed at the Christmas Hotel, a Palestinian Christian hotel located in East Jerusalem, a short walk from the Old City and the Temple Mount. As a result, we heard many more stories than typical visitors to Israel do about the suffering and oppression of Palestinian Christians as collateral damage from the ongoing Islamic and Israeli conflicts. Israel doesn't appear to have set out to oppress and destroy Palestinian Christians, yet they have. With this on our mind, we went as a group to pray, reflect, and lament at the Wailing Wall.

Our next day began with a drive to the highest local point, the top of the Mount of Olives. We had a spectacular view across the Kidron valley looking down upon the Temple Mount and the old fortified city of Jerusalem. Our daylong journey back to Jerusalem included meditating at the place associated by tradition with the Pater Noster, the Lord's Prayer, which Jesus Christ taught his disciples to pray (my rendition):

> *Our Father,* from whom we are descended,
> *who art in heaven,* in a state of eternal bliss,
> *hallowed be thy name,* for it is unnamable.
>
> *Thy kingdom come,* the kingdom of heaven,
> *thy will be done,* not our will but your will for humanity,
> *on earth as it is in heaven,*
> so all the world will be transformed.
>
> *Give us this day,* dwelling among us,
> *our daily bread,* the sustenance of our being,
> *and forgive us our trespasses,* for we will forever fall short,
> *as we forgive those who trespass against us,* as is right.
>
> *And lead us not into temptation,* for we are easily led astray,
> *But deliver us from evil,* as our protector and comforter.
> *For thine is the kingdom, and the power,*
> *And the glory forever and ever. Amen.*

Our descent brought us to the Church of Dominus Flevit. During the Crusades, the Knights Templar built a memorial chapel here, but it was destroyed and replaced by a mosque following the fall of Jerusalem in 1187 CE. Seven hundred years later, the Franciscans acquired a small plot of land near the original site and built this tear-shaped chapel for meditation and prayer for Christian pilgrims in this land. It is part of the Franciscan Custody of the Holy Land.

In Latin, *Dominus Flevit* means "the Lord wept," so the place is associated with Jesus weeping over the fate of Jerusalem. Given all the pain, suffering, and conflict in this Holy Land, we stopped a while in this place to weep over Israel.

Finally, we arrived in the Garden of Gethsemane, where the Church of All Nations has been built to remember the universality of Jesus's teachings on behalf of the marginalized and oppressed. Jesus preached his good news for all nations. We were invited to attend part of a Roman Catholic Mass in the cathedral, but I felt called to leave the tourist-crowded church to go aside and pray. Sitting on a stone bench under a huge and ancient olive tree, I prayed my prayer beads in deep humility, practicing Jesus's Way, the way of love and surrender.

I began to walk the garden in a spirit of prayer, following in Jesus's footsteps. As I meditated ever more deeply, everything fell into place. I knew in my heart I was a beloved child of God. He walked with me, and he talked with me, and he told me I am his own. And the joy we shared as we tarried there, none other has ever known. I have never known the presence of Jesus Christ as fully or fondly as I did in this place.

Jerusalem

We entered ancient Jerusalem through the Lions' Gate to walk the Via Dolorosa, or the Way of Sorrows, which winds through Jerusalem's Old City to the Church of the Holy Sepulchre. The Holy Land guide I purchased helpfully said, "It is not, actually, where Jesus walked. It is where the Church venerates a mystery of Christ's life and a place sanctified by the prayers of the Faithful." Glory be to God.

On the Via Dolorosa, our spiritual pilgrimage of prayer and remembrance is organized around the fourteen traditional Roman Catholic stations of the cross:

1. Jesus was condemned to death in the courtyard of the Roman fortress.

2. Jesus was whipped, flagellated, and given his cross to bear.

3. The tortured Jesus fell under the weight of the cross the first time.

4. Jesus first observed his mother, Mary, in deep emotional distress.

5. Simon of Cyrene was pressed into service to help carry Jesus's cross.

6. Veronica showed compassion by wiping the sweat from Jesus's face.

7. In his affliction, Jesus staggered and fell again, nearly fainting.

8. Jesus called out to console the daughters of Jerusalem.

9. Jesus stumbled and fell a third time, barely able to rise again.

10. Arriving at Golgotha, Jesus was stripped of his garments and ridiculed.

11. Jesus was nailed to the cross through both his hands and his feet.

12. Crying out, "My God, my God, why have you forsaken me?" Jesus died on the cross.

13. Jesus' dead body was taken down from the cross by Joseph of Arimathea.

14. He was laid in a garden tomb with a stone across its entrance.

Yet that is not the end of the story. O death, where is thy sting? The second verse of my favorite hymn at many UU memorial services came to mind: "Swift to its close ebbs out life's little day; earth's joys grow dim, its glories pass away; change and decay in all around I see; O thou who changest not, abide with me." God abides with us even into the valley of the shadow of death.

As the sun was setting, I joined a small group of our pilgrims to make our way to the Garden Tomb. The guidebook said this site was set up "as a place of Christian worship, witness, and reflection on the life, death and resurrection of Jesus the Messiah." We began our walking meditation at the base of a skull-shaped cliff in an ancient stone quarry just outside the northern walls of Jerusalem on the main road to Damascus. I was walking with Jesus, walking with death and resurrection.

All life ends. Death comes. Accepting that we too will die allows us to live more freely. All life contains pain and suffering. All life contains the possibility of joy and transcendence. Jesus taught that he came so that we could have life and enjoy it more abundantly. His death and resurrection are a sign and symbol of the possibility of our own eternal life. Blessed be life.

Walking down into the ancient garden, I saw a small stone bench carved into the rock face outside the tomb. I sat there and meditated upon good and evil, death and resurrection, the presence and meaning of angelic messengers, and the purpose of my pilgrimage. We are spiritual beings taking human form. Our intention, our purpose, our spiritual growth over a lifetime means far more than the length of our lives or the legacies we leave. I was at peace with death.

Our last day in Jerusalem, we visited the monastery where the Christian scholar Saint Jerome studied and drafted his own version of the Bible. His version honored many of the diverse, emerging Christian theologies and perspectives on Christ's salvific role. Jerome is remembered as the author of the Latin Vulgate, which is for Roman Catholics the most influential translation of the Bible and has been a benchmark for many later versions.

Early Christians began gathering stories of Jesus and his sayings soon after his death and resurrection. Many were in Jesus's Galilean Aramaic or Jerusalem's Hebrew. But as the Christian diaspora spread, texts were increasingly in Greek or Roman Latin. By the late fourth century, Christianity, in all its various forms, had spread throughout the Roman Empire. Christian scholars used a multitude of texts in a multitude of languages.

The Christian scholar Origen began assembling every variety of Christian text at the theological library at Caesarea Maritima on the Palestinian Mediterranean coast. This growing ecclesiastical collection eventually included more than thirty thousand manuscripts in different versions and languages. Many of these texts contradicted each other or varied on details of Jesus's life and sayings. Many of them were distinctly gnostic in their teachings.

In the sixth century, Jerome moved from Rome to Judaea. Over the next thirty years of diligent study, he accessed Origen's wide-ranging texts and tried to determine the best rendering in modern Latin. This translation became the Latin Vulgate Bible, and it would be the authoritative translation for the Roman Catholic Church for millennia.

We visited Saint Jerome's Cave, the two-room underground study where he lived and worked. We were searching for the Word of God, for the indwelling divine mystery, for the Spirit of Life, for the light that shows the Way in the darkness.

Palestinians

Leaving the city of Jerusalem behind us, we spent a few days visiting Palestinian Christians in the Judean Hill country, beginning with the little town of Bethlehem. We were now traveling in the territory overseen by the Palestinian Authority (PA), the governing body that grew from the Palestinian Liberation Organization.

These people had an anti-Israeli-government attitude, perhaps understandably, considering all the restrictions the Israelis imposed. The Palestinians feel very oppressed by the strict limits on their freedom of travel, ownership of land, livelihoods, and wellbeing. They are a militarily occupied people with significant constraints on their sense of freedom and their future survival.

Despite Bethlehem's pivotal role in our Christmas story, the city in its modern reality was the most disappointing place we visited on pilgrimage. It felt like theme park tourism. The Church of the Nativity, built by Emperor Constantine in the fourth century, seemed completely devoid of the Holy Spirit. The Shepherds' fields were covered with modern houses. I could no longer sense the Spirit of Life moving there at all. These were only tourist sites. Where were the Magi now? Where was the spiritual magic? Long gone were the humble shepherds watching their flocks by night.

More interesting for me was our visit to the Christian institutions in Bethlehem supported by the Knights Templar: Crèche, the Holy Family Children's Home, which is the only orphanage for babies in the PA territories; the Franciscan Family Centre for orphan children; and Bethlehem University, which trains young Christians for hospitality, nursing, and business jobs in Israel. These holy services feel necessary in a Christian society with a 35 percent unemployment rate. People can't eat, can't live, if they can't find work.

Jesus said to feed the hungry, give drink to the thirsty, clothe the naked, shelter the homeless. And so long as you do it for the least of these, you do this for Jesus. The Templars seem to be doing God's work in the Holy Land.

Before returning to Jerusalem, we stopped at the Bethany Community of the Resurrection and its Orthodox School of Bethany. The school boards fifteen girls from Palestinian Christian families (who cannot daily traverse the security wall blocking the West Bank) and forty-five girls from local Muslim families. Sister Martha, the headmistress of the school, brings a remarkable spirit of hope and optimism to a difficult task and time. Despite the random shootings and violence around them, Sister Martha's program gives these girls a chance at a decent educational experience in an occupied land. She too seemed very much to be doing God's work.

We crossed through the security wall to visit the excavation in Qumran, on the shore of the Dead Sea. Qumran was once the home of a radical Jewish faith community. The video presentation pointed out similarities between the traditions and teachings of the Qumran community and those of John the Baptist. This might suggest he trained first with them, and those teachings then perhaps helped shape some of Jesus's subsequent ministry as well—it appears that Jesus and at least some of his disciples were initially disciples of John the Baptist.

As Judaean religious renegades, the Qumran community rebelled against the temple authorities. The Temple of Jerusalem was ruled by a hereditary elite. As an outsider, Jesus became a religious renegade himself. Renegade heretical wisdom thrives in borderlands.

Next, we stopped at an Israeli Dead Sea beach resort, well below sea level, and enjoyed a beer at the lowest bar in the world. The extraordinarily salty sea makes swimming impossible, the water feels slimy to the touch, and there are health warnings about consuming the liquid, but the mud and minerals of the Dead Sea are said to do wonders for the skin.

For lunch, we headed to the city of Jericho, whose walls archaeologists say never fell down. We enjoyed a delightful Palestinian meal in a wonderful garden restaurant. Then we visited the desert cliff where tradition holds that Jesus was tempted following his baptism. This is a remarkable land, full of divine mystery, with layers upon layers of religious meaning.

The next day, we returned through the security wall to visit two Templar-supported schools in Ramallah: the Arab Evangelical Episcopal School and the Episcopal Technological and Vocational Training Center. These schools maintain high academic standards, and the kids seem full of joy, like normal kids, despite living in an occupied territory. The principal of the school said it is their connection with Christians in Europe and America that allows them to survive and thrive. Such a school serving these Palestinian Christian and Muslim youths, without government interference, makes all the difference in the quality of their young lives.

Leaving occupied Ramallah, we now needed to return to Jerusalem through the restraining wall. On our first attempt, however, we ran into resistance from Israeli border guards. Our bus waited in a long line of vehicles for nearly an hour. Then we were told that our return could not be accommodated at this particular border crossing. We were sent to a larger border crossing about ten miles away, where we waited in another long line.

Then we were told that for our own security, we had to get off the bus, remove all our bags and packages, and join a long line of Palestinians on foot waiting to have their packages scanned and passports inspected after passing through X-ray security checks. This annoyed most of our pilgrims. But then, after two thirds of us had complied, the crossing guards announced we were free to reboard our bus and travel on to Jerusalem.

Renewed and Rebaptized

Back in Jerusalem that evening, the Knights Templar engaged in a Holy Land convent and investiture ceremony. It included solemn affirmations and the wearing of long, white robes with large, red crosses upon them. It took place in the Anglican church on the Mount of Olives. Vows were renewed, and two postulants were invested in the order. After this, we all returned to the Christmas Hotel to enjoy a sumptuous banquet and mystic soul-sharing. As part of the convocation, the Templars awarded me a Jerusalem cross and certificate of merit.

On the twelfth day of this pilgrimage, we crossed over to Bethany, beyond the Jordan and five miles north of the Dead Sea. Since the fifth century, Christian churches have affirmed this as the site of Jesus's baptism by John the Baptist.

I decided to make this the site of my own rebaptism as well. My first baptism at age thirteen, when I professed my belief, was a disappointing experience, so I approached this second baptism without high expectations. I was prepared to accept whatever the Holy Spirit had to offer me.

Mark 1:9–11 recounts that "in those days Jesus came from Nazareth of Galilee and was baptized by John in the Jordan. And just as he was coming out of the water, he saw the heavens torn apart and the Spirit descending like a dove upon him." Perhaps with this baptism, in this holy place, and in this pilgrimage state of mind, something would happen. I surrendered myself to God. Everything is possible with God!

I changed into shorts and a T-shirt at the riverside changing room and made my way across the muddy shore toward the steps that led down into the flowing river's murky depths and bulrushes. A big group left just as I approached the riverbank. I had this spot in the river, at least for the moment, largely to my God and myself.

The river was warm as I silently prayed a prayer of contrition:
Gracious God, my sins are heavy, too real to hide,
   too deep to undo.
Please forgive what my lips tremble to name and my
   heart can no longer bear.
Set me free from a past I cannot change and open to
   a future following your Way.
Grant me the grace and goodness to grow ever more
   in your image and likeness.
Amen.

I immersed myself neck-deep in its waters. And then, at the prompting of the Holy Spirit, I slipped quickly into full immersion while reciting the traditional baptismal formula: *In the name of the Father, Son, and Holy Ghost.* I felt engulfed within and befriended by divine mystery. As I rose up from the waters, it seemed to me as if the heavens opened, the Holy Spirit descended upon me like a dove, and I was raised up to walk in new life. God seemed well pleased.

At age sixty-one, I opened myself to divine mystery in a way I never could have at thirteen. The spirit moved in me and through me. I was a beloved child of God. Born again. I emerged from the river with elation, prepared to continue on with my journey, knowing this love of God in my heart. I was ecstatic!

It appears I was drawn on pilgrimage to the Holy Land to walk in the footsteps of Jesus along the Sea of Galilee, to pray beneath ancient olive trees in the Garden of Gethsemane, and to more fully experience the Holy Spirit in the River Jordan. This was reason enough to have come here on pilgrimage after all.

Next, we traveled south to Mount Nebo, where Moses first viewed the promised land, and had another excellent lunch looking out across the valley toward Jericho. We learned about the death of Moses and the monasteries that have been built upon this mount since the Byzantine period.

We were told Moses came so far in faithfulness to God's call, yet died before entering the promised land. Faithfulness to God is not always rewarded in this life. Yet Moses knew shalom—God's peace, which surpasses understanding. He blessed the Israelites with a blessing he received from God himself (my rendition of Numbers 6:24–26):

May the LORD bless you and keep you;

may his face shine upon you; may he be gracious to you;

lifting you up and giving you peace beyond understanding.

Kindness and mercy are two of the most frequent descriptors for divine mystery in the Bible. The awaited messiah, fulfilled in Jesus, was described as the Redeemer and the Prince of Peace.

Leaving Israel, we crossed over into the kingdom of Jordan. Making our way toward the city of Petra, we passed the memorial to the Old Testament leader Aaron, the brother of Moses. All this was part of ancient Palestine. Despite the boundaries of modern states and racial and religious hostilities, which so often divide the people, this is a holy land.

Our last day of pilgrimage was spent among the archaeological findings of Petra, the ancient capital of the Nabataean kingdom, carved out of limestone cliffs. We entered through the Siq, a narrow, crooked, downward-sloping path through hundred-foot cliffs that create a protected valley.

We explored temples, tombs, and remarkable cave dwellings carved out of the rock by bedouins, the people who until recently lived in these very caves. We then followed the downward-sloping path a couple of miles to the ancient Greco-Roman city center, now being excavated by Brown University. I marveled at the austere beauty of this desert place.

However, I suddenly developed a shooting pain in my right heel, causing me to limp. Perhaps I had been too physically active, too stressed. Or perhaps it was simply the irregularity of the stone surfaces. And now we needed to hike miles back to our bus, uphill, in the desert. Hiking with the intense pain, I might risk dehydration, even fainting, and being left behind.

Fortunately, I was surrounded by friendly bedouins, who are consummate negotiators. After some negotiation, one young man offered to lead me back to the entrance on his donkey for a very reasonable fee. Upon our arrival, I tipped him well, then hobbled to lunch before boarding our bus. From suffering comes the potential for joy; from crisis comes opportunity.

Leaving Petra, we traveled north for a few hours through the desert on the King's Highway. That evening, we enjoyed a final Jordanian banquet as a group before heading to the airport and a night flight back to America.

My Christian mystic soul was ecstatic. I was beloved and deeply immersed in Christian gnosticism. I vowed to continue traveling on pilgrimage with Christian mystics and the Knights Templar—perhaps along the Camino de Santiago, that medieval route through Spain.

A Spiritual Pilgrim's Way

While walking along the shores of Galilee with Jesus Christ at my side, I had meditated on the first four disciples who flocked to Jesus's ministry. Who were these fishermen who dropped everything in order to follow Jesus and, according to the Gospel of John, became the iconic exemplars of what it means to be Christian?

First there was Simon, at least if you follow the synoptic Gospels. Second to join up was his brother Andrew. Third and fourth to join, at least according to the Gospel of Mark, were the brothers James and John. They were the sons of Zebedee, who appears to have headed a well-to-do fishing cooperative. Their mother, Salome, became one of Jesus's first and most devoted female followers.

James is an English translation of the name Jacob, which in Greek is Iakōbos. So James actually shared the name of the supposed patriarch of the twelve tribes of Israel, who reputedly earned this role by wrestling with an angel. This disciple James comes into Christian tradition as James the Great and is remembered as the first apostle to be martyred, in 44 CE. Long after his death, Christian mystics would associate his relics with Santiago de Compostela, the westernmost point of the Roman Empire in Jesus's time. (Iago is another form of James or Jacob.) My interest in James led me to say yes to a Christian scholar's spiritual pilgrimage along the Camino de Santiago—the "Way of Saint James"—to Santiago de Compostela.

From Boston, I flew to Pamplona by way of Madrid. This small city of Pamplona, in a rounded valley, was another crossroads for conquerors. Named after the Roman general Pompey, who conquered the indigenous Basque tribe here in 75 BCE, Pamplona was subject to successive waves of invasion by Goths and other Germanic tribes crossing the French Pyrenees. The city became Christian when conquered by the Arian Visigoths in the fifth century, then converted to Sunni Islam during the Umayyad invasions of the eighth century. Spain would not emerge as a Roman Catholic country until early in the second millennium.

In the fifteenth century, the reconquest of Spain was critical for Roman Catholic Christianity. They needed to populate and protect the ancient, westward pilgrim path across the top of the Iberian Peninsula from the Pyrenees to Finisterre ("Land's End") on the Atlantic coast. In the sixteenth century, Pamplona would become Castilian Spain's strongest outpost at the foot of the western Pyrenees. The German Holy Roman emperor built a pentagon-shaped fort to house his royal troops at this edge of his empire. In the nineteenth century, this pentagon fort and the fortified town featured in the Napoleonic Wars. Today, Pamplona is the center of the most conservative Roman Catholicism in Spain, but it's still possible to walk its ancient fortifications.

Jesus's first disciples followed the Way. Our journey was to travel the Way to where God's breath (in Hebrew, *ruach*) is felt to be present. I would travel the Camino Francés, the ancient "French Way," perhaps the most famous route of the Camino de Santiago. I would journey across northern Spain to experience more deeply and fully the presence of God by walking small parts of the Camino de Santiago in the spirit of pilgrimage. The spirit of Jesus Christ would walk with me.

Many pilgrims hike the nearly five hundred miles of the Camino Francés in under four weeks. They walk an average of nearly twenty miles a day, sleep in inexpensive *albergues* (hostels), and eat as cheaply as possible. For them, the Way requires great bodily exertion and perhaps pain and suffering.

Our particular group, however, consisted of aging scholars and mystics with financial means. Ours would be a physically less arduous journey. We would travel mostly by air-conditioned bus, stay in the nicest hotels along the Way, enjoy spirited academic lectures and discussions, visit famous spiritual sites, feast on excellent Spanish cooking, and sample Spain's finest wines. We would be in heaven.

We would, of course, walk several miles every day. But covering great distances on foot was not the purpose of our travel. We were to walk in transcendental meditation to experience the gnostic presence of divine mystery.

El Camino de Santiago

Aymeric Picaud, a twelfth-century French priest, was the first to describe the pilgrimage route we were traveling. He wrote the first pilgrims' guide for the Camino de Santiago, which is preserved in a manuscript called the *Codex Calixtinus*. In it, he prays for his pilgrimage to the God of Abraham:

> *Be for us our compassion on the walk, our guide at the*
> *crossroads,*
> *our breath in our weariness, our protection in danger,*
> *our albergue [hostel] on the way,*
> *our shade in the heat, our light in the darkness,*
> *our consolation in our discouragements,*
> *and our strength in our intentions.*

Following the *Codex Calixtinus*, pilgrims begin their journey not in Pamplona but in Roncesvalles (Valley of Thorns) and follow the legendary trail to Espinal, across the fertile plains of the Ebro River.

So we took a bus north to Roncesvalles, then set out south on foot. The weather was pleasant, the companionship very enjoyable, and the feel of this ancient pilgrim Way spiritually uplifting.

We began by praying in the Romanesque Capilla de Sancti Spiritus (the Chapel of the Holy Spirit), the eighth-century burial place of Roland. After seven long years of fighting Muslims, Charlemagne and his troops were returning across the Pyrenees. But their rear guard, which included his favorite nephew, Roland, was massacred by Muslims in a final battle. The chanson de geste ("song of heroic deeds") that captures the spiritual significance of this clash of civilizations is the oldest French epic poem to survive. It was already clear to me we were stepping into history by following a Christian spiritual pilgrimage route that was over a thousand years old.

We next passed the fourteenth-century Cruz de los Peregrinos (the Pilgrims' Cross) and descended into a dense, dark woodland said to have been a favorite location for secret witches' covens in the sixteenth century. Shamanic forces were once strong here. Our local guide was named Santiago, so he and I quickly established that we could both be named after the same saint, James the Great. We bonded over this serendipity. He and I fell into step together, temporarily well ahead of the rest of the pilgrims. We walked and talked alone for well over an hour, speaking of human mortality, transience, good and evil, and being of service to the divine mystery. We were soul-sharing.

Walking transformed into pilgrimage. And Santiago, the travel guide, transformed into Santiago Peregrino. It was not unlike the opening scene of the Bhagavad Gita, where Arjuna's chariot driver becomes a manifestation of Krishna. Santiago Peregrino would be my spiritual guide on this journey, and in our local guide he was made manifest.

Eventually, others from our group caught up with us. Santiago and I transitioned back into being just two men walking and talking with our group. But in my heart, I knew this journey of the spirit was already off to a good start. To be a pilgrim is to deeply experience the presence of God or divine mystery. This can lead to inspiration or even help restore health and wellbeing. I was already communing with God.

Our scholarly guide, a Christian scholar and former dean of Yale Divinity School, lectured on the transformative impact of pilgrimages. We were retracing ancient gnostic Christian disciplines of practicing God's presence among us. He said Saint Jerome wrote most elegantly about the mystical experience of God as part of any true pilgrimage. The intent of the spiritual pilgrim is to experience more deeply and intimately the presence of God.

Our scholar said Christian pilgrims have been following this particular ancient Way, the Camino de Santiago, for over a thousand years. For more than a millennium, we pilgrims have sought transcendence, to experience the presence of divine mystery; atonement, to compensate for our sins; and wisdom, to learn something important about ourselves.

This was a deepening of spirituality through self-cultivation. We were practicing the presence of God as a way of being, which involves living between two worlds: the mundane, material world through which we traveled, and the mystical, spiritual world that coexists with it.

We returned that first evening to our Gran Hotel La Perla in Pamplona for a lively evening of tapas, *pintxos*, and simply getting to know each other. The next morning, we would board our bus again.

From our bus windows, we watched other pilgrims set out on foot for the fifteen-mile trek to Puente la Reina. Their journey would include a steep climb up what is locally known as the Alto del Perdón, or the Hill of Forgiveness.

Like all pilgrims, we were seeking atonement as well as wisdom and knowledge. We were thankful, however, when our bus—full of grace and air conditioning—took us through a tunnel beneath the towering hills of penance.

Navarre

We were in Navarre, the northern province of Spain. This part of Navarre has marked the boundaries of various empires and kingdoms in the past and thus has seen much cultural and racial mixing. The Basques; Andalusians; Romans; Visigoths, Franks, and other Germanic tribes; Jews; Arabs; Moors; and Vikings all contributed to the culture and the gene pool. Virtually everyone in Spain has some mix of these various genetic identities in their blood. We encountered a richly varied and diverse people as we traveled the Way.

Puente la Reina retains a medieval feel. We alighted in front of the Iglesia de Santa María de Eunate, or the Church of Saint Mary of the One Hundred Doors. This Romanesque church is one of the jewels built by the Knights Templar along the Camino.

A second church in Puente la Reina, Iglesia de Santiago del Mayor (Church of Saint James the Great), includes a sacred gilded statue of Santiago Peregrino just before it. He has a deeply spiritual aura. Equanimity abounds. At the time, he also looked an awful lot like our local guide.

At the western edge of this medieval village, two major pilgrim Ways converge to cross the Arga River and continue on to Compostela together. We had a delightful lunch in a small pub at the edge of town.

Then our bus skipped ahead fourteen miles to visit the town of Estella. We were grateful for our blessings on the Way. Spiritual pilgrimage requires mindfulness more than physical suffering. Along the Way, we learned how to be with God and open to grace.

Estella was once on the ancient Roman road leading to the gold mines of Spain. High above the Arga, it began as a Roman outpost, became a Frankish pilgrim village, and for centuries was the home of the kings of Navarre. The kings were widely known for their religious tolerance. A Jewish community thrived here, but was expelled in the fifteenth century. We were again surrounded by history—and not all of it good.

In the afternoon, we visited the palace, now a museum and art gallery, and walked a medieval bridge across the river. Most impressive, however, was the steep stone staircase to enter the Iglesia de San Pedro de la Rúa (Church of Saint Peter of the Way), the coronation site for the kings.

Gnostics, in all religious traditions, seek union with the divine. We were on a gnostic pilgrimage. By surrendering to our pilgrim journey, we found union with divine mystery and became part of the body of Christ. As the poet David Whyte writes in his poem "Camino": "The path disappearing and re-appearing even as the ground gave way beneath you . . . pilgrim they called you again. Pilgrim."

We were now traveling through Spain's wine country. We detoured a little to stay at the Villa de Laguardia, a lovely country hotel in the charming medieval capital of the famous Rioja Alavesa wine region. My room looked out over vineyards. As I went to sleep, I left my balcony door open a little to experience some of the softness of the night.

I awoke a little before dawn to a sudden chorus of birdsong greeting the new day. I rose to see the setting crescent moon offset by the morning star as the sky slowly brightened into day. A cock crowed his alarm. I went back to bed for a little more rest, though I wore a smile for the day that was beginning. When I rose again a little later, I watched the misty morning fog rising over the vineyards. Peace and equanimity.

I sensed memories associated with the Knights Templar in these parts. Many of the rural churches and castles were either Templar in origin or copies of Templar buildings. Templar architecture often featured octagonal designs. This represented the Templars' eight-sided Cross Pattee, which represented the mystical symbol of the eight-sided star, which in turn represented the eightfold path to awakening. These multiple layers of meaning are constant reminders of the rich spirituality of this place.

Above the altar, the large beautiful thirteenth-century figure of Christ on the cross seemed to show me a smile of equanimity even in the midst of great suffering. All of life is a spiritual journey, a pilgrimage, if we are open to experiencing it as such. Our challenge is to ground ourselves in Jesus Christ and learn to be spiritual pilgrims wherever we are.

To begin the next day, before setting out on our daily pilgrimage, we offered a pilgrim's prayer of humility and devotion modeled on the Jewish Yom Kippur service:

Birth is a beginning, and death a destination, and life a journey.
from childhood to maturity, and youth to age;
from innocence to awareness, and ignorance to knowing;
from foolishness to discretion, and then, perhaps, to wisdom;
from offense to forgiveness, from loneliness to love, from fear to faith.
Until, looking backward or ahead, we see that victory lies not at some high place along the way,
but in having made the journey a sacred pilgrimage, a walk in the light. Amen.

We enjoyed another scholarly lecture and discussion on Santiago in history and legend before driving to the university city of Logroño. We were now on the far side of the western branch of the great river of Ebro.

We walked the city's old quarter and visited its cathedral, the fifteenth-century Catedral de Santa María de la Redonda. It was a massive and impressive Romanesque structure that housed a small painting by Michelangelo. One could feel the sacred presence of God.

Next, we enjoyed a delightful meal at one of Spain's modern boutique vineyards before heading to our villa for a siesta. This was a pilgrimage style well suited to this aging scholar.

The next morning, I again arose refreshed. Looking out my open window across rustic fields, I watched as the morning mist obscured a solitary mountain on the horizon. A lone wolf yelped in the distance, signaling its comrades. I awoke to life once more, immersed in the beauty of the world made manifest before me. A car honked its horn, a rooster crowed, and I was pulled back into civilization. But the spirit of pilgrimage stayed with me through the day.

Spanish Mystics

Saint Teresa of Ávila and Saint John of the Cross—the sixteenth-century Spanish mystics I encountered and communed with on Mount Carmel—played a large role in developing the Christian mysticism of the Spanish Counter-Reformation. The Spanish Christian church had become secularized over the centuries, as had the Carmelite order to which these two mystics belonged.

Teresa set out to reform her order and, by so doing, reform the church. She serves today as the patron saint of all Spanish mystics. Her younger contemporary and friend, Saint John of the Cross, also worked for reform. His journey would be particularly difficult, but from darkness and difficulty he extracted lightness of being. These two would continue to be my patron saints and guides on this spiritual pilgrimage. They were mystics who described the intimate Way to God.

We began our day in the village of Nájera, once the ancient capital of Navarre. We explored on foot the monastery church where so many kings, queens, and knights of Navarre were buried over centuries. Then we set out on a four-mile walk to the village of Azofra along one of the oldest parts of the Camino.

Our intended route was posted with a sign warning *Paso Malo*, meaning "Bad Way." It appeared to be a narrow path ascending steep sandstone cliffs. But our guide, Santiago, reassured us it was a "Bad Way" for only less than a kilometer, after which we would be rewarded with a hike through gently rolling vineyards for the rest of the Way. Following Brother Lawrence's recommendation, we began in faithfulness, and it led us into joy.

Our path indeed opened into wide country tracks through undulating farmland far removed from human habitation. The stone-border markings showed we were traversing between established places. This was a great day to be alive and to be walking. Teresa of Ávila and her visions accompanied me on the Way.

In the afternoon, we visited with the Cistercian nuns in the town of Santo Domingo de la Calzada, with its historic cathedral and ancient pilgrims' hospital. These enormous, ancient structures suggested that these regions once were far more densely traveled by pilgrims.

For the next two days, we would lodge at the Palacio de Burgos, another luxury hotel. The city of Burgos emerged into history in the eleventh century as the capital for El Cid. A Christian warlord, El Cid beat back the Moors in battle, then encouraged Christian pilgrims to settle all along the Camino to recolonize this part of Spain. Burgos later served as Franco's headquarters during the Spanish Civil War and today remains one of the most conservative parts of Catholic Spain.

We acclimated ourselves to Burgos with a visit to the famous Santa María Real de las Huelgas monastery, which is home to ancient documents including the *Codex Las Huelgas*, a fourteenth-century music manuscript. Then our guides arranged a private, after-hours tour of the Gothic abbey of the Cartuja de Miraflores. Angels have often appeared to me, in one form or another, whenever I most needed them. When we are traveling as strangers in a strange land, our guides are our angels. Our group was grateful for the angels who prepared our way and protected our pilgrim souls.

Early the next day, we visited Catedral de Santa María, also known as Burgos Cathedral. It is the second largest church in Spain, with myriad decorated chapels and a cloister. This began as a thirteenth-century Gothic cathedral but now contains many different architectural styles from different periods. The master masons at work here clearly knew what they were doing. This is a World Heritage site, with its magnificent edifice, its art treasures and artifacts, and its splendidly soaring twin spires surrounded by the bustle of medieval Burgos's ancient stone streets.

Then we drove to the village of Santo Domingo de Silos. Its monastery is a masterpiece of Romanesque architecture. We had a picnic lunch there and listened to the monks' worship through Gregorian chanting. They were singing Psalms as if in the voices of angels. I purchased a CD of their popular 1994 album *Chant* so I could take them with me on the journey. In the afternoon, we walked through a lovely forest leading us to a peaceful valley alongside the Vena River. So many different realities are interlayered here.

The next day, we left Burgos behind and crossed over into the province of León. We would walk an old Roman path from Calzada de Coto to Calzadilla de los Hermanillos, far away from roads, restaurants, or human habitation. We were well aware of the uncertain weather forecast that day.

It began to rain just as we stepped down from the bus. Fortunately, I had brought my umbrella. It helped for the first kilometer or so. But then the gusting winds became so strong that the umbrella was more of a hindrance than a help. We hunkered down, silent and wet, as we made our way several miles to our nearest connection point with the bus. Eventually, the weather cleared, and then we walked in silent meditation on muddy paths. Walking with Jesus, the weather almost didn't matter.

According to my guidebook, the Way we trod had been traveled by Romans seeking Gallaecian gold, by Roman legions traveling between Iberia and Bordeaux, by Caesar Augustus in his campaigns against the Cantabrians, by Christian Visigoths seeking a new homeland, by Muslims seeking an expanding empire, and by Charlemagne recapturing Iberia for Roman Christianity. The route was once known as Vía Trajana and Calzada de los Peregrinos. Today, it is known as a lovely part of the Camino de Santiago.

Of all the uses of this route, I reflected upon how it brought Romans so far west to enslave the Celtic Gallaeci people, mine their gold, and create the wealth of the Roman Empire. It is one of those remarkable coincidences of history—one thousand years later, the Roman Catholic Castilians traveled west across the unknown expanses of the Atlantic Ocean to enslave the Mayan people, mine their gold, and create the wealth of the Spanish Empire. It appears empires are generally built upon the pain and suffering of other people.

In this sense, life is a pilgrimage through a world of wealth and power. Religion often seems to play a greater cultural role than a spiritual one. The Celtic Gallaeci tribes indigenous to this area were called pagans by the Romans, who themselves went from being classicists to Christians before being overrun and conquered by Arian Christian Visigoths, who themselves were perpetually harried and attacked by Viking raiders worshipping the old Norse gods.

Later, the Umayyad Arabs and then the North African Moors conquered these lands for Islam, creating an Andalusian haven for Jewish, Christian, and Islamic scholars to flourish together. But the Moors were then driven out by Frankish troops in the Reconquista, the reconquest of Spain for Roman Catholic Christianity.

Religion and culture are complicated. We lose much when we focus on religion's institutional and worldly powers rather than its ability to foster human flourishing. Mystics know this. We find flourishing by following in pilgrims' footsteps along the Way to salvation.

A Pilgrim's Progress

After drying out over a tapas buffet lunch at a popular pilgrim restaurant, we boarded our bus and traveled on to check in to the Parador de León. This hotel is part of a sixteenth-century complex that was once the Hostal de San Marcos, a monastery and hospital. Another part of this complex, the Convento de San Marcos, once served as the regional headquarters of the Knights Templar. After the Templars were banned by papal decree, the Order of Santiago formed and continued to use this building as their motherhouse.

Our day in León began with a lecture on Compostela and historical sites along the Way. Our scholarly guide introduced us to an eighth-century pilgrim's prayer from the Mozarabic tradition of Christians who lived in the region during the Muslim occupation:

> *You call us from our settled ways,*
> *O God, out of old habits and traditions.*
> *You call us into the land of promise,*
> *to new life and new possibilities.*
> *Make us strong to travel the road ahead.*

Deliver us from false security and comfort,
desire for ease and uninvolved days.
Let your Word and Spirit dwell in us
that you will be fulfilled in us
for the well-being and shalom of all. Amen.

León was first built as a Roman military garrison and base for the Legio VII Gemina, the Roman seventh legion. When the Visigoths captured the city, they made it the capital of the ancient kingdoms of Asturias and León. When the Moors subsequently captured it, they used the city of León as the administrative center for the province of the same name. When Christian forces recaptured the city in the Reconquista, they expanded it greatly. So many layers of civilization were found here.

Here, Roman remains can be seen in medieval city walls. The Romanesque architectural style is prominent in the eleventh-century Real Colegiata de San Isidoro, or the Royal Collegiate Church of Saint Isidoro. High Gothic style is expressed in the soaring thirteenth-century León Cathedral, which includes two remarkable stone towers, a large rose window, and eighteen hundred square meters of medieval stained-glass windows.

León also includes Iglesia de San Salvador del Palat del Rey. Once a Gothic monastery, it became a Mozarabic church during the Moorish occupation of León. Local culture abounds with religious complexity.

The Consistorio Viejo (Old Town Hall) is a beautiful building in the baroque style also dominating León's Plaza Mayor (Main Square). The palace of the wealthy Quiñones family boasts a splendid fourteenth-century Gothic doorway and a fifteenth-century Renaissance tower. The palace of the Guzman family is so magnificent it has been repurposed to seat the León provincial council.

Our group had lunch reservations in the former residence of the count of Sagasta. This was the most splendid Spanish city we had so far visited. But like the city of Burgos, the León we experienced was built upon gold and wealth plundered from South America in the six-teenth and seventeenth centuries, the height of Spain's imperial power and the resulting Spanish Renaissance. We were surrounded by a com-plicated and rich history.

The next day, we departed León on our bus to follow one of the most beautiful parts of the Camino. We walked from the peaceful ham-let of Oncina de la Valdoncina through the treeless, open countryside to the ancient village of Chozas de Abajo. On this sunny early morning, the rich red earth was fecund with agricultural crops and wildflowers. This rural setting felt changeless, even while we knew the crops and wildflowers had changed over the last two thousand years. Still, local farmers lived here and cultivated crops throughout all that time.

We walked in silent contemplation, alone with our thoughts, prac-ticing going with God. As it did in the Holy Land, my old Protestant hymn companioned me: "And he walks with me, and he talks with me, and he tells me I am his own, and the joy we share as we tarry there, none other has ever known." In the warmth of the sun and the heat of the day, I was content just to walk with God.

Our scholarly guide offered a pilgrim prayer from the Christian mystic Thomas Merton:

> *My Lord God, I have no idea where I am going.*
> *I do not see the road ahead of me.*
> *I cannot know for certain where it will end.*
> *Nor do I really know myself,*
> *and the fact that I think I am following*
> *your will does not mean that I am actually doing so.*
> *But I believe that the desire to please you does in fact please*
> *   you.*
> *And I hope I have that desire in all that I am doing.*
> *I hope that I will never depart from that desire.*
> *And I know that if I do this you will lead me by the right*
> *   road,*
> *though I may know nothing about it.*
> *Therefore, will I trust you always*

though I may seem lost and in the shadow of death.
I will not fear, for you are ever with me,
and will never leave me to face my perils alone. Amen.

At the end of our journey walking through space and time, our bus waited to take us to Astorga, to visit the neo-Gothic bishop's palace built by the famous Catalan architect Antoni Gaudí. His late-nineteenth-century work blends neo-Gothic, Muslim, and Renaissance techniques to create a sense of divine mystery. The bishop never did relocate to live in this magnificent structure of heaven on earth, so the town converted it into a lovely small museum dedicated to the Museo de los Caminos (the Museum of the Ways). I was in heaven. Paradise.

We continued on to the city of Ponferrada, which means "Iron Bridge." There, we encountered the most magnificently restored Knights Templar castle I had seen outside the Holy Land. In 1178, Fernando II, king of León and Asturias, invited the Templars to settle on the banks of the Sil River to control the Bierzo area and ensure pilgrims' safety on the road to Santiago de Compostela. So where two popular caminos from the south converge with the northern route, the Templars built an indestructible stronghold above the Sil and an iron bridge for the pilgrims to cross safely. Like many Templar castles, this stronghold's defenses depended on one side upon a moat and labyrinth barbican entrance and on the other side upon a sheer cliff down to the river. From the riverside, they could transport supplies through an easily defended, sharply inclined tunnel-and-pulley system.

The Spanish experience with the Templars was quite different from that of the French, English, or German states. Spanish Templars didn't accumulate wealth and power in order to send knights to Palestine. They were a critical part of Spanish Christianity's defense against Islam. The Knights Templar maintained safety and order in these borderlands between Christianity and Islam. Perhaps because of the impact of Teresa of Ávila, they often allowed women to join as associates of their castles and even full sisters as nuns. And they tended to be more spiritual in their role as religious knights protecting Christian pilgrims, as if they were protecting Christ himself.

Their more integrated and trusted role in the Reconquista is perhaps best seen in Aragon in 1213. Before King Peter II died on the battlefield fighting beside the Templars, he entrusted his five-year-old son and heir apparent James I to the care and protection of Simon de Montfort, the master of Templars in Spain and Provence. After spending his formative years with the Knights Templar, James I would grow up to be perhaps the most militarily successful of the Reconquista kings. He often included the Templars in his plans of defense.

A papal decree on Friday, October 13, 1307, abolished this important religious order of warrior knights, and violent torture and heresy trials followed in France. In the Castile-León region, the Templars were examined by the church and found innocent in 1310.

The Spanish Templars needed to regroup. They gifted twenty of their castles, including Ponferrada, to the mother of the king of Castile, on the remarkable condition that the Templars would continue to use the castles to protect pilgrims. When this approach also became untenable, Ponferrada was then transferred into the safekeeping of the mystical Knights Hospitallers, who absorbed many Templar members and properties throughout Spain.

The Reconquista would last throughout most of the fourteenth and fifteenth centuries. And the Templars—or their knightly successors—were critical to its success. During the early medieval period, what would become Spain was still fragmented between many smaller kingdoms.

They each developed their own traditions of spiritual knighthood, many of them affiliated formally or informally with the Cistercian order of White Monks. These mystic knights included the Hospitallers, the Order of Calatrava, the Order of Santiago, the Order of Montesa, and the Order of the Knights of Christ, who eventually emerged in Portugal. The spiritual knights of Calatrava and Santiago maintained garrison castles guarding and defending key positions in the former borderlands between Christian and Muslim territory well into the sixteenth century.

Returning Home to God

We spent our last night before approaching Santiago de Compostela at the delightful Parador de Villafranca del Bierzo. I woke before dawn and threw the window open to the night air. I noticed a lone campfire on the side of the mountain yonder—pilgrims who decided to sleep raw along the Way. The brightening sky cast into dark silhouette the campers around the fire.

As night turned to day, the birds began singing. I heard distant traffic noises from the faraway highway. Fog slowly crept across the mountains, obscuring the brightening day. I was once again cloud covered, whereabouts unknown, and content. Equanimity and peace abided.

This modest eleventh-century town was built to better accommodate the growing number of pilgrims converging toward Compostela. In the medieval period, it boasted its own castle, three large pilgrim churches, and four large monasteries or convents to house all the pilgrims in dormitory-style housing. We spent the entire morning walking the town, which still has a medieval feeling about it.

Then we packed our bags and drove across the remaining parts of León province to Galicia for a gourmet lunch on the top of Monte do Gozo (Mount of Joy). When we looked down, we saw Santiago de Compostela for the first time in the far distance.

We began our last long walk along the Camino downhill toward Santiago. Our local guide seemed surprised when I was the first of our group to spot and correctly identify the spires of the Catedral de Santiago de Compostela in the distance.

However, as had happened to me increasingly after these many days of intense hiking, the tendons in my swollen ankles began to get all wobbly. They seemed unable to fully support my weight on the decline, giving me the sense that I was about to fall off the trail. Old volleyball injuries tormented my swollen ankles and flat feet. But with Taoist willpower and wu wei mental concentration, I managed not to fall down.

David Whyte described this descent in his poem "Santiago": "the road seen then not seen, the hillside hiding then revealing the way you should take . . . that called you back to the only road in the end you could follow." I walked in gratitude and divine mystery.

Finally, we arrived amidst the bustle and chaos of the main town square, kilometer zero on the Camino. The town square was dominated by the west-facing facade of the cathedral, with the neoclassical Galician government building facing it from the opposite side of the square. In between, on the northern side of the square, was the Hostel de los Reyes Católicos (Hostel of the Catholic Royals). It was built in 1492 under orders of King Ferdinand and Queen Isabella as a large pilgrim hospice. This building served at different times as a royal residence, a hospital, and a monastery. This ancient site is now the Parador de Santiago de Compostela, the hotel where we spent our final two nights in Spain.

Checking in, I received a large key to a room on an upper floor, where my luggage had already been sent ahead of me. The building had various floors built for different purposes at different times. In order to head up to my room, I first needed to descend a set of stone steps to reach another section of the building.

And that was when my left ankle gave out beneath me. The downside of Taoist wu wei mental concentration, it seems, is that pushing too far beyond the body's capabilities may lead it to rebel or simply collapse. I went crashing face-first down a couple of stone steps before I collided with the stone floor. My knees were bruised, my nose bloodied, and I had a growing bump above my left eye, where my head seemed to have hit the hardest.

I was initially dazed but relatively unharmed. No cracked ribs. Nothing seemed broken. Those following me down these steps were aghast and shocked that I had not been more injured by the fall. Yet the growing bump above my left eye was very tender, and it kept getting bigger. I decided to treat it with two bottles of cold beer—one held against the wound while the other was consumed. I was at peace.

I enjoyed an early dinner, with more beer, in a small, open-air café. Then we gratefully boarded our bus once more for it to take us to watch the sunset at Finisterre, the farthest western point of the ancient Roman Empire and the end of our road. We watched the sunset, toasted our pilgrim journey with champagne and strawberries, and stayed to watch the moonrise. It was magical. God was in this place, and now I was capable of perceiving her in all her glory.

David Whyte captured the spirit of this place in his poem "Finisterre": "The road in the end taking the path the sun had taken, into the western sea." We had traveled far, both physically and metaphysically, and we were now at the end. As the sun set, my journey had a feeling of completion. Glory be to God.

We had traveled from the Pyrenees, across the Basque province of Navarre, through the wine country of the Rioja, to the Spanish Renaissance city of Burgos, into the ancient province of León, and now we ended our journey at the westernmost point of Galicia. It was a pilgrimage of the spirit—even though we cushioned most hardships by traveling often by bus, staying in fine hotels, and enjoying great meals and wine. But my spiritual pilgrimages have never been about hardship, but rather about practicing the presence of God. Others may have yielded more spiritual rewards from their travels—or more suffering. But for me, this was enough, for God had traveled with me. I found equanimity. I sought no more.

We spent the next morning exploring the beauty of the cathedral. It is a solemn but joyous place. The ancient *Codex Calixtinus* describes it this way: "All days and nights are celebrated there in constant joy with the same solemnity for the honor of the Lord and the Apostle. The doors of the basilica are seldom closed by day or night."

As it turned out, however, the exterior façade of the main door, the Pórtico da Gloria (Door of Glory), was currently closed and under repair, so we entered through a side door. After all we had experienced, it seemed fitting to enter merely as humble pilgrims.

Inside, the other pilgrims were lining up to ascend a small staircase to hug a statue of Santiago behind the main altar. Instead, we descended a small set of stone stairs into the crypt to touch the stone coffin where the relics of Santiago are reputed to be buried.

This was neither the most beautiful nor the most spiritually enriching cathedral we had visited. Both the Burgos and León Cathedrals were far more spiritually powerful for me. But it was the cathedral at the end of all our striving, and so it held a special importance. We had come a long way to finally arrive here.

We visited the upper levels of the cathedral museum, where ancient documents and tapestries are well preserved. But we cut our visit a little short because pilgrims were beginning to swarm the church in anticipation of the noonday pilgrims' Mass, where a giant, swinging incense burner appeared to be the main attraction. There were over a thousand of us present to mark the end of our many and diverse pilgrimages. All was well.

Segundo L. Pérez López—officially, dean of the Santa Apostólica Metropolitana Iglesia Catedral Basílica de Santiago de Compostela—awarded each of us a certificate of recognition. Mine reads, in part, "To all those who see this certificate of recognition, let it be known that **James Sherblom** has visited the Cathedral and the tomb of the Glorious Apostle Saint James. On such an occasion the Council, prompted by the duty of charity, and in a time of joy greets you in the Lord and prays, with the intercession of the Apostle, that the Father will deign to grant your spiritual requests as well as material blessings. May the blessings of St. James be with you. Given in Compostela after the Camino of Saint James on the 30th day of May in the year 2017."

This had been my journey from fear to faith, from ignorance to gnosis, as I transcended mundane reality and walked with God, experiencing God's everlasting presence alongside me. This is the purpose of pilgrimage. I'd reached equanimity.

Early the next day, I flew back to the US. Now I faced my greatest challenge: living as a perpetual spiritual pilgrim in my own home. Having traveled the world as a pilgrim to Turkey, China, India, South America, Indochina, Palestine, and Spain, could I return home to Concord, where I had lived more than thirty years, and do so with a pilgrim soul?

I explored these questions as I undertook the official training course to become a certified Concord guide. Could I bring this sense of spiritual pilgrimage to Concord's transcendental history and my own Way?

Christian Mystics
BOOK GROUP DISCUSSION GUIDE

Author's Comment

Having grown up Christian, I expected this to be my least surprising pilgrim journey. But instead, it turned out to be the most surprising. The Way of Jesus Christ and other Christian mystics can lead to salvation and redemption, but only if we follow it faithfully.

Questions to Encourage Conversation

1. How does traveling as a guest of the Knights Templar impact the author's pilgrimage?

2. Why is Mount Carmel such an important mystical center for Christian pilgrims?

3. Does it matter that Jesus traveled and taught with Zoroastrians in Tyre and Sidon?

4. Do you find it easier to hear God's still, small voice in grand cathedrals or in quiet places?

5. What do you think is the core message of Jesus's beatitudes?

6. What obligation do the world's Christians have to the oppressed remnant of Palestinian Christians?

7. What makes the twelfth-century Camino de Santiago such a powerful pilgrimage Way?

8. How does the author experience the presence of God on his pilgrimages?

9. What does it mean to go on pilgrimage and come home to God?

Reflection

As a group, reflect upon how such a journey of the spirit might impact your faith or lack of faith.

TRANSCENDENTALIST MYSTICS

What is popularly called Transcendentalism among us, is Idealism. Idealism as it appears in 1842. As thinkers, mankind has been divided into two sects, Materialists and Idealists; the first class beginning to think from the data of the senses, the second class perceive that the senses are not final, and say, the senses give us representations of things, but what are the things themselves, they cannot tell.

—Ralph Waldo Emerson in "The Transcendentalist"

Human Flourishing

There are sacred places to which humans are naturally drawn. Such places lift our eyes to heaven and help us experience transcendentally the divine mystery. Concord is one of those places.

For millennia, indigenous peoples traveled over long distances through the forest—sometimes from as far away as what is now southern Maine—to live for a season close to where I now choose to live transcendentally. Before English settlers came, indigenous people of the Algonquin and Massachusett tribes inhabited the river valley they called Musketaquid. These people had a very different sense of reality and human consciousness. The wildness of this place helped shape their perception of reality.

There is a reason the English colonists chose it for their first inland settlement. There is a reason they called it Concord, meaning "peace" or "equanimity."

Every year, hundreds of thousands of people are drawn here on pilgrimage. For many, it is a historical pilgrimage to where the American Revolution began with the shot heard 'round the world. For others, it is a philosophical and literary pilgrimage to the homes of the nineteenth-century transcendentalists, Concord's second American revolution. For many, it is a nature pilgrimage to Walden Pond to pay homage to Henry David Thoreau.

In Concord, our history, sense of place, literature, and nature combine to create a pilgrimage for the spirit. I live that spirit, often ecstatically, as a transcendentalist author in the wildness of Concord, seeking to transcend self and to become a more fully realized soul.

Whether you approach from the north, east, south, or west, all directions pivot around this axis mundi. Walking, driving, cycling, or paddling in transcendentalist Concord as a spiritual pilgrim can be a journey across space and time. If you come on foot from the north, through Estabrook Woods, you can experience wildness like Thoreau did. If you approach Concord from the east, perhaps through the Great Meadows National Wildlife Refuge, you will experience a profusion of life in all its fecundity. Most days, you'll meet far more wildness than people.

If you approach Concord from the south, perhaps paddling a canoe or kayak, the view from the river gives you a different perspective than the view from the land. If you approach from the west, where I live just beyond the Concord Village, you pass through a more civilized Concord on your way into the wilds of Walden country.

Where you begin, and how you proceed, shapes your experience of the place and your ability to encounter it transcendentally. The goal of the transcendentalist is to convert life into truth through ecstatic experience.

Nowhere is this more apparent than at the entrance to Concord from its northern boundary with Carlisle, along the Old Carlisle Road, now in Estabrook Woods. This land is maintained today much as it was two hundred years ago, thanks to a remarkable series of conservation trusts binding together properties of Harvard University, the town of Concord, the town of Carlisle, and multiple private land trusts. Of Concord's estimated ninety miles of tangled woodland walks, some of the wildest and most remote are in Estabrook Woods. These woods cover over three thousand acres of marked and unmarked trails permanently protected from development.

Beginning in Carlisle Swamp, I make my way south upon the hard-packed dirt of this muddy cart path. It brings transcendence. It is a shady country lane traversing along the higher ground between swampy bogs and crisscrossing occasional brooks and small streams. The irregular stone walls around old fields and homesteads gradually give way to a more forested environment. Wildness exists at the edges of civilization, but especially here in these woods.

This old road is the width of a horse-drawn wagon, and it is made of mud and rocks and protruding tree roots. It has been essentially this way since before the Carlisle Minutemen traveled this road to Concord. The dappled morning light falling upon the mostly new-growth forest casts a narrow rainbow of color entirely within various hues of green and brown. This walking in nature takes me beyond space and time.

The silence of the woods is interrupted by the chatter of birds, perhaps a runner or horse rider or dog walker, and an occasional plane flying overhead. Approaching Botrychim Swamp, I remember Thoreau reported indigenous people living here because of its year-round natural spring. A little farther ahead on the trail is the automobile-size boulder Thoreau called "Indian Rock," a glacial remnant of the last ice age.

At this point, the trail crosses a little brook flowing into the swamp. I step lightly over it. A little farther along, there is a larger stream. I must make my way across wet stepping stones to remain on this muddy path through the swamps. These are the kinds of New England woods I grew up with—these boggy and wet areas that won the moniker of Swamp Yankees for those who thrived in such environments.

The interplay of wood, mud, and water creates a spiritual aura in this small forest preserve, an aura Thoreau noticed in his walks here. It is a deeply spiritual place. In these woods, I embrace paradise. Nirvana. Nearly four-hundred-year-old stone walls, some already ancient in Thoreau's time, border and delimit this old country road. It reminds me that in colonial times, much of this land was farmed or at least kept for wood lots.

At Estabrook Place, where the Estabrook family homestead and farm once stood, the path to the right leads out of the woods onto the grounds of the Middlesex School. A stone marker on the Estabrook Road informs me that I am two miles directly north of the Old North Bridge, which separates this swampy woodland from Concord Village. The old limestone quarries here are in ruins, mostly settling back into the bog, as has the large kiln used to bake and extract the lime for local use as mortar and wall plaster.

As the wind ripples through the trees, it dislodges flurries of rain-drops from last night's storm. One could follow this old road another mile, to where it leads out of the woods at Brooks Clark farm. Here, parts of Thoreau's Walden Pond cabin were used for grain storage and a pig pen.

But I choose to leave this road to follow Esker Trail, as the Carlisle Minutemen did, around the northeastern side of Mink Pond. I climb a short, steep rise to follow a ridge trail between the pond and the swamp. Eskers are found everywhere in the Concord woodlands. Also called serpent kames, they are long, winding ridges of stratified gravel or sand formed by tunneling streams within melting glaciers from the last ice age. They are often high and dry, like railway embankments.

I have now entered a fertile area that once was the campground of fur trappers hunting here a few years before the founding of Concord. When cultivated in the eighteenth century, this area was prized for pro-duction of hay, peat, and cranberries. By the twentieth century, it had gone to ruins, so beavers were allowed to dam and flood it. That created a wonderful bird and beaver habitat, its surface now covered with algae and water lilies. Many diverse uses over time.

I walk in peace above the dappled shores. Iridescent water lilies reflect the bright morning sun. A gentle gray heron views me with equanimity before slowly spreading his wings and sailing across the water to a less public spot. A wild goose honks from the far side of the pond. A large toad suns itself by the wayside. It seems nature makes more fertile use of this land than man ever did. This setting, with its many resonances, is transcendent.

As I cross over another rise, a wide expanse of quiet bog greets the sun's stark rays. Bigger trees felled by storms, and smaller trees felled by beavers, now clog what was once a mill pond.

Between 1820 and 1830, Thoreau's father, John, operated a sawmill on what was then called Saw Mill Brook and is now called Thoreau Pond. He cut cedar trees to make his pencils. Two hundred years later, nothing remains of this early industrial enterprise. But following the sound of cascading water brings me to the site where the old dam stood.

I return to Esker Trail, heading southeast. I immediately cross two fast-flowing streams on wet stepping stones. I am no longer following a cart trail. Rather, this is a narrow footpath that leads most directly toward Punkatasset Hill, where the rebel minutemen gathered themselves that fateful morning of April 19, 1775. Transcendence most often occurs within the matrix of this axis mundi. True lovers of wildness can experience ecstasy here.

If Concord's first revolution was for civil liberty, the second revolution two generations later was for moral and spiritual liberty. Ralph Waldo Emerson and his Concord protégé, Henry David Thoreau, were the primary local literary articulators of this second revolution. Emerson would become my teacher. Thoreau became my life coach.

Thoreau believed our enthrallment to money—ceaselessly working for wages (which he called wage slavery)—limits our human flourishing. Transcendentalists sought novel realities, new forms of human consciousness, and disciplines for self-culture by reconciling German idealism with English romanticism. They sought to create something new and wonderful, to transcend a narrow sense of self. Transcendentalist self-culture lifts me heavenward.

I grew up a middle child, the fifth of ten, and rather poor in Tiverton, Rhode Island. In my family, I was the audacious one, the silly one, the one who attempted big things. I went to Yale but was unable to succeed in that institution's rarified atmosphere. And so I reached a low point in my life journey at the age of nineteen.

At twenty-one, I met—and at twenty-three, I married—Loretta. She would love me, anchor me, and encourage me to great things. I went on long walks in nature, devoured spiritual texts, learned spiritual disciplines, and spent time with my wife and children to restore and maintain my transcendentalist soul, my sense of self, and my equanimity.

Through many and diverse life experiences, I became a twenty-first-century transcendental idealist. Not in the eighteenth-century German style of Immanuel Kant. Nor in the nineteenth-century American style of Ralph Waldo Emerson. Nor even in the twentieth-century *Process and Reality* style of Alfred North Whitehead.

Instead, I became an interreligious mystic transcendentalist. With these three—and many other—antecedents, I found my Way. My intuition and experience of divine mystery mediated what I learned from Sufi, Taoist, shamanic, Buddhist, and Christian mystics.

Sage of Concord

Emerson has always been one of my most important teachers in finding my Way. In the comprehensive biography *Emerson: The Mind on Fire*, Robert Richardson describes key formative experiences for Emerson that felt very familiar to me. He says, "Ralph was the third of six sons. Like some other middle children, he was the silly one."

Poverty would define his childhood. Emerson's father was a Harvard-trained Unitarian minister. But when Waldo was not yet eight years old, the family became destitute upon his father's death in 1811. His mother raised Waldo and his five siblings as a single parent.

Waldo was a precocious, poverty-stricken scholarship student at Boston Latin. He wrote in his journal how he and his older brother William were shamelessly teased at school for owning only one winter coat between the two of them.

Death was also an ever-present reality. In addition to his father's death, an older sister died before Waldo was born, a brother died when he was five, and three of his remaining four siblings would die before him. Life is transient, full of both tremendous joy and great sorrow. Living life transcendentally is to fully experience both the ecstasy of joy and the sorrow of grief.

Waldo was a sensitive boy, composing poetry from the age of nine. His early hardship altered his perception of reality. When he was eleven, his family was temporarily homeless, so he came to Concord to live with his grandparents. It was a seemingly idyllic interlude in a difficult life.

But soon his mother was running a boarding house in Boston. Of course, taking in boarders to help pay the rent was more common in those days. Even his grandparents in Concord occasionally took in boarders, and Waldo would later too. But money would not become his master.

Waldo graduated Harvard at age eighteen and was voted class poet, but he couldn't find a passion for living. He tried his hand at teaching but wasn't very good at it. He had spent over a decade living in Cambridge and Boston in poverty. His journals record his life reaching a low point around the age of nineteen. He wrote: "In twelve days I shall be nineteen years old; which I count a miserable thing." He felt he had not yet accomplished anything of note in his life. Waldo dreamed of making his living as a poet, an orator, or a minister. His brother William was sent off to study theology in Germany, but Waldo was too poor to follow his brother there.

Yet even in despair, Waldo found solace in nature by taking a walking trip through the Connecticut valley. He was an ecstatic nature mystic, perhaps even the first American transcendentalist nature mystic. He wrote in his journal:

*Upon a mountain-solitude a man instantly feels a
sensible exaltation and a better claim to his rights
in the universe. He who wanders in the woods
perceives how natural it was to pagan imagination
to find gods in every deep grove and by each
fountain head. Nature seems to him not to be silent
but to be eager and striving to break out in music.
Each tree, flower, and stone, he invests with life
and character; and it is impossible that the wind
which breathes so expressive a sound amid the
leaves—should mean nothing.*

Since both his grandfathers and his father had been Unitarian ministers, Waldo enrolled at Harvard Divinity School at age twenty-two.
But his Harvard experience was very different from that of the previous
generations. Leading Unitarian ministers and theologians tended to be
sensible people, following their reason and common sense, deeply sus-
picious of mysticism.

But newly available translations of Eastern religious texts, especially the Bhagavad Gita, were increasingly showing the limits of Anglican
Christianity's reliance on reason alone. New transcendental thoughts
were circulating about the role of nature and the nature of God. Writings by Immanuel Kant and Thomas Carlyle on German idealism and
poems by English romantic poets such as Samuel Coleridge and William Wordsworth became a counter-curriculum for intellectually curi-
ous divinity scholars.

Young men training for the ministry were seeking new realities and
new forms of consciousness. Waldo copied Wordsworth's poem "Tin-
tern Abbey" into his spiritual journal:

*Therefore, am I still a lover of the meadows and the
woods, and mountains;
and of all that we behold from this green earth; of all
the mighty world*

of eye and ear—both what they half create, and
   what perceive;
well pleased to recognize in nature and the language
   of sense,
the anchor of my purest thoughts, the nurse, the
   guide,
the guardian of my heart, and soul of all my mortal
   being.

On Christmas Day, 1827, the twenty-four-year-old Emerson met the sixteen-year-old Ellen Tucker, who would prove to be his salvation. He described her as having "the purity and confiding religion of an angel." He finally found a passion for living. At twenty-six, Waldo was ordained as a Unitarian minister—six months later, he married the love of his life.

But their bliss was brief. Ellen was already dying of tuberculosis when they wed. Less than eighteen months later, she was dead. In a letter to his aunt Mary Emerson, he wrote: "My angel is gone to heaven this morning and I am alone in the world."

He made a spiritual discipline of visiting her grave every morning. After a little more than a year of these daily pilgrimages, he even paid to have her coffin reopened to allow him to say a final goodbye, for she was truly gone from his life. However, even if no longer physically available, she would become his muse and the core spiritual companion in his life.

Ellen's death appears to have been a dark night of the soul for Emerson. It broke him free from many of the limitations of his parochial upbringing, and it sparked his resurrection as a freethinking intellectual. As he embraced science and mysticism, he left behind much of Boston cultural constraint, Harvard orthodoxy, and Unitarian common sense.

Emerson was fascinated by science, so went seeking a science-friendly spirituality. Three weeks after Ellen's death, he wrote: "The religion that is afraid of science dishonors God and commits suicide.

It acknowledges that it is not equal to the whole truth, that it legislates, [even] tyrannizes over a village of God's empire, but is not immutable universal law."

Yet Emerson's health declined as he lost his taste for living, including any interest in his ministry at Second Church in Boston. He resigned his pulpit and used his small savings to travel audaciously for seven months in Europe, visiting Rome, Florence, Paris, and London. He met Carlyle in Scotland as well as Coleridge and Wordsworth in England. Like Emerson, Coleridge was a Unitarian minister and a post-Kantian philosopher seeking enlightenment.

Emerson explored the English romantics' experience of nature with Wordsworth and transcendental idealism with Coleridge. His conversation with Carlyle led to their becoming lifelong friends and philosophical correspondents. As he went in search of spiritual companions, the many and diverse antecedents of American transcendentalism slowly gathered for this brilliant but bereft scholar. He was discovering his own unique Way.

Through pain and suffering, he began to turn toward a deeper understanding of divine mystery. In his journal, he claimed: "We dip our fingers in the sea that would make us invulnerable if we would plunge and swim." He wrote to his dear departed wife, "Dear Ellen . . . coming from God's throne, suggest to this lone heart some hint of [God]."

Regarding Christianity, he wrote: "Christianity is validated in each person's life and experience or not at all." God is a mystery. That same summer, he wrote in his journal: "God cannot be intellectually discerned." Herein lie some beginnings of Emerson's transcendentalism.

Then, in 1836, Emerson and Frederic Henry Hedge, who as a teenager had studied Kantian Idealism in Germany, became the center of a group of young, liberal intellectuals seeking to discuss these new views of religion, culture, and society. This small, informal group of radical intellectuals met for the first time at Harvard's bicentennial celebration on September 6, 1836, days after the publication of Emerson's first transcendental essay, "Nature."

The group proclaimed that the sorry state of American intellectual thought was "very unsatisfactory." The group's wide-ranging conversations included Unitarian ministers such as James Freeman Clarke, George Ripley, and Theodore Parker, as well as brilliant young women such as Elizabeth Hoar, Elizabeth Peabody, and Margaret Fuller. Initially, they called their gatherings Hedge's Club, then a symposium. Eventually, they came to call them American transcendentalism.

Emerson read incredibly widely for his era, with frequent references to Hindu and Buddhist texts, Sufi poetry, and Christian mystics. In his first essay on divine mystery, his description of divine mystery as the "over-soul" bore a striking resemblance to the universal soul in Hindu Brahminism. In that essay, he draws freely from Spinoza, Kant, and Coleridge, yet he remains firmly fixed in mysticism, claiming every "man is a stream whose source is hidden."

He also describes this emerging experience of ecstasy in his essay "Nature":

Crossing a bare common, in snow puddles, at twilight,
   under a clouded sky,
Without having in my thoughts any occurrence of special
   good fortune,
I have enjoyed a perfect exhilaration. I am glad to the
   brink of fear . . .
Standing on bare ground, my head bathed by the blithe
   air,
and uplifted into infinite space, all mean egotism
   vanishes.
I become a transparent eye-ball; I am nothing; I see all;
the currents of the Universal Being circulate through me;
I am part or particle of God.

Subsequently, in "The Method of Nature," Emerson draws upon Kant, Schelling, Carlyle, and Coleridge to describe a dynamic pantheism with parallels in Pythagorean, Neoplatonic, and Zoroastrian philosophical traditions. For Emerson, transcendentalism was a uniquely American manifestation of the perennial philosophy—the Way to achieve ecstatic union with the One. He drank deeply from the living waters of mystics ancient and modern.

Emerson found a very satisfactory mix of scientific mysticism in the sixth-century BCE writings of Anaximander of Miletus, Pythagoras of Samos, and Zoroaster of Babylon. Emerson saw Anaximander, Pythagoras, and Plato as prototypical idealists rather than materialists, as were Kant, Coleridge, and later Whitehead. Emerson was articulating and adding his own contribution to what he felt was a noble philosophical tradition.

Ultimate reality is beauty that can be scientifically defined. Richardson writes:

> *[Emerson's] new interest in science was stirred by Pythagoras's teaching that reality is mathematical, that the fundamental principles of things are numbers, and that beings are bound together by laws as by numbers. It was Pythagoras who gave the name cosmos—meaning order, harmony, and, by extension beauty—to the world, who taught that moderation is the essential characteristic of virtue, and that [self-culture] is the means to obtaining it. It was Pythagoras who insisted that the soul is an emanation of the divine.*

Shortly after I turned thirty, Loretta and I moved to Concord and became Unitarian Universalists and transcendentalists. For the next twenty years, however, most of our time and energy were devoted to furthering our business careers and raising our children.

I ceased to consider myself philosophically limited to Christianity, so I sought instruction also in the disciplines of Hinduism, Buddhism, Confucianism, Taoism, Islam, and shamanism. Christianity was still important to me. I didn't leave it behind so much as add these other paths to my journey of enlightenment. This emerging sense of being a spiritual pilgrim and sojourner in life eventually led me to ordained Unitarian Universalist parish ministry. And then, like Emerson, I would leave ministry behind to become more fully my authentic self.

Emerson reflected on what he called narrow religious sectarianism. He wrote:

> *I suppose it is not wise, not being natural, to belong to any religious party. In the bible you are not directed to be a Unitarian or a Calvinist or an Episcopalian. Now if a man is wise, he will not only profess himself to be a Unitarian, but he will say to himself I am not a member of that or of any party. I am God's child, a disciple of Christ, or in the eye of God a fellow disciple with Christ.*

Emerson came to believe that Jesus, though qualitatively different from other human beings, was merely a fully realized human being, and that a loving God could never be cruel or wrathful but rather would universally save all his children. Emerson confessed in his journal, "I have sometimes thought that in order to be a good minister it was necessary to leave the ministry. The profession is antiquated. In an altered age, we worship in the dead forms of our forefathers."

Later, in his essay on "Representative Men," he said, "Our colossal theologies of Judaism, Christism, Buddhism, Mahometism [Islam], are the necessary and structural action of the human mind." That is divine mystery; we cannot conceptualize the bigness of God. Yet transcendentalism creates a reverence for life and shows the Way to human flourishing.

In "Mystics in All Religions," Freeman Clarke declared Emerson the prime example of an American mystic. In fact, everything I learned from traveling with twenty-first-century mystics in different parts of the world was, to some extent, anticipated by Emerson. This included the power of resilience, surrender, gratitude, and generosity.

God is a divine mystery humans can never fully comprehend. Through interreligious perspectives, I learned to awaken to the ultimate nature of reality, to live among wildness, and to love ecstatic transcendentalist mystics.

Concord's Wildness

To experience how transcendentalists encounter Concord's wildness, you could approach the village from the east. This path is partially preserved today along the Reformatory Branch Trail, named after a late-nineteenth-century rail spur built along an esker ridge path between meadow and swamp.

Beginning at the Bedford town line, for the first mile or so, you'll have the Great Meadows National Wildlife Refuge on your right. This marshy area was known even in colonial times as the Great Meadow. It is a sea of green grasses, water lilies, cattails, and wildflowers along the river. Punkatasset Hill rises up before you on the north side of the river.

The Great Meadows today are a naturalist's heaven. From its viewing tower, you can observe two dozen species of birds, including red-winged blackbirds, Canada geese, ducks, snowy egrets, and great blue herons. In spring, the shallow water is alive with tadpoles and minnows, an inland sea of water lilies, and occasionally even a swift-moving muskrat.

As the trail moves to higher ground, you encounter bicyclists and butterflies. You eventually come to where the poorer people eked out a living at the edge of the swamp in colonial times.

John Jack, the first previously enslaved African American to own land in Concord, built his homestead at the edge of the Great Meadows. Born in 1712, Jack worked four decades as an enslaved farmhand owned by Benjamin Barron, a Concord yeoman farmer. After Barron died in 1754, Jack worked for wages, allowing him in 1761 to purchase his freedom along with four acres of plowable land at the margins of Concord society. It was a fruitful life, if not always a free one, as George Tolman told the early-twentieth-century Concord Antiquarian Society:

> *Later he bought a lot of two and a half acres in the*
> *Great Meadow, upon which he built his house,*
> *and the spot has been occupied by [African*
> *American] families ever since, until a few years*
> *ago. He supported himself by working out for*
> *the farmers at odd jobs, haying, pig-killing, and*
> *the like, and by going around among the farms*
> *in the winter cobbling shoes.*

Daniel Bliss, Concord's most prominent pre–Revolutionary War lawyer, was a good friend of Jack's and served as executor of his estate when Jack died in 1773. In his will, he bequeathed to Violet, a previously enslaved black woman, "all his lands . . . a cow and calf, a good pair of oxen, some farming tools, a bible and psalm book and seven barrels of cider."

The town voted to allow this formerly enslaved person to be buried in Concord's Old Hill Burying Ground–but only if his grave was placed on the back side of the hill, facing away from the village church. Yet his friend Daniel Bliss wrote a remarkable epitaph on Jack's gravestone:

> *God wills us free; man makes us slaves.*
> *I will as God wills; God's will be done.*
> *Here lies the body of JOHN JACK*
> *A native of Africa who died March 1773, aged*
> *about 60 years.*
> *Tho' born in a land of slavery, he was born free.*
> *Tho' he lived in a land of liberty, he lived a slave.*
> *Till by his honest, tho' stolen, labors, he acquired the*
> *source of slavery,*
> *which gave him his freedom; tho' not long before*
> *death, the grand tyrant,*
> *gave him his final emancipation and set him on a*
> *footing with kings.*
> *Tho' a slave to vice, he practiced those virtues*
> *without which kings are but slaves.*

A succession of often-related African American families lived around Great Meadows throughout the eighteenth and nineteenth centuries, on land few others found worthwhile to build upon. Caesar Robbins, who fought in his owner's stead in the French and Indian War, was probably standing with the Concord militiamen on Punkatasset Hill that 1775 morning. In 1823, two of his children, Susan and Peter, built a substantial two-family house on this same site. It is known to this day as the Robbins House, and it has been relocated to a nearby site as a museum.

Susan Robbins Garrison became a founding member of the Concord Female Antislavery Society. Her daughter, Ellen Garrison, went on to be Concord's leading African American scholar, teacher, and activist. Peter Hutchinson, a distant relative by marriage, lived in this house in Thoreau's time. He served local farmers by slaughtering their pigs—a sort of work few others would willingly undertake.

A little farther along the trail, on high ground overlooking Borden's Pond, was the dry campground of the Nipmuc tribe. These are the oldest signs of human habitation in the Concord area, going back at least eleven thousand years. As late as the eighteenth century, they were still used transiently by remaining members of that tribe. For many years, anyone with a sharp eye could find their leaf-shaped spear points, arrow heads, and grinding mortars there. This spot is located just north of Moore's Swamp, which is today home to Blanding's turtles, great blue herons, ducks, woodpeckers, and great horned owls.

Much of the rest of Moore's Farm is rolling hills or protected marshland. It was a favorite walking and reflection locale for nineteenth-century transcendentalists. Picture this scene on a sunny Sunday afternoon: Margaret Fuller sprawled on the grass, reading a book in German. Nathaniel Hawthorne happens along and sits down beside her to talk metaphysics. Henry Thoreau ambles through, leading the Alcott girls on a huckleberry hunt. Finally, Emerson, on his Sunday afternoon walk, stumbles upon them. They all decide to retire to Emerson's house for an early tea. This was the transcendental experience of serendipity in wildness in the village of Concord.

In the 1860s, this part of Moore's Farm was converted into one of the first garden-style cemeteries, which they named Sleepy Hollow. The cemetery ridge overlooking Moore's Swamp is now called Author's Ridge, and it has become the final burial ground for Emerson, Thoreau, Alcott, and Hawthorne. Their transcendental spirit of life is still very much present in this place.

From this small ridge, we can descend toward Minute Man National Historical Park and Old North Bridge. As we do so, we pass by the relocated Robbins House. We also pass by the Old Manse, where Emerson composed his first essay, "Nature." Hawthorne's *Mosses from an Old Manse* was directly inspired by the home, a great nineteenth-century writer's retreat.

The Old Manse looks much as Hawthorne described it 175 years ago. You still enter its yard by passing "between two tall gateposts of rough-hewn stone." Hawthorne described how "the glimmering shadows that lay half asleep between the door of the house and the public highway were a kind of spiritual medium, seen through which the edifice had not quite the aspect of belonging to the material world." Hawthorne was enchanted and transcendentally transformed by Concord's wildness.

Nathaniel Hawthorne spent the first three years of his married life living with his wife, Sophia, in this enchanting home. Previously, it had been Emerson's grandparents' house. It was also the home of various Unitarian ministers for seven decades.

Hawthorne was in awe of its sacred nature. He wrote, "Nor, in truth had the old Manse ever been profaned by a lay occupant until that memorable summer afternoon when I entered it as my home. A priest had built it; a priest had succeeded to it; other priestly men from time to time had dwelt in it; and children born in its chambers had grown up to assume the priestly character." This house was a center for the flourishing of human consciousness.

The Old Manse is at the northern edge of the village. While Hawthorne lived there, Emerson was living in his somewhat grander house on the eastern edge of the village. While they saw each other regularly and would sometimes go walking together, Hawthorne was skeptical of the Concord transcendentalists. Early in his Concord sojourn, he sardonically remarked upon the many and strange spiritual seekers making pilgrimage to visit Emerson, the sage of Concord. Yet after three years of living in Concord, Hawthorne's writing had taken on a transcendental quality. This Old Manse set Hawthorne firmly on his path as an author.

A friend of mine recently gave me a behind-the-scenes tour of the restored Old Manse. We toured the garret attic, where visiting clergy, the household slaves, and the older children all slept. We found graffiti left by Waldo marking his own time spent living in the house, as well as graffiti from his father's growing up there. We also found a message etched by Nathaniel and Sophia in a window.

It is a building as rich with character as Concord itself. Hawthorne called it a kind of fairyland and observed, "In fairyland there is no measurement of time." The house still has a special, timeless quality about it, partly because of the many lives that passed through these rooms and partly because of the rich history that surrounds it. You can rest here in equanimity with the spirit of this place and experience peace and joy by living fully engaged with life's wildness.

Through engagement with nature, Emerson, Thoreau, and Hawthorne sacramentalized their world. Each reflected some aspect of the ancient nature deity Pan and a love of fairyland, which lifted them out of mundane reality and humdrum time. Joseph Campbell, the great scholar of myth and magic, said, "Sacred space and sacred time and something joyous to do is all we need. Almost anything then becomes a continuous and increasing joy. What you have to do you do with joy. I think a good way to think of sacred space is as a playground. If what you're doing seems like play, you are in it." This axis mundi is conducive to sacred playing.

Just beyond the Old Manse were the farm's orchards and fields by the Concord River. Hawthorne said these fields were on a former indigenous people's village. He wrote, "The site is identified by the spear and arrow heads, the chisels, and other implements of war, labor, and the chase, which the plough turns up from the soil." Hawthorne described in detail the eighteenth-century battleground of the American Revolution, but he saved his most transcendental description for the river. He wrote, "We stand on the river's brink. It might well be called the Concord, the river of peace and quietness; for it is certainly the most unexcitable and sluggish stream that ever loitered imperceptibly towards its eternity—the sea." Hawthorne said the river was so quiet it was often difficult to know which way it flowed. All was equanimity.

As I walk the paths of Concord, I am mindful that I am myself descended from the Pilgrim John Alden, who helped pacify and destroy the indigenous people of this land. But I am also descended from the patriot Abner Goodale, who fought with the rebels at Concord's Old North Bridge; the loyalist Peter Collicutt, who fled to Canada during the American Revolution; and many other good and complicated men and women. Our personal histories are deep and richly interlayered.

Yet as an increasingly mature spiritual being, I can sometimes transcend self, greeting the world in perfect exhilaration, like Emerson's "transparent eyeball," which is "part or particle of God." Or as Margaret Fuller wrote, "I saw there was no self: that selfishness was all folly, and the result of circumstance; that it was only because I thought self [was] real that I suffered; that I had only to live in the idea of the all, and all was mine . . . I was for that hour taken up into God." Fuller was a Gnostic mystic.

When my kids were little, we used to play "pooh sticks" on the Old North Bridge. Here's how you play: Each person finds a stick. At a signal, you all drop them simultaneously from the upriver side in the middle of the bridge, hoping to drop your own stick into a slightly swifter northeasterly flowing current. Then, as the slow-moving water swirls and eddies around the bridge pilings, you race to the downriver side of the bridge to see whose stick floated out first. We played this game over and over again, making silly sport of the slow-moving current. It brought transcendent joy!

Thoreau also had a playful spirit in relation to time and distance. Louisa May Alcott called him "Concord's Pan." Choosing time spent among the sunny meadows and shaded woods of his childhood over mercantile endeavors became a large part of Thoreau's self-definition. Thoreau never had much money, so he learned to simplify his life and make do with less. He taught that when a wise man "has obtained those things which are necessary to life, there is another alternative than to obtain superfluities; and that is, to adventure on life now, his vacation from humbler toil having commenced." Thoreau's measure of a man was how frequently his money allowed him to take a vacation from humble toiling in order to simply experience life to its very depths.

Yet like other New England villages of its time, Concord has a history of slavery, of disenfranchising the poor, and of killing the indigenous people. The Robbins House is now a small museum to Concord's black history. Only now in the twenty-first century has Concord begun to more fully acknowledge its history of enslaved blacks serving as domestic servants and farmhands, of runaway slaves traveling the Underground Railroad, of free blacks forced to live on the margins of white society. Concord has yet to come to terms with its part in the genocide of the indigenous people living in this place. A mystic must live between two worlds, two realities.

Thoreau's intent was to be fully transcendentally conscious of life in all of its meanness and all of its glory. As he declared:

> *To anticipate not the sunrise and the dawn merely, but, if possible, nature herself! How many mornings, summer and winter, before yet any neighbor was stirring about his business, have I been about mine . . . It is true, I never assisted the sun materially in his rising, but, doubt not, it was of the last importance only to be present at it.*

For me, my vacation from humbler toiling didn't really commence until I turned sixty and retired from parish ministry. Only then did I have the spaciousness to become an authentic, spiritually mature human being.

Now I too live transcendentally, sometimes ecstatically, as a spiritual pilgrim. This sense of transcendence is often indistinguishable from oneness with God.

Transcendentalist Concord

Life circumstances made Emerson into a spiritual pilgrim and sojourner. He developed his ideas in public lectures and moved to the Old Manse in Concord to better contemplate how to live his life. Two years later, he began receiving an inheritance from his dead wife's estate—which in today's terms would be roughly $750,000. That, along with his growing lecture income, allowed him to make a life. Emerson would never be rich, but he invested well, and never again would he be poor. Being a person of independent means became part of his self-identity.

He courted and wed Lidian Jackson of Plymouth. They purchased a large house on the main road just east of Concord Village. It had been a Boston merchant's summer house, which locals called the Coleridge Castle, but the newlyweds renamed it Bush House. They hired a housekeeper and cook and frequently entertained large dinner parties. From time to time over the years, Emerson's mother, his siblings, his children, and Henry Thoreau would also live there. This house would become the vibrant unofficial headquarters of American transcendentalism.

The village of Concord that welcomed Waldo and Lidian had about two thousand residents, most of whom were white Anglo-Saxon farmers. There were twenty-eight formerly enslaved people of color, a somewhat smaller number of poor Irish Catholics, and a few indigenous people, most of whom were transitory migrants. People who were not White Anglo-Saxon Protestants (WASPs) mostly lived on the margins of the village or in the less desirable, uncultivated forest and wastelands beyond the village proper. They were distinct from the WASP Concord villagers.

Less than 10 percent of the white males were college educated, mostly at Harvard. They worked as ministers, teachers, merchants, surveyors, and clerks. Most everyone else were farmers or day laborers. Richardson writes, "There was a cotton mill, employing forty-two persons, thirty of them women . . . [and] two sawmills, two gristmills, a bookstore and bindery, six warehouses and a bustling carrying trade. . . . Before the coming of the railroad in 1845 the trip to Boston by cart, carriage, or horse took about two and a half hours."

The year after they married and moved to Concord, the Emersons' first child, a son they named Waldo, was born. Emerson wrote, "Last night at eleven o'clock a son was born to me. Blessed child! A lovely wonder to me, and which makes the Universe look friendly to me . . . The truth seems to be that every child is infinitely beautiful, but the father alone by position and duty looks near enough to see." Emerson encountered divine mystery gazing into his young son's eyes.

Weaving his spiritual life out of the experiences he encountered as well as out of his new financial security helped Emerson live transcendentally. He would become the quiet benefactor of his relatives and oft-struggling friends. At one time or another, he financially helped his mother; his brother William; his friends Alcott, Fuller, Hawthorne, and Thoreau; and many others.

Among the greatest joys of my life were the births and childhoods of my daughter and my son. I loved being a family-centered householder for the twenty years they lived with us. During those years, I was also engaged in building entrepreneurial businesses. There were many triumphs and failures, great happiness as well as deep suffering–all leading ultimately to equanimity.

Over decades, I developed resilience, ego surrender, gratitude, and generosity of spirit. From our abundance, we financially assisted friends, family, and good causes. Our joys and sorrows were woven finely together, but once we were financially secure, we could live transcendentally. This was my form of self-culture as a twenty-first-century transcendentalist.

It appears Coleridge introduced Emerson to the German ideal-ist notion of *Bildung*, or self-culture. Coleridge wrote, "To reform a world, to reform a nation, no wise man will undertake; all but foolish men know, that the only solid, though a far slower reformation, is what each begins and perfects in himself."

As early as 1830, Emerson began to give popular lectures on self-culture, how to develop oneself into a more cultured and hu-mane human being. He suggested young people seek to find their unique place in the world, read widely, keep a spiritual journal, prac-tice contemplation in solitude to develop mindfulness, and take long walks in nature.

In his essays, Emerson clearly described his experiences of the mystic path. He wrote, "This path is difficult, secret, and beset with terror. The ancients called it *ecstasy* or absence—a getting out of their bodies to think. All religious history contains traces of the trance of saints." As he encountered ever more spiritual teachers of the past, he drew upon mystics of all the ages.

Emerson's universalizing of the spiritual journey, along with his growing mystic experiences, led him to conclude that "the history of Jesus is only the history of every man written large. The names [each person] bestows on Jesus, belong to himself—Mediator, Redeemer, Savior." We are born to be children of God. As such, we are life's mediators, redeemers, saviors.

However, self-centeredness is a major impediment to cultiva-tion of the soul. Self-culture then becomes essential to spiritual growth. The transcendentalists believed surrendering self through engagement with nature and its wildness was necessary for living transcendentally.

On May 25, 1838, Emerson turned thirty-five, which he de-scribed as midway toward the three score years and ten of a full and meaningful life. His life began to take on new forms. In November, he was adopted by a brilliant protégé, Henry David Thoreau, newly graduated from Harvard. The following February, Lidian gave birth to their second child, a daughter, whom they agreed to name after his first wife, Ellen, his muse and spiritual companion. That baby Ellen would also grow into the muse and spiritual companion role in Emerson's old age. Henry Thoreau became Emerson's constant walking companion. They would walk through the woods, around Walden Pond, and sometimes as far as the cliffs above Fairhaven Bay. That next April, Thoreau recorded such a walk in his journal: "Warm, pleasant, misty weather which the great mountain amphitheatre seemed to drink in with gladness. A crow's voice filled all the motes of air with sound." These shared mystical experiences in nature helped bond them to each other. They experienced divine mystery in encountering wildness. They grew, like Rumi and Shams, to be great spiritual companions.

Over the next twenty years, they would spend so much time together. They exchanged thoughts and experiences so often that it became increasingly difficult to know where ideas originated—from Emerson's science and reason or Thoreau's embracing of experience. Richardson writes:

> *Emerson's ideas on poetry, history, self-reliance, and*
> *friendship show up in Thoreau's journals and many*
> *of Thoreau's subjects appear in Emerson's journals.*
> *It's sometimes impossible to say who took what from*
> *whom. Emerson talked about sauntering just as he*
> *came to know Thoreau. Emerson owned land at*
> *Walden Pond, took almost daily walks there, and felt*
> *a proprietary interest in the place.*

Emerson cherished Walden Pond, but Thoreau became famous for describing it.

They shared so constantly and freely that many of their thoughts were a collaboration, with Emerson gradually becoming more comfortable relying simply upon his experience, and Thoreau relying increasingly upon scientific observations. They matured intellectually and spiritually together, even while serving as a kind of yin-yang counterbalance to each other. But New England Unitarian common sense was often scornful of their mysticism. In August 1841, the *Christian Register*, the Unitarian magazine, went so far as to describe this American transcendentalism as synonymous with hocus-pocus mysticism. In response that winter, Emerson delivered his lecture "The Transcendentalist" at the Boston Masonic temple.

Emerson noted that mystic experiences are ecstatic, ephemeral, yet still subject to scientific reason. He said mystics live between two worlds and have a "double consciousness," with two understandings of underlying reality. He wrote, "One prevails now, all buzz and din; and the other prevails then, all infinitude and paradise." The mystic lives as much as possible in infinitude and paradise, reaching beyond the mere senses to encounter transcendence.

This lecture, along with his writings on the over-soul, helped shape my understanding of spirituality when I discovered Emerson in the early 1970s. It would be another forty years, however, before I realized how great were the similarities between our life experiences and our spiritual journeys. As Emerson might have put it, we were both just representative mystics. There is much of my story in his, and his in mine, as we each made our Way as a mystic soul.

What Emerson called self-reliance, I came to call resilience. Emerson saw self-reliance, or resilience, as the spiritually audacious core discipline that eventually ensures success in all other endeavors. He wrote in his journal,

> *A great genius must come and preach self-reliance. Our*
> *people are timid, desponding, recreant whimperers.*
> *If they fail in their first enterprises they lose all heart.*
> *If the young merchant fails, men say he is RUINED*
> *... A sturdy New Hampshire man or Vermonter*
> *who in turn tries all the professions, who teams it,*
> *farms it, peddles, keeps a school, preaches, edits*
> *a newspaper, goes to Congress, and so forth, in*
> *successive years, and always like a cat falls on his*
> *feet, is worth a hundred of these Boston [timid] men.*

As a nature mystic, Emerson's favorite meditation practice was to take long walks through the woods and around Walden Pond. He became enraptured in nature. Concord's particular form of transcendentalist meditation is deeply connected to nature. One winter, he wrote,

Pleasant walk yesterday, the most pleasant of days. At Walden Pond, I found a new instrument which I call the ice-harp. A thin coat of ice covered a part of the pond but melted around the edge of the shore. I threw a stone upon the ice which rebounded with a shrill sound, and falling again and again, repeated the note with pleasing modulation. . . . I was so taken by the music that I threw down my stick and spent twenty minutes in throwing stones singly or in handfuls on this crystal drum.

Yet his was an equanimity in the midst of both joy and suffering. In September 1841, Emerson's step-grandfather, the last tie to the Revolutionary War generation, died. Then, in January 1842, Thoreau's older brother John died from lockjaw. And that same month, Emerson's five-year-old son, Waldo, died of scarlet fever. Joy and death never seemed far apart.

Emerson and Lidian, as well as their relationship to each other, were forever changed. Lidian increasingly turned toward the Christian God for comfort, while Emerson increasingly stared into the abyss. It was many years before Emerson's playful and silly nature would return, and then mostly with his grandchildren. Lidian's health went into steady decline.

Thoreau's grief over his brother's death led him to spend over two years at Walden Pond, in what he called an experiment in learning to live fully engaged with life. From joy arises suffering, and from suffering new opportunities for joy. This is the inevitable yin and yang of human life: joy and sorrow are always woven fine together. We can't have one without the other.

Change is the only constant. Following the American Revolution, Concord underwent an enormous change, from rural village to county seat. In the next forty years, the country's population tripled. Massachusetts emerged with one of the highest average-per-capita incomes on the planet. Freed from constant toil, lyceums sprang up in every small town, every farmer became a philosopher, and interest grew for lectures and transcendent books. The time was ripe.

Thoreau had been born in 1817 on his maternal grandmother's rural farm on Virginia Road, a winding way outside Concord. In Thoreau's lifetime, the Industrial Revolution transformed life in Massachusetts, not entirely for the better.

By 1850, the American population would quadruple again, partly through a massive influx of immigrants. Most were desperately poor Irish immigrants. Income inequality would soar. Anti-Irish prejudice and contempt were a source of much friction in this small New England village. The Irish were often treated no better than the freed blacks or indigenous people.

Thoreau wrote about the growing poverty among the marginalized and oppressed of Concord society. He was an advocate for the formerly enslaved and for desperately poor immigrants as well as impoverished indigenous people. And he was a sharp critic of those WASPs, clinging to their formerly comfortable lives, living mundane lives of quiet desperation in the village.

Generally, transcendentalists were socially engaged mystics endeavoring to enact racial, gender, economic, political, and environmental justice. They embraced social reform in education, women's rights, cooperative living, and the abolition of slavery. The entire Thoreau family, especially Henry, were leaders in Concord's abolitionist movement.

Thoreau was prominently involved with the Underground Railroad and was a public speaker with Frederick Douglass against the Fugitive Slave Act. This led to his involvement with John Brown's violent and unsuccessful attempts to end slavery in America.

Thoreau preached civil disobedience—but not nonviolence in the face of evil. For transcendentalists, spiritual seeking and action for social justice are two aspects of the same commitment to truth. They believe that by first transforming ourselves, we prepare the way to transform society as a whole. This is transcendentalist self-culture.

Paddling Musketaquid

Approaching Concord's wildness from the south or west is best done paddling on the rivers. The Algonquian indigenous people called this ancient river system Musketaquid. It is a land defined by its sandy esker ridges and its plentiful waters.

While the long, low sections along the Sudbury River are still largely marshes or swamps, the downstream meadows and fields along the Concord River have been gradually filled in and transformed into dry land for housing. The neighborhood in which I have lived for over thirty years might best be designated the Musketaquid Fens, a fertile area between the confluence of the Assabet and Sudbury Rivers that forms the Concord River. Once the Lee Farm, much of the area experiences some seasonal wetness. Our house is a little over three miles from Walden Pond and less than a mile above the confluence of the Assabet and Sudbury Rivers.

Our street ends at the Assabet. The colonists simply called it the "north river" (with the Sudbury being the "south river"). But the indigenous people called it the Assabet, for its clean, faster-moving waters, which brought minerals and life to the meadows. It is a spirited little river.

In Thoreau's day, the areas north and east of Concord were more settled and civilized then those areas southwest of Concord. Thoreau wrote dreamily about exiting Concord Village over the South Bridge, walking west along the Old Marlborough Road. In his day, it was a rural dirt road following the southeastern shore of the Assabet. Today, the road traverses heavily settled suburbia.

Walking west, once you reach the Assabet River National Wildlife

Refuge in the town of Stow, you can still find a little over a mile of this old rural dirt road preserved. Walking there is transcendental! In the west is wildness, at least if you bring it with you in your soul.

In 1993, we bought my mom a house seven miles west of us on Lake Boon in Stow. That was when I noticed that this small lake emptied into the Assabet. So, one Saturday I put my kayak over the dam and made my way downriver along the Assabet, through Stow and Hudson. I then paddled over into Maynard, where I traversed dirty industrial areas and needed to portage around two industrial dams and over the Damon Mill dam in West Concord. Finally, I arrived at the end of our street. That daylong kayak trip was an ecstatic adventure across space and time.

When I sit at my computer in my home office, I look across our backyard into a small forest of green, whose boggy terrain and deciduous trees remind me of my childhood home. Across from our small wetlands is a horse farm. These undisturbed wetlands provide an animal corridor down to the river. As a result, our backyard is frequented by groundhogs, birds, many deer, an occasional fox, and even peahens roaming from the neighboring farm. We have a sense of living in nature less than a mile outside the original Concord Village.

Kayaking is a form of moving meditation for me. It begins as I walk out from our Chinese red front door, past our lichen-covered Chinese stone lion sentries. Heading down our street, carrying my one-person kayak, I pass increasingly massive suburban houses. I shift the weight of my kayak as I pass the last fire hydrant and enter the woods, walking beneath the evergreens of new-growth forest. By the time I'm on the river, with only bird sounds to distract me, my heart rate slows, and I paddle gently with the current. I paddle with equanimity.

As I circumnavigate rocky shoals and fallen limbs, the edge of Barrett's Mill Farm, the final destination of the British troops on April 19, 1775, appears on the river's northern shore. I am already drifting between Concord's two revolutions: the eighteenth-century civic fight for freedom and the nineteenth-century transcendentalist reimagining of the role of reason and nature in spirituality. This tranquil final mile of the Assabet River is mentioned often in Thoreau's journals, as if he were paddling off into paradise, free of mundane toil and strife. Nirvana.

Hawthorne wrote, "A more lovely stream than this, for a mile above its junction with the Concord, has never flowed on earth—nowhere, indeed, except to the interior regions of a poet's imagination." This is why it's still home, or at least a pilgrim's destination, for transcendentalists today.

On the far side of Barrett's Mill Farm, the Spencer Brook empties into the Assabet from Anglers' Pond, temporarily widening the river to create a great swimming hole. Coming up on the southwestern shore, I pass what had been the site of the Leaning Hemlocks, a favorite nineteenth-century place for walking and picnicking along the river. It was much celebrated in the writings of the transcendentalist authors. Hawthorne wistfully wrote:

> *At one spot there is a lofty bank, on the slope of which*
> *grow some hemlocks, declining across the stream*
> *with outstretched arms, as if resolute to take the*
> *plunge. In other places the banks are almost on a*
> *level with the water; so that the quiet congregation*
> *of trees set their feet in the flood, and are fringed*
> *with foliage down to the surface.*

Water pollution, combined with climate change, has left this section of the river mostly empty of life. But even thirty years ago, when I first paddled it, it had an abundance of fish, water bugs, birds, and turtles. Hawthorne once described:

> *Ducks that had been floating there since the preceding*
> *eve were startled at our approach, and skimmed*
> *along the glassy river, breaking its dark surface*
> *with a bright streak. The pickerel leaped from*
> *among the lily-pads. The turtle, sunning itself upon*
> *a rock or at the root of a tree, slid suddenly into the*
> *water with a plunge.*

The river next turns east through marshland and swamp. Nashawtuc Hill rises before us. Nashawtuc, which in Algonquian means "hill between rivers," is a glacial drumlin rising 250 feet above the Sudbury and Assabet Rivers, just before their confluence.

Many indigenous people once lived within easy walking distance of Nashawtuc Hill most of the year. They spent their summers along the Atlantic coast, where they began interacting with European fishermen and explorers early in the sixteenth century. As autumn approached, the indigenous people would travel back up the Merrimack and Concord Rivers to spend the rest of the year near Nashawtuc Hill.

In the fifteenth century, members of indigenous tribes numbered in the tens of thousands in this area. However, after European contact, a plague broke out among the indigenous people, decimating their numbers. Over the following years, smallpox outbreaks continued to kill off those who had survived the earlier plagues. By the late 1620s, European warfare, enslavement, and diseases had reduced their numbers over 90 percent, to just a few hundreds of indigenous people.

In 1632, William Wood—an English explorer, adventurer, and propagandist—published a pamphlet in London encouraging WASP emigration to Massachusetts. He included a map showing the confluence of these three rivers, which he, like the indigenous people, called the Musketaquid. He described empty meadows and fields for the taking, standing ready to be easily cultivated, as if God intended the land for Englishmen.

Simon Willard was an English beaver-fur trapper who in the 1630s was living in this area among the indigenous people. In September 1635, the General Court of Massachusetts Bay Colony sold Willard and a group of recently arrived English settlers and investors a six-square-mile parcel of land to form Concord at Musketaquid. It was largely built upon the abandoned site of a village of the Massachusett tribe. The investors made peace with the indigenous people but bought the land from the king's agents.

Most of the colonists initially settled on the east side of the Sudbury and Concord Rivers, bordered by the South Bridge on the Sudbury and the North Bridge on the Concord. But Willard chose to make his home on the side of Nashawtuc Hill, near the village site of the few remaining indigenous peoples in the seventeenth century.

Today, Nashawtuc Hill has some of Concord's most expensive and exclusive homes. Yet from the top of this small hill, on what is now known as Willard Common, you can look out across the entire Musketaquid river valley, with Concord Village and First Parish in Concord spread out there before you. You can delight in the wildness of this ancient and beautiful land.

By the end of the seventeenth century, the last fifty-eight indigenous people were rounded up by colonial soldiers and imprisoned near Boston Harbor. Those who did not die were sold into slavery. This is perhaps Concord's original sin. We often try to tell the story differently, but the Anglo-Saxon colonists coming to this land led to the indigenous peoples' deaths and destruction.

In the early nineteenth century, a few Penobscot families occasionally lived in the undeveloped parts of Estabrook Woods, the Great Meadow, or near Walden Pond. One indigenous woman eked out a living weaving and selling baskets made of native materials.

As he walked Musketaquid, Thoreau dreamed of a time and culture more attuned to nature's wildness. He wrote, "There on Nashawtuc was their lodge, the rendezvous of the tribe, and yonder, on Clamshell Hill their feasting ground." He imagined a time when the indigenous people were loving, feasting, and walking through the woods. Over twenty-five thousand specimens of their stone weapons and cooking implements have been found in this area.

Thoreau and his older brother, John, would rise early to saunter over to Nashawtuc Hill to watch the sunrise over the Musketaquid river valley and commune with the ancestors they imagined lived here for thousands of years before them. Thoreau often dreamed of walking in the footsteps of Tahattawan, the chief of one of the tribes that welcomed the English. Thoreau frequently found many stone arrowheads, and he imagined Tahattawan had used them in his hunting. Thereby, Thoreau communed with the spirit of this place.

As my kayak approached the Assabet's end, the north bank of the river was entirely muck and marsh. The south bank, thanks to Nashawtuc Hill, remains high and dry straight out to its low promontory point, a rock formation known as Egg Rock. When the rivers run high, they can flood the fens behind the point, leaving Egg Rock as its own small, egg-shaped island at the confluence of the three rivers.

The rock face bears an 1885 inscription, made for the 250th anniversary of Concord's state charter. It says, "On the hill Nashawtuc at the meeting of the rivers and along the banks lived the Indian owners of Musketaquid before the white men came." It is mute about what happened to them.

To preserve at least a little of the feeling of the ancient Musketaquid, the Concord Land Conservation Trust has permanently conserved the Davis and Sherwood Red Maple Swamps to the river's north; part of an area known as the Old Calf Pasture across the river to its east; and French's Meadow, which includes many acres, to its south. This was the axis mundi, sacred center, of the world of the local indigenous tribes and of Thoreau when he lived just a very short walk up along the Sudbury River. Given where my family has put down our roots in Concord, it also remains an axis mundi for me. All my travels, wherever I roam, bring me home here.

If I paddle up the Sudbury, it takes me along the campus of Concord Academy and past the homes of Concord's most prominent nineteenth-century abolitionists, located as they were in the neighborhood between Concord Center and the train station. Continuing upriver, I pass Concord's popular South Bridge canoe and kayak rental establishment, always busy on a summer day. I next pass the Old South Bridge and metal railroad bridge, bringing us past Emerson Hospital. Just beyond the hospital is the current site of Newbury Court, the assisted-living complex where my mother lived the last twelve years of her life.

Throughout the nineteenth century, this ancient mound was known as Clamshell Bank and was Concord's most prolific precolonial archaeological site. Based upon the mounds of clamshells that have been discovered, archaeologists estimate that as many as twelve thousand native people might have joined in these feasts.

Continuing up the Sudbury past the Nut Meadow Brook brings me past Conantum and eventually out into Fairhaven Bay. A placid pond in the river, Fairhaven Bay is a mile west of Walden Pond and was one of Thoreau's favorite places to end the day. So much wildness can be seen and experienced in this six-square-mile heaven on earth.

Alternatively, I could head downstream along the Concord River. After a short bend in the river, I would encounter the Old Manse on my right, immediately followed by a replica of the Old North Bridge—arguably the sites where Concord's two revolutions began. Then the Minute Man Visitor Center would be on the hill on my left, with Punkatasset Hill clearly visible behind it. The Great Meadows National Wildlife Refuge would occupy a long stretch of the river on my right. And if I were to stay on this river, leaving Concord, it would eventually take me to the Merrimack River—and from there, paddling with equanimity to the sea.

Concord Village

However, many people today enter Concord by car from the west, first encountering the Concord rotary and then the Concord state prison. The prison is Concord's most racist institution. There, working-class white guards watch over the imprisoned souls, who are predominantly poor men of color. In a town known worldwide for freedom, white supremacy still holds sway in so many ways.

While many approach Concord Village from the west by car, I prefer to do so on foot. From my house in the Musketaquid Fens along the river, reaching the village requires only a little meandering. I first set out along the animal corridor, but I quickly sink into muck and mire. I next try walking along the south bank of the Assabet, toward Egg Rock.

Thirty years ago, I could trek that route with little difficulty. Today, though, I find my way blocked by marshy ground, briar patches, and redirected flows of water caused by the massive new construction of houses on the back side of Nashawtuc Hill. After several attempts, muddy and scratched, I return home to try another way to walk along the Assabet.

I walk out to Elm Street, and then one block east to Musketa-quid Road; from there, I turn left onto Simon Willard Road. I can make my way along dry paths through Simon Willard Woods to the river less than a quarter mile from my home. I can then follow the abandoned Reformatory Branch Rail trail over Concord Land Conservation Trust property to visit the Leaning Hemlocks site. Clearly marked trails easily lead me along the river and out to the promontory of Egg Rock, where I can watch midday traffic on the river. The trail then leads along French's Meadow to where the old rail bridge once crossed the Sudbury River.

The Reformatory Branch Trail picks up again on the east side of the Sudbury River, along the southern edge of the Old Calf Pasture. If I follow it across Keyes Road, it will take me all the way past the North Bridge to the Great Meadows; or, instead, I can follow the Mill Brook back toward Concord Village.

The Mill Brook today flows slow and shallow behind the First Parish meetinghouse, then drops underground to cross Main Street. Just past Main Street Markets and Café, it reemerges into a quiet brook that meanders next to the town's visitor center and largest public parking lot.

A lovely wooden footbridge is hidden away here in the heart of the town. It crosses the Mill Brook and travels through the Chamberlin Park, a little hidden pocket park. This hidden path emerges up alongside the Christian Science church.

Walking back along the Lowell Road brings me to what remains of the Concord town common, now known as Monument Square. It is surrounded by Concord's Colonial Inn, Concord Town House, the Roman Catholic church and rectory, Old Hill Burying Ground, the

First Parish meetinghouse, Wright's Tavern, and the Masonic hall. This common has been Concord's civic and spiritual center for nearly four hundred years. Like most seventeenth-century New England villages, Concord was laid out along familiar patterns. Concord had a large, grassy common with its meetinghouse, with houses beneath the esker ridge along the Bay Road that led through the wilderness to what would become the town of Lexington, and eventually Boston Harbor and the Massachusetts Bay. It is now the Lexington Road.

More houses and shops ran perpendicular along Main Street. The colonists dammed the Mill Brook at the site of an indigenous people's fish weir to create a millpond with enough water pressure to mill wheat and corn flour. Later, as the seat of Middlesex County, Concord used its shrinking common land for its growing public purposes.

Of the six square miles the founders of Concord laid out for the village, less than two square miles at the center were given over to houses, shops, the common, and village activities. This central village was surrounded by fields, which the farmers drained and ditched to grow all the food the town consumed in a year. Surrounding these cultivated fields were the large, marshy meadows, often left in their watery conditions. Enormous quantities of marsh grass were grown for livestock and for domestic needs. This was a tidy little English village in the midst of a dark and wild wilderness.

Wood-burning and water were the major sources of energy in colonial times. This meant that an even bigger area nearby needed to be given over to woodlots to provide the many cords each household burned. Beyond the village, fields, meadows, and woodlots were large areas of wasteland, deemed unfit by topography, conditions, or distance from the commons to be worth cultivating. These were often left in a semi-wild state of nature.

The Massachusetts Bay Colony was founded in 1630 as a theocracy, and Concord has always been a deeply spiritual place. In July 1636, the First Parish Church in Concord was founded. It was located within the meetinghouse, the town's first—and initially only—public building. The meetinghouse was in the eastern corner of the burial ridge on the north side of the Bay Road.

As the town grew, a bigger assembly hall was needed, so in 1673, a larger, square meetinghouse was built across the street, overlooking the millpond on the southeastern corner of the common. This new meetinghouse could accommodate worship services, town meetings, public addresses, and the county courts. From 1673 to 1719, the meetinghouse was used for weekly worship as well as town meetings and county government.

Gradually, other public buildings—schoolhouses, taverns, hotels, and stores—were added around the common. Beginning in 1719, the Middlesex County offices—including the courts, living quarters, and jail—frequently changed locations around the common. From 1789, they occupied what is now the Holy Family rectory.

At the end of the eighteenth century, Middlesex County constructed a new courthouse opposite Concord's Colonial Inn. Then, in the first half of the nineteenth century, the county offices moved to a building on the current site of Concord's Town House. Concord's changing public buildings reflect the changing nature of the local government over centuries. The common, in its greatly shrunken form, is now called Monument Square for its war memorials.

Thoreau lived most of his life within a stone's throw of this shrinking town common, either in a red brick house near the common or in the various houses his family rented or owned along the upper part of Main Street. All roads led to Concord. Concord was his Rome.

The meetinghouse was renovated and expanded again in 1791. For the first time, a church steeple and a bell were added, but it was still used for both the town's religious and secular purposes.

For years, church and state had been intimately intertwined. But this all began to change as the Constitution of the Commonwealth of Massachusetts was ratified in 1780 and as the former colony became part of the United States of America at the end of the eighteenth century. And after the 1833 disestablishment of religion in Massachusetts, the long and tedious process of separating church and state, civic and spiritual, began on the town level.

This is the era from which Thoreau and Emerson emerged. Thoreau was baptized at First Parish, then watched his aunts break away to form the Trinitarian Congregational Church, Concord's second church. He then watched his friends build Concord's First Universalist church—the building is now the Roman Catholic church. But by that time, the young college graduate had resigned from First Parish. He would henceforth find his connection to divine mystery in the wildness of nature and through the pilgrim journey of his own soul.

Finally, at a 1850 town meeting, there was a vote to create Concord's first townhouse for all secular purposes on the former site of the county offices. That building originally included the town offices, the town records, the public library, and classrooms for intermediate and high school students. It also featured a large second-story town hall for public meetings and lectures.

First Parish, with its roots still tied to the original town meeting-house, saw its own changes during this time. The congregation remodeled its sanctuary in 1841 and reoriented the church to face Lexington Road, rather than the shops on the Milldam stretch of Main Street. Following a devastating fire in 1900, they rebuilt the entire building for a fifth time. With each transformation, it became a more suitable gathering space for religious and spiritual uses.

Town and church had finally, amicably, parted ways. And encountering divine mystery in Concord's wildness would become an increasingly secular pursuit—spirituality without the need for religion.

When you stand before the fifth First Parish meetinghouse, take a moment to reflect upon its changing role over the centuries. Notice the partial remains of the bell from the fire that destroyed the fourth meetinghouse. This bell rang to call the townsfolk to important meetings.

Perhaps sit for a while in the left front balcony of the sanctuary, where Emerson regularly sat glowering as poor Reverend Barzillai Frost delivered his seemingly inadequate Sunday sermons. Richardson writes, "Frost's style was abstract and dull . . . Emerson was driven frantic as he sat and listened." Thoreau went to the woods; Emerson stayed and complained.

Pick up a volume of *Singing the Living Tradition*, the 1993 UUA hymnal used each Sunday for worship. Notice its seven readings from Tagore, six from Emerson, five from Lao-Tzu, and only one from Thoreau. Sense its overwhelming focus on the celebration of life, transcendence, seasons of nature, transience, and mystical songs. Or turn to the back for meditations and prayers, wisdom from the world's religions, Jewish and Christian teachings, humanist teachings, and readings for ceremonial occasions.

As UU minister Reverend Doctor Jonipher Kūpono Kwong says: "We take refuge in all that is holy. We take refuge in sacred teachings throughout the ages. We take refuge in our community of faith and in the interdependent web of life." Unitarian Universalists often take refuge in the Spirit of Life.

If you exit the meetinghouse from the religious education wing, you can walk the congregation's meander labyrinth used for spiritual reflection. I often lead groups through the labyrinth as a form of Unitarian Universalist mindfulness walking meditation:

> *Focus with your heart,*
> *guiding your steps toward your goal,*
> *undeterred when the path leads out into wildness.*
> *Walk with equanimity, even when the way forward*
> * is unclear.*
> *This path is leading you into your Way, your Truth.*
> *Pay attention to the twists and turns,*
> *Bringing you ever closer, and then further away.*
> *This is the Way of the mystic. Know thy Self.*

Walking east from the meetinghouse along Lexington Road, Thoreau would have passed Revolutionary-era houses and trees. Many of them, thanks to the Historic District Commission, still line that ancient roadway today. Concordians live in our history and in our present moment.

Just east of the common, there are stone steps down into a sunken parcel of conservation land across from Heywood Meadow. It was once the easternmost part of the old millpond, before it was drained and filled in the nineteenth century. Walking mindfully, we can experience transcendental echoes of the indigenous and early American mystics who traveled these paths before us.

Walking Walden Country

If Thoreau entered the woods behind Emerson's house, it was less than a two-mile walk to the cabin site on Walden Pond. This is a path Emerson and Thoreau often walked. Now called the Emerson-Thoreau Amble trail, it is perhaps the prettiest and most meaningful trail in the town of Concord. Despite Concord's modern transition into a wealthy Boston suburb, this trail retains a transcendental feeling. I often walk it ecstatically as a spiritual pilgrim.

The trail begins at the southeast corner of Heywood Meadow, traversing overgrown, marshy fields that once had been cultivated for growing food. But when the 1845 railroad line made transportation faster and less expensive, it put many Concord farmers out of business.

Our trail roughly follows the meandering path of the Mill Brook. Invasive shrubs and wildflowers are joined by a dizzying array of moisture-loving plants and briars. Thoreau claimed credit for introducing the lovely but invasive watercress that grows abundantly in the Mill Brook even today. Thoreau was not an environmentalist in the modern sense, but he loved fecundity and wildness.

The trail circumnavigates the Concord police and fire station before crossing over the Mill Brook. It travels along the border of a still-worked field. The trail touches the edge of Walden Street before turning southeast to avoid the Concord community gardens, public housing, and the new Concord District Court. The skyline views include some of Concord's largest and oldest hardwood trees, which turn glorious shades of yellow, orange, and red every autumn.

The trail turns onto a wide cart path and passes the now-vacant building of the Concord Ice Company before traversing another wooden bridge across the ditch draining Hugh Cargill's Stratton Farm.

Cargill was a wealthy late-eighteenth-century Boston innkeeper who retired in Concord to become a gentleman farmer. On his death, he bequeathed his farm to the town of Concord for the benefit of the poor. In *Walden*, Thoreau mentions traversing "the present dusty highway, from the Stratton, now the Alms House Farm, to Brister's Hill."

Our trail now crosses over into the Hapgood Wright Town Forest. We have left the formal domain of Concord Village and are entering tangled woodlands. Just a few steps beyond civilization, you can feel the wood's wildness.

Despite marshy areas continuing off to the left and the right, we are following an esker ridge path that is elevated and drier. There is a pleasant change in vegetation as a result. It has wildness enough for me to surrender to the spirit of this place. I focus my breathing and thoughts, living life fully and engaged, living transcendentally. I breathe more deeply. A weight has been lifted from my spirit. I am at home in the forest.

I become one with the woods. This part of the wildness journey brings me a sense of peace and happiness. As Thoreau observed in his journal:

> *We do not commonly live our life out and full; we do
> not fill all our pores with our blood; we do not
> inspire and expire fully and entirely enough,
> so that the wave ... of each inspiration, shall
> break upon our extremest shores, rolling till it
> meets the sand which bounds us, and the sound
> of the surf come back to us. ... We live but a
> fraction of our life. Why do we not let on the
> flood, raise the gates, and set all our wheels in
> motion? He that hath ears to hear, let him hear.
> Employ your senses.*

I wander beneath pine trees. Their needles carpet the ground, and the dappled sun breaks through between the dark trees. The trail comes to a T junction. It is best to turn left, deeper into this small forest. I am now in the uncultivated world that Thoreau loved in his day. Wildness occupies my consciousness. We are made for wildness at the borders of civilized society.

The reedy brook feeding this swamp wasn't dammed until well after Thoreau's time. Now, this way brings us down to Fairyland Pond. In my own Way, I ritually sacramentalize this space and time as I transcendentally travel through it. This nearly three-acre shallow pond casts an affective spell.

Beavers are quite active downstream of the pond, which has transformed into their swampy habitat. You can sometimes find their houses and come upon their gnawed tree stumps. But here, upstream, the lovely pond is maintained through an ingenious beaver-foiling innovation: the inflow and outflow water is channeled under the dams. That way, humans can enjoy the lovely forest pond, and the industrious beavers can enjoy their swampy, wet habitat.

Fairyland Pond is fed by Brister's Spring, making it one of several hidden fountainheads of the Mill Brook. The spring is located above the top of the pond, near where our trail ascends steeply up Brister's Hill. As it crosses the hill, the trail finally leaves the Musketaquid valley watershed and enters into the westerly-flowing Walden Pond watershed.

We are once again transcendentally crossing through space and time as pilgrims. We have left behind the cultivated parts of Concord Village, with its businesses, houses, fields, meadows, and woodlots. Now we have entered what in the eighteenth century was considered wasteland, uncultivated and worthless woodlands, between the towns of Concord and Lincoln.

Thoreau remembers this hill as the home of Freeman Brister, a previously enslaved African American who kept an orchard on this dry ridge. His wife fetched all their water from the spring below and carried it up the steep hill. Back breaking work and a daily choir.

In the 1990s, a developer tried to build an office park over the abandoned orchard, alongside what is now the busy commuter highway

Route 2. In response, Walden lovers—including, importantly, Don Henley of the Eagles rock band—raised millions of dollars through the Walden Woods Project to buy up and conserve this part of Walden country. I'm told they said they were seeking to preserve Concord's "wilderness," but I think they meant "wildness."

The trails they built here provide a lovely walk through where Brister's orchard once stood. There are plaques with quotes from Thoreau and others, including "in Wildness is the preservation of the world." At the heart of the nature park, they built a meditation circle that by itself is well worth the visit. Exiting the Walden Woods Project land, the trail then crosses Walden Street and Route 2 to enter into the Walden Pond State Reservation.

The wilds beyond Brister's Hill were part of the uncultivated woodlands where the poor and marginalized sometimes lived as squatters. Irish immigrants lived here or in a shantytown along the railroad lines. When enslaved African American workers were released into freedom, they often received permission to live in these woods as well. And indigenous people passing through Concord often squatted in these woods temporarily.

Thoreau would have crossed down the Old County Road and then a few thousand feet farther to his cabin site. Today, the park has Do Not Enter signs directing us around the edge of the park, along Walden Street. When Loretta and I first adopted Concord as our home in 1986, this route along Walden Street passed a trash dump and a run-down trailer park. In modern times, the dump has been transformed into a composting site and transfer station with acres of solar panels, and the state park has absorbed the now-defunct trailer park. Disorganized and uncultivated wastelands gradually turned into carefully curated wildness.

The Emerson-Thoreau Amble quickly reenters the woods to take us toward Thoreau's bean-field and his experiment in living in the woods. Of his bean-field, Thoreau wrote, "I came to love my rows, my beans, though so many more than I wanted. They attached me to the earth." For Thoreau, hoeing his beans was a transcendental experience. His beanfield became the size of two football fields and earned him $8.71 profit.

When Emerson purchased fourteen acres a mile southeast of Concord—a woodlot by Walden Pond—Henry immediately wanted to live freely at the pond. His nearest neighbors were the marginalized and dispossessed. He wrote, "East of my bean-field, across the road, lived Cato Ingraham, slave of Duncan Ingraham, Esquire, gentleman, of Concord village, who built his slave a house, and gave him permission to live in Walden Woods." Also, "Here, by the very corner of my field, still nearer to town, Zilpha, a colored woman, had her little house, where she spun linen for the townsfolk."

Thoreau wrote fondly of Brister Freeman , his wife Fenda, and the poor Irish living in hovels and shacks along the railroad tracks. He seemingly felt freer living among the marginalized and oppressed then he did among the churchgoing WASP villagers and farmers.

Walden Pond

Each year, over half a million visitors make their pilgrimage to Walden Pond. They come from around the United States and from around the world. Often having read Thoreau's transcendental descriptions in *Walden*, they seek to experience it for themselves. They are seldom disappointed.

Thoreau's moving to the pond may have been a form of penance for surviving after his brother died. Thoreau was a spiritual pilgrim, a sojourner from ordinary life, at the pond. Yet he remained very much open and eager to what life had to teach him. He wrote, "I have traveled a good deal in Concord; and everywhere, in shops, and offices, and fields, the inhabitants have appeared to me to be doing penance in a thousand remarkable ways."

But Thoreau had no need—nor patience—for guilt or penance as quiet desperation. Rather, he simply embraced his life fully in all its goodness and meanness. In his journal, two days after settling at the pond, Thoreau wrote, "I wish to meet the facts of life—the vital facts,

which are the phenomena or actuality the gods meant to show us—
face to face, and so I came down here. Life! Who knows what it is,
what it does?"

Thoreau had spent the previous summer living in the quiet
camp of a saw miller in the Catskill Mountains. Now he wished to
experience the same wildness here as a spiritual pilgrim in Concord.
Thoreau's experiment in living at Walden Pond was his form of self-
culture to transcend self-centeredness.

It was often a mystical experience. He wrote about becoming
ecstatically immersed in nature. He remembered,

> *Regularly at half-past seven, in one part of the*
> *summer, after the evening train had gone by,*
> *the whip-poor-wills chanted their vespers for*
> *half an hour, sitting on a stump by my door, or*
> *upon the ridge-pole of the house. They would*
> *begin to sing almost with as much precision as*
> *a clock, within five minutes of a particular time,*
> *referred to the setting of the sun, every evening.*
> *I had a rare opportunity to become acquainted*
> *with their habits.*

Writing in *Walden* of his time living in the woods, he also recalled:

> *As I came home through the woods with a string of fish,*
> *trailing my pole, it being now quite dark, I caught*
> *a glimpse of a woodchuck stealing across my path,*
> *and felt a strange thrill of savage delight, and was*
> *strongly tempted to seize and devour him raw; not*
> *that I was hungry then, except for that wildness*
> *which he represented.*

In wildness, Thoreau found the preservation of the world. Yet I
should caution: the transcendentalists' distinction between wilderness and wildness often confounds those who embrace their writings. The word *wilderness* implies being untouched and unchanged

by human activities. Such wilderness was long gone in Concord by the early nineteenth century. *Wildness*, however, implies nature untamed by humans. And in nineteenth-century Concord, there was much wildness. Even today it is in our midst—if we can but see it.

Some environmentalists mistakenly claim Thoreau said, "in wilderness is the preservation of the world." But in fact, he had an important metaphysical point to make: it is in wildness that the world is transformed, as is our relationship to the world. We can engage such wildness only if we give up our illusions of control, surrender our egos, and enter as coequal participants rather than masters or dominators of nature. We are in and part of such wildness.

The woods around the pond reflect wildness at every season of the year. In springtime, the bursting forth of new and vibrant life is glorious as one circumambulates the pond. On warm summer afternoons, the nearside beach is swarming with families and swimmers. During the height of fall leaf-peeping, the glorious colors of leaves puts death in a proper perspective. And the thick winter ice, beloved by skaters and ice fishermen, makes for a wonderful ice-harp if we skip stones, as Emerson once did. There is real beauty in every changing weather condition, time of day, and season.

Water flows downhill from the higher grounds around the visitor center and parking area, through the pond, under the railroad tracks, and over to Fairhaven Bay. Walden's sandy soil is a perfect conduit for this slow-moving underground stream. Walden Pond is Massachusetts's deepest lake. And thanks to sandy filtering of moving water, it is often its clearest lake, though most days it's not half as clear as it was in Thoreau's time.

Thoreau graduated from college in 1837, during one of the worst recessions in the country's history. Initially, he could not find a job. He lived for six weeks that summer with his college roommate in a temporary hut on the shore of the nearby Flint's Pond. Then he became a Concord schoolteacher, but evidently was no better at it than Emerson had been.

The recession of 1837 lasted seven years. America was finally emerging from a deeply depressed economy when Thoreau again took to the woods, this time with a higher purpose and transcendental intent. That spring of 1845, Henry built a small, bare, ten-foot-by-fifteen-foot cabin by the pond. It cost only $28.12 ½ cents.

Here is why it was so cheap: In early spring, Thoreau heard that an Irish day laborer living near the pond was moving his family west in order to avoid debts he owed his landlord for his rent and fuel the previous winter. The Irishman had built a shanty too small for his large family and too heavy to take with them, and he feared the landlord would confiscate it to settle his debt. Thoreau offered to buy and relocate this shack to a site on Emerson's land before the landlord knew what had happened.

Then, in the beginning of May, he raised the frame of his cabin with the help of some friends. He scavenged whatever materials he could from various farmers and neighbors and paid cash only for everything else. Thus, Thoreau managed to build a small cabin in the woods, with a woodshed but no outhouse, for 5 percent of the cost of a normal house.

The cabin might have passed as a mere toolshed or perhaps a clubhouse for boys. He compared it to the wigwams of the indigenous people. But the simple accomplishment of building the modest cabin brought Thoreau great joy. It would be his happy place! He was equally pleased with his worn-out, unfashionable clothes, which he used to make a strong statement against the emerging materialism of his time.

He could live ecstatically in Concord as a simple spiritual pilgrim. Living at the pond put Thoreau in touch with a simpler and more embodied Way of being:

> *Once or twice, however, while I lived at the pond,*
> *I found myself ranging the woods, like a half-*
> *starved hound, with a strange abandonment,*
> *seeking some kind of venison which I might*
> *devour, and no morsel could have been too*
> *savage for me. The wildest scenes had become*

*unaccountably familiar. I found in myself, and still
find, an instinct toward a higher, or, as it is named,
spiritual life, as do most men, and another toward
a primitive rank and savage one, and I reverence
them both. I love the wild not less than the good.*

However, Thoreau didn't completely withdraw from society while living at Walden Pond. He still remained actively involved with life in Concord. He raised beans and potatoes for his fellow townspeople and sometimes worked as a carpenter, gardener, and surveyor. He was a frequent fixture at Concord social occasions—despite his eccentric clothes.

He also wrote the first draft of his book *A Week on the Concord and Merrimack Rivers.* Like Emerson, he went on the lecture circuit, speaking about life in the woods, though he never made much money at it.

He had frequent visits from Hawthorne, Emerson, the poet Ellery Channing, and Bronson Alcott. Many other visitors would travel out from Boston. They often marveled that he could live on so little. However, none offered to try it themselves.

As active and social as he could sometimes be, Thoreau also relished his solitude. He could, like Chuang Tzu, dry his hair resting in the ground of being. In fairyland, there are no limits to sacred space or sense of time. As he wrote in *Walden:*

*Sometimes, in a summer morning, having taken my
accustomed bath, I sat in my sunny doorway
from sunrise until noon, rapt in reverie, amidst
the pines, hickories and sumac, in undisturbed
solitude and stillness, while the birds sang around
and flitted noiseless through the house, until by the
sun falling in at my west window, or the noise of
some traveler's wagon on the distant highway, I
was reminded of the lapse of time.*

In the Bhagavad Gita, Krishna teaches Arjuna to transcend the ego through self-culture. In *Walden*, Thoreau describes a similar experiment in living. In the 1840s, Emerson often found his grounding in his study; Hawthorne, in the Old Manse; and Thoreau, in his cabin by the pond. These three each transcended self through their particular forms of self-culture.

All three, like many German idealists and the English romantics, also adopted walking in nature as their spiritual practice. Thoreau raised sauntering to a high art form. He walked long distances in every season, in every weather, and everywhere. He could set out in a westerly direction shortly after dawn and find himself already in Fitchburg, some twenty-three miles away, as night fell. From dawn hikes to afternoon saunters to moonlight strolls, walking became his primary self-culture to transcend the ego and become one with God. This has now become my primary spiritual practice as well.

On July 12, 1847, Henry David Thoreau turned thirty. That September, Thoreau moved back into his room at the top of the stairs in Emerson's house, while Emerson left on a lecture tour to England.

His manuscript for *A Week on the Concord and Merrimack Rivers*—which was dedicated to his deceased brother, John—could never find a publisher, so after four years Thoreau borrowed funds from friends to publish a thousand copies of the book on his own in 1849. He was now an author. He sold his cabin for scavenged parts.

Living as a Spiritual Pilgrim

Walden Pond has become part of my own spiritual journey. On pleasant days, I meditate at the former site of Thoreau's cabin or wander along the pond's rocky shores and azure waters.

I circumnavigate Ice Fort Cove, once the site of Walden Pond's shantytown for poor Irish immigrants. I then traverse the railroad's Deep Cut Woods. This is where, in the late winter of 1847, Thoreau watched hundreds of Irish laborers, each "armed with a double-pointed pike-staff," harvest vast quantities of large blocks of Walden Pond ice to be shipped by rail to Boston and beyond. It is said Walden Pond ice made its way by steamship to New York City, New Orleans, Bombay, and Calcutta.

Following the American Civil War, the whole western end of the pond was clear-cut, and a rail station was constructed. This broad expanse was used first for religious revivals, then it was turned into a large amusement park bringing thousands of visitors to what they called Lake Walden. In the 1870s, sometimes as many as thirty-five railroad cars would arrive on a summer day. These day-trippers, out to enjoy the wild, were unaware of, and uninterested by, where Thoreau's sojourner cabin had once been.

Some days I cross over the railroad tracks and make my way to the cliffs overlooking Fairhaven Bay on the Sudbury River. It was one of Thoreau's favorite short saunters. Crossing the railroad tracks at the southwestern corner of Walden Pond, I am careful to look and listen both ways. Trains travel fast here, far from any road or junction. But this section of track is relatively straight, so you can hear the trains from far away. The clickity-clack is a frequent sound at Walden.

Once I cross over, out of the state park, three trails lie before me on the far side of the tracks. If I go to the left, this trail will connect me with Lincoln's extensive trail system, and there will be a great view of Fairhaven Bay from the top of Mount Misery. If I go to the right, this trail will lead me meandering toward the lower Sudbury River, arriving just upstream of the historical site of indigenous people's clam feasts on the river.

But, as usual, it is best to take the Middle Way. This trail passes between bogs and wetlands, over small hills, and through shady dales. It descends into a broad and straight wooden path, ideal for mountain bikes and horses. It is the most direct route through the Adams Woods conservation land to paradise.

When this trail ends at a T junction, I turn right and look for the sign marking the Fairhaven Trail. This trail wanders the edges of the Fairhaven marshes and eventually leads to a gorgeous overview looking across Fairhaven Bay. This was one of Emerson's and Thoreau's favorite places from which to watch the late-afternoon sun shimmer across the surface of the bay and set over the Conantum neighborhood of Concord. The transcendentalist poet Ellery Channing waxed eloquent about the beauty of this overlook.

I stand here, just above where I paddled upriver days before. Then I begin my long walk home, with both my transcendental teacher and my transcendental life coach by my side. I am at peace.

Seeking to break life open, to suck all the marrow out of its brittle bones, I have fasted on mountains in Vermont, traveled to Turkey with Sufis, hiked mountains in China with Taoists, subjected myself to shamanic mysteries in South America, and traversed the mystic Ganges and the Mekong Rivers. I have walked with Buddha and Jesus, experienced the oneness with divine mystery, and wrestled with Pythagoras and Zoroaster. I have traveled the world as a spiritual pilgrim.

And now I have returned home again. I have found a peace that surpasses understanding and an equanimity in life.

From the Buddhist perspective, I have discovered that from *dukkha*, or suffering, comes forth *sukha*, or equanimity. Or as Rudolf Steiner writes,

> *We must eradicate from the soul all fear and terror of what comes towards [humanity] out of the future. We must acquire serenity in all feelings and sensations about the future. We must look forward with absolute equanimity to everything that may come. And we must think only that whatever comes is given to us by a world-directive full of wisdom.*

Our future is uncertain—never more so than today. But I rest on the bosom of God, within the inexplicably interconnected Spirit of Life that gives meaning to my spiritual journey.

I have great empathy for those people who trust only the realities they can sense directly through sight, sound, or touch. I understand why they sense that the earth is flat, that the sun literally rises and the moon shines. For them, God doesn't exist in such a reality, as God is not perceivable solely through our senses.

I have even greater empathy for those who employ both their senses and their reason in framing their reality. They know the earth is round and circles around the sun. And they know the moon's glow is merely reflected sunlight. A reason-based religion, however, can either affirm or deny God's existence, because we can rationally explain these experiences with or without the concept of God.

But having traveled with mystics and having practiced their spiritual disciplines, my consciousness has been greatly changed. I have no doubts about the existence or love of God. I am part and particle of God. I employ my senses, my reason, and my intuition. Together, they lead me to know myself as a beloved child of God. And sometimes when in a deeply meditative state, perhaps while walking in the wilds of Concord, I experience the inexplicably interconnected ecstasy of complete and total union with the divine. This is my source of peace and equanimity.

I continue to discover new wonders and adventures in Concord while walking around White Pond, the October Farm, the Old Rifle Range, and the Wright Woods. Friends have introduced me to the privately owned Hundred Acre Woods, the Farmers Cliff trail leading into Estabrook Woods, the wildness surrounding Massport trails near Hanscom Field airport, and so many other hidden treasures both public and private. With over ninety miles of trails in Concord, one could walk daily here for decades and still have more transcendental treasures to discover.

Yet I wonder, how many people have lived in Concord much of their lives and have never discovered even a small portion of the treasures this axis mundi holds? Residing in the tameness of their homes, most people miss the wildness of the woods. Thoreau would say they are trapped in a consumerist existence, which ignores the transcendental wildness surrounding them.

When I regularly circumnavigate Walden Pond, the patterns in the pure water reflect back to me the Ganges and the Mekong. This cold, deep kettle pond attracts the world to our axis mundi. I have no higher aspiration left than to say, with Henry, that I have traveled widely in Concord and have known life for what it is and what it can be, in the company of mystic saints.

I have so many traveling companions—of this world and no longer of this world—who have achieved union with divine mystery and helped me on my Way. As I walk the woods of Concord and meditate while meandering, the spirits of Waldo and Henry travel with me, but so do those of Michael, Jesus, Immanuel, Bernard, Hildegard, Francis, Meister, Teresa, Mirabai, Kabir, Siddhartha, Jacob, Mary, Hafiz, Ibrahim, Rumi, Shams, Ismael, Chuang Tzu, and Odin. I am well and richly blessed. Becoming spiritually grounded in God was never merely an intellectual exercise. These were mystic journeys of awakening.

Yet no longer do I feel the need for great and distant pilgrimages, for now I can simply still my monkey mind and experience the presence of the divine. Rumi described it as becoming so hollowed out and full of God that the breath of God plays you like a holy lute. Dear God, let your holy breath play through me.

My favorite image, however, is Hafiz's intimate description of this state of being: "God and I have become like two giant fat people living in a tiny boat. We keep bumping into each other and giggling."

Thoreau's lifelong pilgrimage ended in 1862. He died of tuberculosis at age forty-five and was buried in his beloved Concord.

Emerson, in writing Thoreau's eulogy, said,

> *Mr. Thoreau dedicated his genius with such entire love to the fields, hills, and waters of his native town, that he made them known and interesting to all reading Americans, and to people over the sea. . . . His soul was made for the noblest society; he had in a short life exhausted the capabilities of the world; wherever there is knowledge, wherever there is virtue, wherever there is beauty, he will find a home.*

In this delightful eulogy, Emerson's one criticism was that Thoreau preferred leading a huckleberry party more than making a significant contribution to the world.

Now I am home, having far outlived Thoreau. I am fast approaching the age of Waldo's greatest fecundity as a public lecturer. Having lived most of my adult life in Concord, I am now also a spiritual pilgrim of the world, traveling widely—including in Concord. Every day, in every way, I try to embrace my life more fully.

I have been humbled and privileged to travel an ancient path and draw on living waters in my spiritual journey toward awakening and enlightenment. I have become a pilgrim soul. To quote one of my favorite UU hymns: "Sing out praises for the journey, pilgrims, we, who carry on. Searchers in the soul's deep yearnings, like our forebears in their time. . . . Stand we now upon the threshold, facing futures yet unknown. Hearth behind us, wayside hostel built by those who knew wild roads." Having traveled many wild roads, my pilgrimages became my Way.

To paraphrase Henry: O blessed serendipity, that I have lived my life in precisely the right place, and in the nick of time. For everything changes, and life is so precious and fleeting and deserving of transcendental experiences.

I am awake—no longer needing to be international strategy consultant, chief financial officer, chief executive officer, venture catalyst, parish minister, or doctor of ministry. I am content to live transcendentally, walking the wild woods as Huckleberry Jim, embracing ultimate reality as it embraces me.

Perhaps one day you'll join me.

Transcendentalist Mystics
BOOK GROUP DISCUSSION GUIDE

Author's Comment

One path to spiritual awakening is to travel the world as a pilgrim—even if only by experiencing such a journey through a memoir. You can embark from the comfort of your favorite armchair and then return to wherever you call home and know it for the first time. During the thirty-plus years Loretta and I have lived in Concord, I have traveled the world on spiritual pilgrimages, and now I am home.

Questions to Encourage Conversation

1. What is so special about Concord that the author calls it an axis mundi?

2. Why does the author enter Concord from the north along the Old Carlisle Road?

3. How does that route contrast with paddling the rivers from the south?

4. What is the difference between wildness and wilderness?

5. Do you perceive the transcendentalists as romantic idealists?

6. To what extent are you a nature mystic?

7. Is there someplace you know so well, it can be your spiritual home?

8. What simple accomplishment brings you such joy as building the cabin did Thoreau?

9. What place or experience most often brings you a sense of transcendence?

Reflection:

As a group, reflect upon how you will live differently for having read this book.

POTENTIAL FURTHER READING

Islamic

Barks, Coleman. *The Essential Rumi.* New York: Quality Paperback, 1995.

Barks, Coleman and John Moyne. *The Drowned Book: Ecstatic and Earthy Reflections of Bahauddin, the Father of Rumi.* San Francisco: Harper Collins, 2004.

Ladinsky, Daniel, translator. *The Gift: Poems by Hafiz.* New York: Penguin, 1999.

Ladinsky, Daniel, translator. *I Heard God Laughing.* New York: Penguin, 2006.

Nicholson, Reynold, translator. *The Mathnawi of Jalaluddin Rumi.* Kindle edition. Amazon Digital Services, 2015.

Nicholson, Reynold, translator. *A Rumi Anthology.* Oxford, England: One World, 2001.

Chinese

Ames, Roger and Henry Rosemont, Jr. *The Analects of Confucius.* New York: Ballantine, 1998.

Ames, Roger and David Hall. *Dao De Jing.* New York: Ballantine, 2003.

Arcones, Pedro Ceinos. *Sons of Heaven, Brothers of Nature: The Naxi of Southwest China.* Kunming, China: Papers of the White Dragon, 2012.

Hinton, David, translator. *Chuang Tzu: The Inner Chapters.* Berkeley, CA: Counterpoint, 1998.

Lin, Derek, translator. *Tao Te Ching.* Woodstock, VT: Skylight Paths, 2012.

Lin, Derek. *The Tao of Joy Every Day.* New York: Penguin, 2011.

Shamanic

Campos, Don Jose. *The Shaman and Ayahuasca.* Studio City, CA: Divine Arts, 2011.

Eliade, Mircea. *Shamanism: Archaic Techniques of Ecstasy.* New York: Pantheon, 1964.

Elkin, A. P. *Aboriginal Men of High Degree.* Rochester, VT: Inner Traditions, 1994.

Lawlor, Robert. *Voices of the First Day.* Rochester, VT: Inner Traditions, 1991.

Buddhist

Anālayo. *Satipaṭṭhāna: The Direct Path to Realization.* Cambridge, UK: Windhorse, 2014.

Chodron, Pema. *Living Beautifully: With Uncertainty and Change.* Boston: Shambala, 2013.

Dalai Lama. *How to See Yourself as You Really Are.* Edited and translated by Jeffrey Hopkins, PhD. New York: Atria, 2006.

Easwaran, Eknath, translator. *The Dhammapada.* Berkeley, CA: Blue Mountain Center of Meditation, 2001.

Hanh, Thich Nhat. *Old Path White Clouds.* New Delhi, India: Full Circle, 2015.

Hindu

Easwaran, Eknath, translator. *The Bhagavad Gita.* Berkeley, CA: Blue Mountain Center of Meditation, 2007.

Easwaran, Eknath, translator. *The Upanishads.* Berkeley, CA: Blue Mountain Center of Meditation, 1992.

Eck, Diana. *Darśan: Seeing the Divine Image in India.* New York: Columbia, 1996.

Harvey, Andrew, editor. *Teachings of the Hindu Mystics.* Boston: Shambala, 2001.

Christian

Cutsinger, James. *Not of This World: A Treasury of Christian Mysticism.* Bloomington, IN: World Wisdom, 2003.

French, R. M, translator. *The Way of a Pilgrim.* New York: Quality Paperback, 1998.

Moore, Thomas. *The Soul's Religion.* New York: Perennial, 2003.

Talbot, John Michael. *The Way of the Mystics.* San Francisco: Jossey-Bass, 2005.

Transcendentalist

Hecking, Rebecca James. *The Sustainable Soul.* Boston: Skinner House, 2011.

Oliver, Mary. *New and Selected Poems.* Boston: Beacon Press, 1992.

Robinson, David, editor. *The Spiritual Emerson*. Boston: Beacon Press, 2003.

Thoreau, Henry David. *Walden*. San Diego: Canterbury Classics, 2014.

Trapp, Jacob. *The Light of a Thousand Suns*. London: Rider and Co., 1973.

Interreligious Mystics

Gurdjieff, George. *Meetings with Remarkable Men*. New York: Dutton, 1963.

Otto, Rudolf. *Mysticism East and West*. New York: Living Age Books, 1957.

Ouspensky, P. D. *In Search of the Miraculous*. Orlando, FL: Harcourt, 2001.

Ouspensky, P. D. *Tertium Organum*. New York: Alfred Knopf, 1981.

Shield, Benjamin and Richard Carlson, editors. *For the Love of God*. Novato, CA: New World, 1990.

Watts, Alan. *The Joyous Cosmology*. Novato, CA: New World Library, 2013.

Multireligious Collections

Harvey, Andrew. *The Essential Mystics: The Soul's Journey into Truth*. Secaucus, NJ: Castle Books, 1998.

Ladinsky, Daniel. *Love Poems from God*. New York: Penguin Compass, 2002.

Mitchell, Stephen. *The Enlightened Heart*. New York: Harper Perennial, 1989.

Selby, John. *Seven Masters, One Path*. New York: Harper Collins, 2003.

ACKNOWLEDGMENTS

I am grateful to my friends and family—especially my wife, Loretta, and our two audacious children—for their love and support as I have traveled an awesome and sometimes scary path to spiritual awakening. The key, pivotal event in my life, which made all the rest of this blessed life possible, was meeting and marrying Loretta when we were young and traveling this spiritual journey together. She is the love of my life, the wind in my sails, my anchor in the storm, and my best friend. We are blessed to have found nirvana together. As always on the Way, I walk in serendipity. As a result, all will be well.

There are no words adequate to describe the mystic experience. We are talking about the inexplicable and unknowable. The process of converting my spiritual life into readable text continues to stretch me in remarkable ways. I remain amazed and thankful for the genius of my publisher, Amy Quale.

My editor, Angela Wiechmann, has once again used praise, careful critiques, fact-checking, and candid comments to catalyze and help me create a far better book than I otherwise would have. Angie has been a blessing and a pilgrim soul to accompany me on this journey of converting my life to Truth.

My spiritual journey of awakening was made possible by many mystics, manifestations of divine mystery, and pilgrim souls who preceded or guided me on my Way. A few of them were Antony of Egypt, Bernard of Clairvaux, Hildegard of Bingen, Francis of Assisi, Meister Eckhart, Brother Lawrence, Teresa of Ávila, John of the Cross, Mirabai, Kabir, and Chuang Tzu. A mystic's life is a varied and splendid thing. Also helpful on my journey were Jacob Trapp, the Benedictines, UU mystics, Gaia, Mary Oliver, my dark night of the soul, and my men's group,

My guides included Hafiz, Al-Haqq, Ibrahim, Rumi, Madonna, Muhammad, Shams of Tabriz, and Ismael. I had adventures with Changzu, Confucius, Alan Watts, Buddha, *tiandi*, Derek Lin, *wu wei*, Pachamama, Dhyani Ywahoo, Odin, Pythagoras, Zoroaster, Imbabura, Pukyu Pamba, the Achuar indigenous people, Daniel, Robin, and Alice. It remains a great and wonderful adventure! My teachers included Thich Nhat Hanh, monkeys, Rabindranath Tagore, Kali, Ganesh, Lord Krishna, Jack Kornfield, Budai, Naga, Father Peter, Jesus of Nazareth, and the Holy Spirit. I traveled with the Knights Templar, Saint Jerome, Simon Peter, Saint Andrew, Santiago Peregrino, Ralph Waldo Emerson, Immanuel Kant, Thomas Carlyle, Henry David Thoreau, wildness, and Nathaniel Hawthorne. I am a grateful and blessed spiritual pilgrim.

ABOUT THE AUTHOR

Reverend Doctor Jim Sherblom is a transcendentalist, author, mystic, theologian, entrepreneur, investor, company creator, venture capitalist, spiritual seeker, and laughing buddha. Jim holds a BA from Yale, an MBA from Harvard, and Master of Divinity and Doctor of Ministry degrees from Andover Newton Theological School.

Jim grew up in the middle of a very large, very poor family in Tiverton, Rhode Island. His acceptance to Yale brought this small-town boy into a maelstrom. Meeting and marrying his wife, Loretta, brought him transformed into the wider world. After graduating with highest honors from Harvard Business School, he began his career as a strategy consultant with Bain & Company, working in Boston, London, and Munich.

Jim was a founder of the Massachusetts Biotechnology Council and served as its president. His industry roles include serving as senior vice president and CFO of Genzyme Corporation and as chairman and CEO of TSI Corporation. As founding managing partner of Seaflower Ventures, he has been involved in the creation of six biotechnology and health care companies and was an early investor in at least twelve more.

At midlife, he was called into divine mystery. Through a series of vision quests and theological studies, he emerged as a spiritual teacher, preacher, and friend of God. He was called to parish ministry, serving as a senior minister at First Parish in Brookline, Massachusetts, for eleven years.

Since retiring from parish ministry in late 2015, Jim devotes full time to his writing and traveling with mystics. He mostly writes about spiritual matters, especially his travels with mystics, pilgrims, and spiritual seekers. He lives a transcendental existence in Concord, Massachusetts, with his wife Loretta. His favorite and most frequent deep spiritual practice consists of walking meditation in Walden Woods or around Walden Pond. Jim and Loretta are the proud parents of two grown children.